D0343763

MR NASTASE

MR NASTASE

Ilie Nastase

with Debbie Beckerman

CollinsWillow

An Imprint of HarperCollins*Publishers*

First published in 2004 by
CollinsWillow
an imprint of HarperCollins*Publishers*
London

1 3 5 7 9 8 6 4 2

A CIP catalogue record for this book is available from the British Library

ISBN 0 00 718141 8

Set in Sabon by Rowland Phototypesetting Ltd,
Bury St Edmunds, Suffolk

Printed and bound in Great Britain by
Clays Ltd, St Ives plc

The HarperCollins website address is www.harpercollins.co.uk

PHOTOGRAPHIC ACKNOWLEDGMENTS

All inside photographs supplied courtesy of Ilie Nastase with the exception of the following: **Associated Press** page 5, 12bl; **Central Press Photos** 7t; **Corbis** 6b, 13b; **Daily Telegraph** 7b; **Evening Standard** 13cl; **Getty Images** 14cl; **Hulton Archive** 9, 10cl, 12br; **Magnum** 13cr; **Mirrorpix** 6c, 11cl; **Presse Sports** 7cl, 7cr; **Rex Features** 14cr; **Time Life Pictures/Getty Images** 11t, 14t; **Wimbledon Lawn Tennis Museum** 13t. While every effort has been made to contact the copyright holders of the photographs included in this book, there may have been omissions. The Publishers will endeavour to rectify any outstanding permissions on publication.

To Jean-Luc – you'll be always in my heart

CONTENTS

ACKNOWLEDGMENTS

from Ilie Nastase

There have been so many people who have shown me kindness and encouragement over the years. I cannot hope to thank them all, and I am sorry if I have forgotten somebody in the following list. It could have gone on for many more pages:

Nathalie, Nicky, Charlotte and Alessia, for giving a reason to my life.

My parents, who never interfered with my tennis, and for giving me so much love.

My brother, Constantin, who influenced my career, and my three sisters Ana, Cornelia and Georgeta.

Ion Tiriac, who protected me and who accepted me as I was. I think you understood me better than anyone!

Adi Dassler and his son Horst Dassler, for believing in me for more than thirty years.

Claus Marten, thank you for continuing to believe in me, as the Dassler family did.

Jean-Luc Lagardère, for being like a second father to me, and to his wife Bethy Lagardère – the biggest sports fan.

Colonel Medeleanu and Colonel Chivaru, for bribing me with chocolate to prefer tennis instead of football.

Stefan Georgescu, coach of the Romanian Davis Cup

team, for supporting me in all 146 Davis Cup ties I played for Romania.

Ion Gheorghe Maurer and Corneliu Manescu, for making easier for me the Communist years.

Fred Perry, who I admire and love.

René Lacoste, Toto Brugnon and Marcel Bernard, for helping me to play my first Roland Garros in 1966.

Pancho Gonzales, for his inspiring tennis and temper.

Nicola Pietrangeli, first for his friendship and for his tennis style.

Manolo Santana, my clay-court idol and friend.

Roy Emerson, the strongest tennis player and the funniest of all Aussies.

Vitas Gerulaitis, great buddy of mine and a great person.

Gerry Goldberg, for being a constant friend throughout twenty-five years.

Harry Hopman, for coaching me and Ion for the tie against Great Britain in 1969.

Bill Riordan, for getting me started in the USA and for the financial support at the beginning.

Peter Lawler, for putting up with me for such a long time.

Peter Worth, for believing in me at nearly sixty.

Bambino, for protecting me and making me laugh.

Kirk and Ann Douglas, for their friendship and hospitality.

Muhammad Ali, the greatest sportsman ever.

My tennis friends Jimmy Connors, Bjorn Borg, Adriano Panatta, Manuel Orantes, Pierre Barthès, Guillermo Vilas, Stan Smith, Rod Laver, Ken Rosewall, Fred Stolle, John Newcombe, Tony Roche, Peter McNamara and Paul McNamee.

Mansour and Frédérique Bahrami, thank you for always being there for me.

Arthur Ashe. Wish you were still here.

To the Wimbledon Committee, for keeping me young by not making me a Wimbledon member.

Christian Bimes, for making me feel at home during Roland Garros, and for our long friendship. Caroline, thank you for keeping him young.

Sting, for giving me the opportunity to meet Amalia.

And to my wife, Amalia, the best thing that's happened to my heart.

PROLOGUE

'Give me all those flowers, please,' I asked the flower seller.

She wrapped the colourful mixture of red, white, and yellow roses up carefully, imagining the pleasure the lucky woman would have when she received them. I didn't explain but handed over the money and ran back into the hotel dining room. I crept nervously up to the man they were intended for, trying to hide behind the huge bouquet as I did so. When I got to his table he turned round, saw the flowers, saw me, smiled, and then laughed. I was forgiven.

The night before, the man in question, Arthur Ashe, had been driven so crazy by me at the 1975 Commercial Union Masters tournament in Stockholm that he had walked off court, mid-match, screaming and shouting, something he had never been known to do. By leaving the court, he had been instantly disqualified. I knew I had gone too far this time in the lead-up to that incident, and, as I hate people to stay angry with me, I knew it was time to make up with Arthur. I had tried to apologize the evening before, but he had brushed me aside and refused to talk to me, so now I was trying again, hoping that this time we could be reconciled.

The scandal I had created was even bigger because Ashe was the most gentlemanly, composed player on the tour. He had never lost his temper and had recently been one of the main people involved in drawing up a Code of Conduct for the players. This outlined which offences were punishable by what fines and explained when a player should be disqualified. It was ironic therefore that he, of all people, should be the first to receive the ultimate punishment, because these rules had been written with players like me in mind, not him.

Arthur happened to be one of the players that I got on with best, even though he was so different from me. Years ago, I'd started to call him Negroni, explaining that in Romanian it doesn't mean 'nigger' (as people often thought) but a little black kid, dressed nice. So he said: 'I like that, I like that, but only you can call me that.' He was also very different from the other players: he was involved in politics, in the fight against apartheid, and he was bright. He was the only one to read a book before a match. You never saw other players doing that. I liked him because he always talked sense; he would ask me questions about life in Romania, about politics there – we could have a proper discussion, not just about tennis.

The night before the match, I'd seen Arthur dining a couple of tables away from me with his blonde Canadian girlfriend, and I'd gently teased them: 'You two look cute, you look like salt and pepper.' At the bar, later on, I'd teased him a bit more, just to prepare him for the encounter. 'Tomorrow night I do things to you that will make you turn white. Then you will be a white Negroni.' Arthur laughed, because he knew what I was like. I wasn't trying to needle him, like boxers before a fight. We both knew that if I did something in the match, I would upset him. But when it happened it was almost stupid.

I had won the 1st set 6–1, playing with ease and calm, then Ashe had fought back to win the 2nd set 7–5. The 3rd set, I'm still behaving really well but lose my serve and find myself 1–4 down. I'm serving at 15–40 down. Lose this game and it's all over, Arthur just needs to serve out for the match.

I'd been heckled by this guy in the crowd during the game, and every time I tried to serve he'd start shouting at me. I just couldn't ignore him, so I'd shout back. At last, I served, only for Ashe to catch the ball in his hand. Apparently, a ball was rolling between the two ball boys at my end during my serve, so Arthur said he had not been ready. The umpire told me I had two serves. I protested, arguing that Ashe hadn't indicated he wasn't ready. The crowd started to whistle and jeer, and the heckler behind me was carrying on. It was then that, for some reason, I thought I would slow up play. 'Are you ready, Mr Ashe?' I taunted, as I got ready to serve. I bounced the ball again a few more times, with the heckler still shouting out as I did so, then I asked Arthur again: 'Are you ready, Mr Ashe?' I don't remember how many more times I said this, but it must have been quite a few. Suddenly, with no warning, he starts waving his arms in the air and marching to his chair. He's screaming: 'That's it! I've had enough!' and he just takes his rackets and leaves. I'm left standing there, really surprised because I'd never seen Ashe behaving like that. There was total chaos on court, and the public was getting really mad. Nobody knew what to do.

Normally, I should have been awarded the match because he had left the court, but I felt bad about winning like that. Back in the dressing room, I stayed out of Ashe's way but I could hear him ranting in his corner at the officials. It turned out that the tournament referee, Horst Klosterkemper, was about to disqualify me anyway when Ashe walked off, so the tournament committee were now in a crazy situation where they had two disqualified players.

The end-of-season Masters tournament had gathered

together the top eight players from the Grand Prix series of tournaments and had split them into two round-robin groups. The top two from each group then went on to the semifinals. By disqualifying us both from the match, we still had a chance of getting to the semis, if either of us won our two remaining matches in our group. So it seemed like a good solution at the time. But when Ashe was told of their decision, he went berserk. The tournament committee then met again at once. After more heated discussions, they decided, given Ashe's reputation on the tour and the fact that he was president of the players' union, the Association of Tennis Professionals (ATP), that he should be given the match after all and that only I should be disqualified.

The final decision was not reached until eleven o'clock that night, but when they told me I was not upset or surprised. I didn't think that what I had been doing on court would get me into so much trouble – I certainly never wanted to be disqualified – but once it happened I was not angry. I accepted it and just thought, 'OK, now I have to win two more matches to get to the semis', which is exactly what I did.

I felt bad, though, about what I had done to Arthur because he was a good friend of mine. So it was natural for me to want to make it up to him afterwards. The flowers had been my idea alone. It was important that he forgave me; and Arthur of course was too great a man to let a tennis match get in the way of our friendship. It had never been my intention to drive him crazy, despite what some people thought, because my problems on court were hardly ever planned. Yes, I was often called Mr Nasty, but I could also be Mr Nice as well.

CHAPTER ONE

1946–1959

I could have been a Russian.

My story begins not in Bucharest, Romania, but beyond the mountains of Transylvania, in what is now the independent republic of Moldova, a country squeezed in between the Ukraine and Romania and that was formerly part of the Soviet Union.

My mother, Elena, was born there in 1907, but she and her younger sister were orphaned during the First World War. In fact, I have no further details of who they were brought up by because my mother never spoke about her childhood. I only discovered that she had lost both parents when her sister revealed this to me shortly before her death a couple of years ago, and, as my mother had long since passed away, I was unable to find out anything more about her early years.

My father, Gheorghe, was born in 1906 in Ramnicul-Sârat, which means Salty River, and is a town about 240 km from Bucharest in the mountainous Muntenia region of Romania. He met my mother in 1925, when he came to Moldova to work as a policeman for the national bank, the Banca Nationala a Romaniei (BNR). He worked all his life for this bank. Within a year, they were married and my eldest brother Volodia was born. By 1933, they had two more children, Ana born in 1930 and Constantin three years later. In those days, though, medicine was not as developed as it is today, and when Volodia fell ill, aged eight, nothing was available to help him. I don't know what he died of but I think he had the sort of illness that today would simply have been cured with antibiotics.

I have no doubt that losing a child is the worst thing that can happen in life, so I can only imagine that losing their first-born child must have hit my parents hard. This may partly explain the nine-year gap between Constantin's birth and the birth of their next two children, Cornelia in 1942 and Georgeta in 1944. Barely a few weeks after Georgeta's birth, however, the Russians started making their way towards Moldova. It was then that my father decided to take the entire family back to his home town of Ramnicul-Sârat. He had found work in the BNR branch of the town and felt the family was safer there than in Moldova. Sure enough, within two weeks, the Russians had invaded and Moldova became part of the Soviet Union.

My parents did not stay long in Ramnicul-Sârat and, by 1945, my father had again managed to get himself transferred, this time to Bucharest. So I look back now and realize that, had he hesitated for a couple more weeks, my family would have had to stay in Moldova, I would have been born a Russian and tennis history would have been quite different. Too bad, eh?

By the end of the Second World War, Romania's own pro-Nazi government was overthrown and Stalin had appointed a Communist government. Soon after, the king was deposed and my country became the People's Republic of Romania. Communism had arrived. So it was against that background that my mother gave birth to me on 19 July 1946. I was an enormous 5 kg baby, and my father told me many years later that my mother had not actually wanted another child: she already had enough mouths to feed. But he insisted and insisted – poor woman – so it was agreed that I would definitely be their last child. Given how much I weighed at birth, she was hardly going to change her mind. So maybe because of this, and maybe because, having already lost one son, my mother was happy to have another baby boy, she may have indulged me a bit more than my brother and sisters. I won't say any more than that because I can already hear the amateur psychologists exclaiming with excitement that this explains everything: I simply wasn't disciplined enough as a child. All I can offer as a defence is that there wasn't anything, such as toys, food or money, that my mother or father could spoil me with. We weren't poor but we weren't comfortably off either. But I think when you have so many children, you simply relax about discipline and attention by the time you get to the last one. As long as he is safe and healthy, you worry less about whether he has done all his homework perfectly or has gone to bed at the right time every night. So I don't think I was spoiled so much as protected.

We lived in an idyllic setting for a child. My father had been given a house in the grounds of the Progresul Tennis Club, which belonged to the bank (it had originally been the king's club as well), so, as well as being a policeman for the bank, he also took care of the grounds of the club. The tennis club happened to be the main national club, where tournaments and Davis Cup ties were played. It is in beautiful grounds, the size of Roland Garros in the old days, and the courts are situated among alleys bordered by huge old plane trees and great big expanses of grass.

Our house itself was a cream-coloured bungalow at one end of the club, next to the football club that also belonged to the BNR bank, and I shared a bedroom with Cornelia and Georgeta, who everyone called Gigi, though we used to spend as much time as we could outdoors. As a family, we owned very little other than the basic items of clothing and furniture, but that was not unusual in Romania in those days.

You have to consider that there was no television until the mid Fifties, and we did not own one until I bought our first one ten years later. In any case, in the early days of television, they only showed Russian and Romanian stuff and the odd very bad American film. Nothing that you would want to watch, in other words. So until we got a TV, we would listen to our enormous Russian radio, which my father used to hit regularly to get it going again when it decided to stop working, which was very often. We didn't own things such as a camera, either, which is why I do not have a single photograph of me as a child, something I am very sad about because I can't show my kids what I looked like when I was little. So all the material goods that we now take for granted were absent in our household during my childhood. But as any person will tell you who has grown up in this way, what you don't know you don't miss.

What I did have, though, was freedom. We lived in an enclosed environment – and the grounds were guarded by police because the club belonged to the national bank – so I could run around all day in total safety. I would climb, and fall out of, the many fruit trees in the grounds, and would chase my sisters endlessly and get up to all sorts of stupid games. I remember, when I was five or six, falling over during one of our chases, and a piece of wood piercing my knee from front to back. Screaming and in pain, I was carried home, where a friend of my mother's just removed the wood with one sharp movement. With my sister Gigi, we would practise jumping off the flat roof of this building that was about 3–4 m above the ground. One day, when I wasn't looking, my sister thought it would be funny to push me off and see what happened. Instead of landing on all fours, like a cat, as I usually did, I landed flat on my face and flattened my nose completely. My mother beat her up after that.

But my earliest memory was when I must have been about three years old. The seating around the main stadium court just consisted of open wooden benches, rising up above the court. I remember I used to run around naked a lot – it was summer and hot – and I liked to clamber up to the top corner of the stadium's seats and watch the tennis, naked. On this occasion, Romania was playing a Davis Cup tie against France, and the ground was full. People were excited to be able to see great names like Benny Berthet playing. So there I was, happily watching the action when I realized I badly needed to go to the toilet. Unable to hold myself, I started to pee and everything started to dribble between the stands. At first, people below thought it was raining until they realized what it was that was dripping on to their heads. Some guy came running up and started to scream and beat me up, and my mother rushed up and beat the hell out of me too. That was my first court-side scene. And, even then, the punishment didn't put me off.

When I was four, my brother hired me as his sidekick to help sell Turkish delight to the fans who went to the nearby soccer stadium to watch matches. Constantin has always been one to spot an opportunity to make a bit of extra money, so he'd buy this Turkish delight and sell it at a profit to the captive audience. I'd have to nip over the busy tram lines that separated the Progresul Club from the soccer stadium, carrying not only the sweets but also big jugs of cold water – we'd offer a glassful as well to offset the cloying taste. I suspect we weren't really allowed to engage in this sort of entrepreneurship as it did not really fit in with Communist thinking.

By the Fifties, food shortages were severe in Romania and, even though Ana and Constantin were also working, we only had just about enough food for us all. I remember my father queuing for basic foods such as bread and, although we never actually went hungry, others certainly did. The one thing we were most lucky about was that the authorities allowed us to keep a cow and a goat in the grounds of the club, which meant we always had enough milk. My mother would regularly get me to hand bowlfuls of milk to children on the other side of the fence separating the club from the street, and I have to say that the image of these hungry children has stuck with me to this day.

But it was because we had these animals that this absurd legend began to circulate when I first joined the tennis circuit, that I had once been a shepherd boy, although God knows how I could have kept sheep in a city-centre club. Even so, I lost count of the number of articles about me in the early years that stated this 'fact' as the Gospel truth. The intention, I guess, was to make out that I had only just emerged from a cave and that my story literally was a rags to riches tale.

By the time I was five or six, I had started at the nearby kindergarten, where I was allowed to go by myself, although the grass was so tall that you could not see me walking through it. I also used to spend a lot of time watching tennis but had yet to pick up a racket. My brother, who is thirteen years older than me, was a good tennis player who went on to play tournaments abroad and Davis Cup for Romania.

I would admire his rackets, although they were still too heavy for me to pick up, but there was never any question that I might start to play. Actually, I think that was the best thing for me because, if I had started when I was three or four, as so many kids now do, I would probably have got bored with tennis by the time I was a little older and would have moved on to something else. My mother never said: 'Go and watch them in the Davis Cup, try to learn from them.' I would just run up over the little grassy hill that separated our house from the courts and watch the players for hours on end, subconsciously taking in all their movements, simply because I enjoyed watching. I never thought of it as a learning process.

I was extremely skinny when I was young, largely because I was unable to stay still for very long. When I was six, I was very ill with bronchitis and pneumonia, and my father – fearing that I might suffer the same fate as Volodia – scooped me up, took me to the governor of the bank, put me on his desk and pleaded with him to get me some medicines. This had the desired effect because the guy signed at once to allow me to be prescribed some antibiotics. But even so, I remained scrawny right through childhood and adolescence. Even in 1970, aged twenty-four, I still only weighed 70 kg, which is not very much for my height of 1.85 m.

Around the age of six, I started to play tennis a bit, not with a real racket but with a sort of wooden bat. I would hit endlessly against a wall that was directly below a chocolate factory that backed onto the club, and occasionally the women who worked there would throw sweets out to me. Needless to say, that encouraged me to go there more regularly and to play for hours on end. I would still watch the club members whenever I could, but I remember thinking, even at that age, that I could probably beat most of them if I was given a chance. Because the grounds were also next to the soccer club, I would often wander onto the pitch, juggling a ball at my feet and the bat and a tennis ball in my hand. The soccer ball was sometimes just made of old pieces of material tied up and stuffed into a sock and I would kick it around until basically it disintegrated. Still, I loved running around doing both things at once. It was all just one big game.

Unfortunately, my huge, safe playground was taken away from me when I was eight: my two eldest siblings had left home, so we had to move house to make way for others. Our new home was a ground-floor, two-bedroomed apartment in a small, grey block of flats nearer the city centre. I had to share a room with Gigi and Cornelia. With its windows that were barely above street level and no garden, the apartment was bleak compared to our bungalow, and I hated it at first.

The street became my playground, and my main pastime with my friends was to play soccer for hours on end. We also liked to run over to the US ambassador's residence, which was not too far away, and rummage through the bins, picking out anything that was American or that smelt good. What we were really looking for was Coca-Cola bottle tops, which we would then place on the tram tracks. When they had been well flattened by the trams, we would retrieve them and play a game of chance. This involved flipping the tops like coins and the one whose top came out with the Coca-Cola sign on top would win both coins. You could, if you were lucky, accumulate quite a lot of these prized symbols of Western decadence.

My current wife, Amalia, tells me that, thirty years later, under Ceauşescu, with the country in massive debt and food shortages a daily occurrence, she and her friends used to play an almost identical game. They would collect Pepsi bottle tops (by then, for some reason, Pepsi had overtaken Coca-Cola in appeal) and the one who had the most tops was the most important. So nothing had changed, and, either way, it goes to show that if you deprive kids of these sorts of things, they will just come to want them even more.

The only good thing going for our new apartment was that it was literally over the road from the school that I went to from the age of eight to seventeen. So I used to jump over the fence at lunchtime, grab a piece of bread with sugar on it for lunch, which was sometimes all we had to eat, then run back and spend the rest of the breaktime playing soccer with my friends.

The school was mixed and had about 1,000 pupils. Until we were eleven, there was no school uniform so I used to wear the same blue tracksuit every day. My mother would wash it every three days in our huge bath, because we did not have a washing machine. She would then hang it up to dry and hope that it was dry the next morning for school, which was not always the case. The tracksuit was like wearing jeans and a sweat shirt now for kids. Similarly, the only shoes I had as a child were tennis shoes. But then, what other shoes would I have needed at that age? I wasn't exactly going to parties.

School was something that I put up with. In primary school I was constantly being punished, sometimes for things that I did not even do. Because I was so shy and never dared look the teacher in the eye, I always looked guilty. The teacher would then pull my ear, which made me mad, or hit me round the head, which made me madder. But one of her favourite punishments was to get me to kneel in a corner, for hours on end, on upturned walnut shells. Weird, I know. And painful, too, I can tell you. By the end, my mother would be summoned in almost every day to see this mean old teacher, and she would try to tell me to behave, but somehow no amount of threats or punishments seemed to work. Do you detect a pattern for the future?

In secondary school I continued to be uncommitted to work. I'd get by – no more. We studied French, which I hated at the time, because we had a teacher who spat all the time when he spoke and who was never satisfied if you didn't say the word exactly right. He was Romanian, by the way. Anyway, he managed to put me off that language, which is a shame because if I'd known I would marry a French woman I might have paid more attention.

We were also forced to study Russian, and, as a result, it was universally the number one most hated subject. In fact, we hated anything to do with Russia and any influence it had over our country. I will say, in his favour, that one good thing Ceauşescu did was to remove Russian from the list of obligatory subjects to study at school. We were also the only Eastern bloc country never to have Russian soldiers on our soil, so somehow, in these small ways, we managed to keep our independence just a little bit. But our leader at the time, Gheorghiu-Dej, headed up a Stalinist regime and was more friendly with the Russians than Ceauşescu ever was. In fact, I remember vividly the day that Stalin died: sirens went off all over the city; trams, trains and buses came to a halt and everything stopped while we had a minute's silence and we all pretended we were very upset. They used to make us chant a slogan at school that said: 'Stalin and the people of Russia bring us liberty.' It rhymes in Romanian (*Stalin şi poporul rus, Libertate ne-a adus*), so it was meant to be a nice, catchy thing to chant. But no one was fooled. My parents, my brother and elder sister remembered life before Communism and they knew this current regime did not mean liberty. This wasn't the right way to live. So even at a young age I knew this chant was not true.

I was still getting into trouble at school, not for anything really bad, but for just making a nuisance of myself, pulling the girls' hair – that sort of thing. Then one day, something happened. I must have been eleven or twelve, and the teacher was about to punish me for whatever it was I was supposed to have done, when the guy who'd actually done it owned up. The teacher was about to hand out the punishment to him, but I said: 'No, it's OK, punish me anyway.' 'No,' she said, 'you haven't done it.' 'Yes but it's OK, punish me, it's always me anyway.' I was so used to it by then that any punishment didn't mean anything any more. I treated it as a joke. Maybe if tournament directors and tennis officials had realized this, they would have not bothered to go through all those later fines and suspensions, and spared everyone a lot of problems.

Because we no longer lived at the Progresul Club, I was having to play tennis and soccer at the Steaua Club, about twenty minutes' walk away from where we lived. The Steaua Club (which means Star) is the Army Club in Romania, and my brother played tennis for them. I was obsessed with soccer and tennis, and so I happily went down every single day, after school, to play both for hours and hours, practising tennis wherever and whenever I could, ball-boying for anyone who wanted me and generally hanging around as much as possible. Sometimes I would get up at 6 a.m. to ball-boy for members of the club. Nothing else mattered but those two sports and, between the ages of ten and thirteen, I played both nonstop.

With soccer, however, I used to come home battered and bruised all over (I played inside right, the number 8 shirt), and my mother was getting more and more unhappy about the state of my legs, which were usually a nice mixture of red and blue cuts and bruises. Tennis at least had the advantage of not risking broken bones every time I played a match. On the other hand, soccer was very good for my tennis because it helped with the coordination, the speed around the court, the footwork, and the balance.

So, until I was in my teens, I could not decide whether to be a footballer or to devote myself to tennis. It was not a question of a career or money because, in those days, it was clear that there was no money in tennis. My brother, despite being a Davis Cup player and despite bringing back exciting tales of foreign travels and the odd packet of chewing gum, was still having to work as an electrician to make ends meet.

From the age of eleven, I had a coach, Colonel Constantin Chivaru, who was an ex-tour player himself, a Davis Cup team member with my brother, and it was he who persuaded me to devote my time to tennis. He never changed my technique, though, because he could see that it was very instinctive and natural, and he realized that it would do more harm than good to give me formal coaching. Because he didn't want me going off to play soccer, he would bribe me with chocolates and encourage me to keep practising – not that I needed much encouragement. So, for a while, there was quite a lot of friction between him and the Steaua soccer coach as each fought for my loyalty and commitment.

During this whole period, my parents never once pushed me in one direction or the other. They had never done a stroke of sport in their lives and they never showed the slightest interest in my sporting career, so they were the least likely to know what to advise. All they worried about was where on earth my future lay, because it was clear that I was never going to do more than the absolute minimum amount of school work. Frankly, they didn't even know what I was up to in sport. My father used to tease me. He'd say: 'What are going around with that guitar for? You're not going to do like your brother?' He didn't actively discourage me, but probably if he'd encouraged me to play I would have done the opposite, because it always upset me – and, yes, it still does at times – when someone told me I had to go and do something. So I can definitely say that my parents were the total opposite of pushy tennis parents. They never went near a court. But, in my mind, I knew that I wanted to do sport. I didn't care what it led to – I just knew I could not imagine doing anything else. It was just a question of which one I was going to choose, tennis or soccer.

In the end, tennis won because I just enjoyed it more and I knew deep down that I was better at it. And when you are good at something, you get emotionally involved in it. I suppose I stopped being emotionally involved in soccer. Also, in tennis, I could get noticed more: if I won it was all down to me, and if I lost it wasn't because ten other players had let me down. I could play the match my own way, unlike soccer where there is a team to consider. Although, I have to admit, I did tend to do as I wanted a bit too much on the soccer pitch as well: I'd hog the ball, to the extent that some players would shout: 'Hey, did your mum give you the ball? Is that why you won't let it out of your sight?'

My first tennis tournament was when I was eleven or twelve, and it was not a success. I played this kid who quickly beat me 6–0 in the 1st set. That was too much to bear, so I put my racket down and started to chase after him round the court until I caught him. 'What's wrong with you?' he said. I immediately started to cry and then screamed back: 'Nobody's going to beat me 6–0,' and promptly started to hit him on the head. He still beat me 6–2 in the next set, but it had started already: my first on-court tantrum. And it was not the last time I cried after a match, either.

My brother and my coach could see I had a lot of talent but they did not know whether that was going to be enough because I was so skinny. At that age, I used to run like a rabbit, chasing balls all over the place, whether they were in or out, and would return absolutely everything, using big, loopy shots. It used to drive my opponents crazy. But, with no television, I'd never seen top-level tennis, other than the odd Davis Cup tie, so I did not know how else tennis could be played, especially not when I was twelve or thirteen. The notion of clay-court tennis versus, say, grass-court tennis, or serve-volley versus back-of-the-court play had never even entered my mind. All I had was a treasured photograph of Roy Emerson that I had cut out of a tennis magazine brought back by my brother from one of his trips abroad. In it, Emerson was hitting a high backhand volley, so for years I only had that to go on when trying to work out how to hit that shot. But really, I didn't have a clue, I just played instinctively, because my technique was never taught to me.

When people look back at their lives, they realize that certain events along the way were crucial to the direction that life eventually took. Some are down to good luck – and I believe that to be successful we all need a bit of luck – others to conscious decisions. In my case, the first key event that shaped my life occurred when, aged thirteen, I won the National Championships for my age category. Held in a city called Cluj, this was a big win for me but, best of all, I was given my first ever new racket – a beautiful Slazenger. I was unbelievably excited. That decided it. I realized tennis could be good for me and, from then on, I worked hard and was determined to get better.

The other thing that happened to me that week was that I saw, for the first time, the man who was to become the biggest influence in my life for the next ten years, Ion Tiriac. Aged twenty, he was seven years older than me and he had just created a big upset by beating the longstanding Romanian number 1, Gheorghe Viziru, to become National Champion, a title he retained until I took it from him eight years later, in 1967. Because I was so keen to stay on after my win and soak in the atmosphere of the tournament, I asked to ball-boy the senior final. Ion of course does not remember seeing me run around the court retrieving balls for him. Frankly, why should he, I was a mere bean-pole ball boy. But watching the National Champion play was a big thing for me, and it showed me, once again, what I should be aiming for.

That was when I realized that tennis was going to be my life.

CHAPTER TWO

1959–1966

Paris in 1966 was good to me.

Despite winning in Cluj, my life did not change much for the next few years. Nowadays, a kid who wins a national title starts to travel to as many junior tournaments as possible. He is ranked from the age of eight or nine, and he has agents looking to sign him up before you can say 'match point'. Instead, I went back to the Steaua Club, practised hard, and played a few tournaments here and there.

One of my biggest regrets today is that I was not able to play junior tournaments around the world, because I am sure that I would have learned to compete earlier and to handle the pressure of matches better if I had been playing the juniors. And this would have improved my subsequent results. It used to really hurt me when I read in the papers that players such as the Czech Jan Kodes or the Russian Alexander Metreveli, who I played in tournaments when we were teenagers, were regularly touring abroad, getting valuable experience. The Australian players also used to go travelling for weeks at a time from the age of about sixteen, learning how to compete.

I, meanwhile, was stuck at home, the Romanian Tennis

Federation being unable to send me overseas to get experience, through lack of money. Strangely, although I knew I wanted to keep playing tennis, I never had a grand master plan that I was going to build a career from it, even when I was fifteen or sixteen. I loved the sport. I was passionate about it. I knew I wanted to keep playing it, but I never thought further than that. Planning in fact has never been my strong point, and there was nobody around me who could help me to plan. I certainly had no idea that I might actually live from my winnings. Tennis in those days was strictly an amateur sport, certainly for people who came from Communist countries, so there was no notion of playing yourself into money.

On court, during practice, I used to like to have fun but I also had a temper because I hated to lose. My temper, I think, is something to do with the Romanian temperament. Contrary to what most people think, we are not Slavs but Latins. Our language closely resembles Italian (and is now the closest living language to Latin), and we get into heated arguments very easily. But although I lost my temper and cried and screamed regularly during practice matches, I did not cheat. Anyone who thinks that I may have grown up in an environment where this was common is wrong. There was no point in cheating, because you'd just get found out by parents and coaches who were watching and beaten up by your opponent.

I did, however, like to complicate things by playing drop shots, lobs, finishing the point the way I would like. I wanted constantly to make the ideal, perfect, point. So if I missed a drop shot once or twice, I would keep playing it until I made it. It used to drive my coach, Colonel Chivaru, absolutely crazy. Later, it drove Ion Tiriac even more crazy, because I would insist on doing this in real matches. Ion would sometimes try to talk tactics with me the day before a match, saying: 'Don't try to drop-shot that guy too much, he's very fast.' That was dangerous because I didn't like being told how to play. I liked to play the game my way – that's what made me happy. So I'd go out, do the opposite of what he'd said, and drop-shot the guy for the hell of it, just to see how many times I could beat him. I'd then go back to Ion 'You see how much I made him run? He ran like a yo-yo!' 'But you lost three sets to love,' he'd growl, tearing his hair out. 'Yes, but God I made him run for his win,' I'd reply, beaming.

Finally, aged seventeen, I left school and entered the Army, the only choice for someone in my situation. Normally, military service would have lasted sixteen months, but luckily, because I was already playing for the Army Club, it was reduced down to a couple of nights in barracks and a ceremony where I had to swear allegiance to the colonel of the regiment. I had to be given the words to read because I had no idea what I was swearing to. After that I was free to keep playing tennis all day, every day. I am happy to say that a rifle never passed through my hands, although this did not prevent me from being immediately promoted to the rank of lieutenant (obviously not because of my good soldiering skills). I was also given a nice uniform and, even better, a pay rise.

I used that extra money to buy my first bicycle. I was thrilled, because now I could get around town much faster. I would cycle to the club, practise, then cycle off to a canteen-style restaurant where sportsmen were able to go. The Ministry of Sports gave us vouchers so that we did not have to pay. On any given day, there would be a great mix of different sportsmen – cyclists, soccer players, gymnasts. Tiriac and I would usually have lunch there, and he would often have breakfast there in the morning as well. He would think nothing of demolishing twelve or fourteen eggs. He would eat like an animal, just like his future protégé, Guillermo Vilas. Neither of them put on any weight, though, because they were doing so much training. After a few days with my brand-new bike, which had cost me almost one month's salary, I pedalled up to the restaurant, left it against the railings, did not lock it, and never saw it again. It was stolen from under my nose.

The only downside to my life as a so-called soldier was that my hair was cut to within ½ cm of its life. So it was as a shaven-headed recruit that I was packed off for my first trip abroad, to play a tournament in Sofia, Bulgaria. I was unbelievably excited. Far too excited in fact to be worried by the bumpy plane ride in the old twin prop Ilyushin that took me there. Nowadays, turbulence in planes frightens me a lot. It's the one thing that panics me in a plane, far more than the supposedly more dangerous takeoff and landing. But, back then, I barely noticed. My head was, literally, above the clouds.

Tiriac was also on that trip, and he had obviously been asked by the Federation to keep an eye on me. He had this incredible aura about him, and for the first few days he barely even looked in my direction. He'd turn up to watch my matches, but I could tell he wasn't very interested in what else I was up to. After all, I was an unbelievably shy and naïve seventeen year-old, whereas he was an established twenty-four-year-old international player. It must have been embarrassing to drag me around with him.

After the tournament in Sofia, I was able to travel to a few other tournaments in Communist countries such as Hungary, Czechoslovakia, and Estonia. But mainly I practised a lot, and, when the weather got too cold and snowy (Bucharest is covered in snow for at least two months every winter), Tiriac and I would get sent to training camps high up in the Transylvanian mountains to get fit and, in my case, to fill out. That I hated. Unlike Tiriac, I have always been bored by physical training and gym work, so I just could not take all those exercises seriously. These camps were like army camps. They'd be full of athletes from every sport: some were huge great boxers and weightlifters, who only showed up my scrawny body even more. I hated the whole time I was there, particularly as nothing I could do seemed to fill me out and I'd come home as thin as ever. Tiriac used to say that I looked as though I was walking on my hands, because my legs were as thin as my arms. He'd then poke my ribs and wonder where on earth my muscles were. Obviously none of this did much good for my confidence.

In 1965, aged nearly nineteen, I was finally allowed to travel to the West. The Federation had obviously realized that it was worth sending me abroad, and, from the start, they gave me total freedom to go wherever I wanted (or, at least, to wherever I could get invited). This really was a gift from God. I was always aware of how fortunate I was to be granted such freedom, which was not available to other sportsmen from Romania – and from other Communist countries – who were very restricted in their travel. Of course, I was also aware that this freedom could be taken away. But, by being able to travel and do my sport to a high level, I had access to a better life and to one that my countrymen could never hope to have. Being a promising tennis player, though, did not make much difference to my everyday life in Romania. I still lived at home, and, although we did not have the diversity of food of the West, we did not have the food shortages that we had suffered in the Fifties. So apart from receiving a bit of extra food and regular amounts of chocolate, the main advantage was that, in that Cold War period, I was suddenly gaining the freedom to come and go as I pleased outside the Iron Curtain.

The first few trips I made were to countries such as Egypt and India. Hardly places that symbolized the glamorous Western lifestyle, but, in the beginning, the only thing I thought about was tennis. I had no time or money to go exploring very much beyond the club. In Egypt, Tiriac and I would play for several weeks in a row, going from one tournament to another. I loved Egypt, the people were so kind, and the club in Cairo – the Gezira Club – was a beautiful English club with a great tradition going back a hundred years. The tournament there was the start of the European circuit, and good players would come and play.

That first year, I played the Australian Ken Fletcher. He was an excellent doubles player who won the Wimbledon men's and mixed doubles titles. In my match with him, my shoes were so bad that I had no grip at all, and I was slipping and sliding all over the place, like I was on ice. There was only one thing for it: off went the shoes. After that, it was easy. Game, set, and match to me. Fletcher couldn't believe it. He'd been beaten, not only by some skinny unknown Romanian but also by one who was wearing socks as well. I'm sure he drowned his sorrows with a few beers that night.

We would get two Egyptian pounds (20p) a day in pocket money, enough to buy two pairs of shoes. OK, so they were Egyptian shoes but they were still shoes. We would be given one free meal a day at the club, and we would supplement that by buying all the exotic fruit, such as oranges (for us these were exotic), which cost so little out there. We would usually stay in small, very basic hotels or with English families, who took good care of us. But once or twice, because we had basically run out of money, Ion decided it would be good to sleep on the beach. It was hot, he figured, so we washed at the club, bought food and ate dinner on the beach and settled down to sleep outdoors. Why not? Well, actually, it was terrible, that's why not, with sand getting everywhere inside our clothes, so luckily he soon went off that idea.

My game around that time was unorthodox and relied heavily on my speed and anticipation around the court. I had a very loopy forehand, no serve, and no power in my shots. I just used to run everything down. This made my opponents mad, but there was not much else I could do. I also loved to drop-shot, lob, and try out crazy shots that my opponents were not expecting.

Because I'd never been shown how to hold a racket, my grips were not perfect, particularly the backhand grip, and this did not give me the ideal backhand, like Laver's or Emerson's. I also held (and still do) the racket so that the end was in the palm of my hand, rather than emerging beyond. If you look at photos of other players, you can usually see the tip of the racket handle, whereas with me you cannot. The advantage was that I could play with much more wrist, and, throughout my career, this enabled me to get shots back with the much heavier wooden rackets that everyone used – shots that other players could not return. Consequently, I developed both a very strong wrist and great touch.

As for the anticipation, you cannot teach that to anyone. All I knew was that I had a sixth sense, particularly at the net, about where the ball would go. If you put me with my back to the net and hit ten balls, eight times out of ten I would turn the right way to hit the ball. Martina Hingis was the same, and that's partly what made her such a great player. Nowadays, players so rarely come to the net that they cannot have that anticipation. They will stay in the middle and wait for the shot to be hit before moving, whereas I would start to move as the shot was being hit – and sometimes even before – because I was usually right about which direction it was going in.

Slowly, my experience grew and I began to win a few matches and to do well with Tiriac in doubles. At first, he told me he would have preferred to play doubles with other players – even my brother who was closer in age to him than I was – because I was not helping his results, but gradually we started to improve on court and to get closer off court. His influence over me began to grow and, at that time, I used to lap up everything he said and copy everything he did. He would look after our spending money and give me just enough to buy something to eat – another great way to stay skinny – although if I really wanted to buy myself a T-shirt or something, and we had enough money at the end of the week, he would allow me to do so. Usually, though, he made very sure that I did not spend all my money at once and that I saved what I could, not that there was usually much left over. But it was advice that I have carried with me to this day. He'd say it was better to put the money in the bank, where it would grow slowly but surely, than to invest it in something crazy which might or might not work.

When it came to tennis, Ion was also the first to recognize that his success was down not so much to talent as to sheer hard work and determination. This was fine, except that he was sometimes so determined to win at all cost that it became very well known on the tour that he would use various tricks to obtain an advantage over an opponent. Tricks such as staring long and hard at him when he'd won a good rally, or breaking up his rhythm either by slowing down or speeding up play between points. Gamesmanship was a word that Ion knew well, and many people think that he deliberately taught me all the tricks in his book. I suppose in some cases he did, but in others I just watched and learned. If it worked for him, then I might use it on a later occasion, though I was not always conscious that I'd seen Ion use it first.

In those early years, I was happy to work hard and practise for hours. I did not see it as 'work', just as total enjoyment. If ever Tiriac had to go rushing off court during a practice session to make a phone call or whatever, he would return a quarter of an hour later to find that, to amuse myself, I had been hitting lobs to myself, jumping over the net to retrieve them, then hitting another lob back over, jumping the net again, and so on, trying to see how long I could keep the rally going without the ball bouncing twice. It was all just a game.

Although I was totally at ease on the tennis court, I was still hopelessly shy off it and didn't say much to anyone. I took the view that no-one was interested in what little I had to say. Winning gives you confidence in yourself as a person, and as I was not winning anything I was not confident. As for women, I was physically incapable of looking any of them in the eye, still less to lay a finger on them. God knows I was interested and I liked looking at them, but I was still not able to go any further. In Romania, I had had a few fumbles with one or two girls but that had never led to anything, partly because I was away a lot and partly because I felt so unattractive. Skinny and with no muscles to speak of, who on earth would want to go to bed with me, I thought? I avoided what I assumed would be a humiliating refusal by never putting myself in the situation of asking.

My two trips to Roland Garros in Paris, in spring 1966, proved to be a breakthrough for me, both professionally and personally. As a child brought up to play clay-court tennis, Roland Garros was my Mecca. It was the biggest tournament for Europeans, and the one that I had dreamed of playing and occasionally that I had even dared to dream of winning. Walking through those historic gates, seeing the distinctive grey concrete stadium, knowing that those French Musketeers had won here so many times, thrilling the crowds for years, all this was unbelievably exciting. Unlike today's players, I have always been fascinated by the history of tennis, by the great champions of the past and how they managed to play. Even when I first started to travel – and maybe because as a child I had been starved of information about tennis – I had nothing but respect and admiration for everything these past champions had achieved, even though their style of play and equipment were totally different. Despite that, they played fantastic tennis. When you think that, not only were players such as René Lacoste playing in long trousers, but also their rackets did not even have leather on the grip. They played with just wooden shafts. Incredible. I don't know how they held the racket. That's why a visit to the Roland Garros museum, which opened in 2003, is a trip all tennis fans should make, to appreciate how exceptional these champions were.

So when I was selected to play Davis Cup for Romania against France in Paris, I could not wait. As anyone from a Communist country will tell you, it was always made clear that representing your country in any sport was the highest honour for any citizen and what really mattered to the country was not what you achieved as individuals but what you achieved as a team, in our case in the Davis Cup. Nothing else really received the same amount of recognition.

The Davis Cup tie itself went by in a blur, but the best bit about the three days was that René Lacoste kindly gave me some matching Lacoste outfits. Never before had I been in matching clothes. I would usually play in whatever clothes I could lay my hands on, even though these were not always in a small enough size for me. The days of my big Adidas sponsorship deal were still far away. Usually, I was a mis-match of Fred Perry and Lacoste shorts and shirts. This time, though, I was in gleaming new all-white Lacoste and this made me very proud. I had also been given four new Slazenger rackets, which again for me was a lot. I felt I was finally joining the big time.

There was a big crowd – or, at least it felt big because I was not used to playing in front of so many people – and the stadium itself felt enormous as well. The only courtside ad was a small sign for Coca-Cola, in contrast to the year I won the French Open, in 1973, when the new sponsors, the Banque Nationale de Paris (BNP), put up their signs in all corners of the court. In 1966, I remember feeling very scared when I walked out onto the Court Central for the first rubber. Although I lost both my matches (and we lost the tie 4–1), I won a couple of sets in one of my singles and Tiriac and I lost the doubles only in five sets. I must have played reasonably well because I impressed both René Lacoste and Toto Brugnon, one of the other Musketeers. So much so that they encouraged me after the tie was over and said they would put in a good word for me so that I would be invited to play the French Open the following month. They were as good as their word, and, sure enough, the invitation came through shortly after. I was eternally grateful that they gave me a chance, because in those days young players relied on such acts of kindness to get them into tournaments.

One month later, I was back at Roland Garros, this time playing my first grand slam tournament. This is a huge step for any player, anyway, but for me it was an even bigger one because I had never even played a junior grand slam event. I was going into the experience totally cold. Yet, I was just one month short of my twentieth birthday. More incredibly, I did not play my first US Open until 1969, when I was already twenty-three. Compare that to today's players, who have usually peaked by that age, and you get an idea of quite how late I started my proper career.

In those days, the Romanian Tennis Federation organized all our travel and hotels. During the two weeks of the French Open, Tiriac and I were checked into a small hotel, called Le Petit Murat, near the Porte d'Auteuil and the Bois de Boulogne, where the Stade Roland Garros is situated. Despite having to share a double bed with Ion and having to tramp down the corridor to the bathroom, I thought this hotel was great. Opposite was a restaurant, Chez André, where we would have dinner every night. The owner was a typical Frenchman with a yellow, unfiltered Gauloise permanently hanging out of the corner of his mouth. His set menu never changed: we'd have either *tête de veau pressée* (a sort of terrine made from veal's head) or *oeuf mayonnaise*, followed by *steak frites* or *poulet frites*. And all for a few francs. Also near the hotel was a cinema, and if we weren't playing we'd go twice a day to the movies. Tiriac and I used to love going to watch films, usually action ones because it was less important to understand all the words. We have been to cinemas all over the world, from Bombay to Philadelphia. This is one of the main ways we learnt our English, though some might argue, given my English, that I can't have been paying too much attention to the dialogue.

I managed to pass two rounds in the singles, which was not bad, before being beaten by the South African-born Cliff Drysdale, who by then was a naturalized American. But really I was just so happy to be playing that I wasn't all that disappointed. For the first time, I was seeing some of the great names of tennis, such as the Spaniard Manolo Santana and the Italian Nicola Pietrangeli. I also shared the same changing rooms as them, practised on adjoining courts, and ate at a nearby table. Some of them, like my hero Roy Emerson, even said 'hello' to me, although usually I was barely able to mumble 'hello' back because my English was so bad.

In the doubles, Tiriac and I began a run of victories that, against everyone's expectations and certainly ours, brought us to the men's doubles final. For a first grand slam tournament, I couldn't believe it. I managed to get a call through to my parents in Romania to tell them my exciting news, but, as was typical of them, they were very low key about it all. Throughout my career, they never showed the slightest interest in what I was up to. Even at my peak, my father would sometimes casually say: 'Someone told me you won a tournament,' but he wouldn't actually ask what I'd won. They never came once to watch me, even when we played our Davis Cup final in Bucharest in 1972. Occasionally, they'd see me on television but more by accident than by intention. It's strange, I know, but they simply weren't interested. They were pleased with what I did, of course, but they never thought of supporting me by coming to see me. I understood what they were like, though, and maybe it would have put more pressure on me if I'd had to worry about them at tournaments.

Because we were not even seeded, Tiriac and I would be scheduled on the farthest outside courts at Roland Garros. We would stand at the back door of the changing rooms, which looked out onto those courts, and we could see the matches finishing and work out when we were due on. Then we'd trot out and play in front of a handful of people. So suddenly to be in the doubles final, on Centre Court, was a big difference. Thank God I'd played the Davis Cup tie the month before, or I would probably have died of nerves. Our opponents were the American Davis Cup pair Clark Graebner and Denis Ralston, and they were too strong for us, beating us in straight sets, 6–3, 6–3, 6–0, but I was so happy to have made this big step that I didn't care too much about the score.

Getting to the men's doubles final called for a celebration, but our small daily allowance would not stretch to what we did next. We had a Romanian friend called Gheorghe, who lived in Paris and who had supported us throughout the tournament by buying us dinner and things. So that evening he and Tiriac decided to take me to Les Halles.

'Come on, there's a good bar there, we meet some nice girls, there's a nice hotel above.'

Fine, I thought, as long as I don't have to pay for the drinks. So off we go. Sure enough, the bar's fine and the girls are beautiful.

'Which one do you like?' asks Ion.

'Well, all of them,' I reply, innocently.

'No, stupid, which one do you want to sleep with? What did you think they were all doing here, going up and down the stairs like that?'

Gheorghe is falling about laughing by this time, and I'm in total shock.

'Who's going to pay?' I worry.

'It's OK, Gheorghe has everything sorted,' answers Ion, irritated that I was even thinking about this.

So eventually I pick out a pretty girl. She has long dark hair, typical Sixties' make-up, with lots of black eyeliner. And up we go. I'm so nervous I can hardly swallow. She asks how I am ('How do you think I am?' I feel like saying), but as I don't speak much French I barely answer back. I start to get undressed . . . and try not to think of what I would have done with the money if Gheorghe had just given it to me. I can tell you that the going rate here was worth about a week's room rate at Le Petit Murat.

I'm not going to say any more about my first experience with a woman – not surprising, surely? – except to say that I was out before Ion. When he eventually padded back down, he looked at me, raised his thick eyebrows expectantly, and all I did was smile like hell and raise my thumb.

So that's how I got laid first time. Not original, I know, but, hey, quite common in those days when nice girls did not always do as much as you would like them to. Anyway, I can think of worse ways to lose one's virginity. Plus, as I have already said, I was so shy, I was having problems even getting physically close enough to a girl to look her in the eye. Usually, I'd look somewhere over her left shoulder. The truth is, when you have no money, your looks aren't great, your body's too thin and you don't speak the local language, let's face it, you're not a great catch. Even I could see that. And Ion was getting to a stage of despair seeing me eye up the girls and never make a move. So I think he did us both a favour by getting that hurdle out the way in a pretty painless fashion. After that, it's fair to say that I quickly started making up for lost time.

All in all, Paris in 1966 was good to me. I'd taken two huge steps forward in my life, one professional, one personal, and both had been fantastic. It's no wonder that, from that moment on, Paris became my favourite city in the world and the one, after Bucharest, in which I feel the most at home.

CHAPTER THREE

1966–1969

'Have you ever seen this fucking guy play?'
asked the Spanish Davis Cup captain.

My next stop after Paris was to the unknown shores of England. I had heard so much over the years about Wimbledon and its famous grass that I had no idea what to expect. I had also been told how bad the food was, how traditional the tournament was, and how you had to bow to all members of the royal family. Such a big deal was made of this last thing that I was really scared I might come face to face with the Queen one day, not recognize her, and forget to bow.

For many tournaments, Tiriac and I had to write to the tournament referee, or director, hoping that he would give us an invitation. There were no official rankings – not like now, when it's very clear which players can get into the draw of a tournament. At my level, I had to send what was, in effect, my CV, making a case for why I should be asked to play their tournament. It was like applying for a job except that, instead of being interviewed, my past performance in recent events, or in their event the previous year, would be examined. Of course, if you knew the tournament referee personally, or if you had sent a nice note to the tournament director's wife, thanking her for everything she had done for you that week (you hoped she could remember who you were), then you might be looked at more favourably next time around. Similarly, if you were put up at the home of a tournament volunteer, as often happened in some countries such as India, it was important to thank them for their hospitality. We soon got used to sending off these notes in broken English and hoping that they led to something the following year. One way or the other, a lot of invitations to young players such as myself worked by personal recommendations.

Luckily, by 1966, Tiriac's status in tennis was such that he was starting to get invited to tournaments without having to ask. At one stage, he was one of the top players in Europe, so they would even offer him a small financial guarantee, in the region of $200 (although it was illegal at the time), to come and play their event. He would then say: 'You give Ilie $100 as well. If not, I'm not coming.' Never one to beat about the bush, was Ion. And because tournaments began to notice that we often got better crowds watching us play than watching others play singles, they paid up and we started to get invited a bit more often.

When it came to Wimbledon, though, it was another matter. Captain Mike Gibson ruled the roost, in those days. A typical, buttoned-up Englishman, whose career had been in an army quite different from the one I knew in Romania, he was known to be fond of whisky. When players asked me, in the months before the tournament, whether I was playing Wimbledon, I'd say: 'Yes, I hope so,' and they'd reply: 'Don't forget to buy Captain Gibson a bottle of whisky.' I got the impression that, every year, he must have received dozens of bottles and that they always went down well – and quickly.

England was totally bewildering to me, although I didn't stay long, because my Wimbledon, both in singles and doubles, was over in a few days. Tiriac and I shared a small room in a £1 a night bed & breakfast on the Cromwell Road, in West London. The road is a noisy four-lane highway, with lorries and buses thundering past our window day and night, and our accommodation was near the British Airways terminal (now a big supermarket), just before Earls Court Road and the flyover that takes you out to Heathrow. The following year, 1967, we moved up-market and splashed out on separate rooms in a B&B near Gloucester Road, a bit further into town, though still on that terrible Cromwell Road. I didn't make it to a proper hotel in London until 1969.

I remember finding the whole business of driving on the left very scary and had to be really careful crossing the road. As for Wimbledon itself, the first time I saw the grass I was totally confused. It looked like a carpet. I didn't think it was possible to play on it and I couldn't work out what was the real tennis, the one on clay or the one on grass. My 1st round opponent was the Brazilian Thomas Koch, a useful player but one who only ever managed to beat me on this one occasion, losing to me eight times in total in later years.

I was scheduled on an outside court, number 9, one of those where there are just a couple of benches for spectators to sit on and a constant movement of people walking around. Unfortunately, the chair umpire was a guy who had been a line judge during my doubles final at Roland Garros a couple of weeks before. I think I had thrown a ball at him or something during that match. Whatever it was I had done, he didn't say anything at the time, but when it came to my match against Koch he went for it. He gave me a grand total of forty-two foot faults. That was it. I lost every service game and lost the match 6–2, 6–0, 6–0. He had upset me very much, but that first year I had decided to say nothing and do what I was told, so I did not complain. Once I got good, though, I would never stand for that sort of treatment again. In any event, I wanted to disappear fast after that match, and I left the tournament without once having bowed to anyone royal.

After that, the Romanian Tennis Federation thought it would be good for me to learn a bit more how to play on grass, so they sent Tiriac and me to India for couple of months at the beginning of 1967. The trouble was, the official surface there wasn't grass – it was cow shit. Literally. They'd get the cow shit, spread it out over the court, and wait for it to dry. So it was more like dried earth than anything that grew in south London. We didn't care, though. We played on anything, anywhere. Over the next three years, we visited the length and breadth of India, from Amritsar, with its beautiful golden temple, to Bombay, from Calcutta to New Delhi. It was so hot that matches would be played early in the morning. Despite this, and because tennis was very popular in India at the time, fans would turn out in their thousands to cheer and encourage their top players, Premjit Lall and Jaidip Mukerjea, who were two good players. So there was always a great atmosphere at these tournaments.

We would often stay with families who were keen on tennis. They could be from any nationality, it did not matter to us. Mainly, they were either local Indian families or expatriate English ones, though we did once stay in a police station. The rooms were above the actual station and we could not hear what was going on below, but it still meant we had to walk through the police station itself, past strange-looking people, every time we left our rooms. The English families led a typically colonial lifestyle: afternoon tea was served by the Indian servant, and English-style, well-cooked roast beef was often on the menu at dinner. The Indian families were also nice to stay with, although we avoided eating the curries. This sometimes made things difficult at dinner time, and I remember once having nothing but fried eggs and Coca-Cola for about two weeks, in an effort not to catch anything terrible.

One evening, in Calcutta, we went to a party and I was very shocked, because they came round with plates and food and everyone ate with their hands, something I certainly was not used to doing. I realized it was a tradition there to eat like that, and, as I did not want to offend my hosts, I just got on with it and dug in with my fingers too. I had learnt, early on, that when in Rome . . .

It reminds me of the story told me by the French Interior Minister Dominique de Villepin, who I know well. President Chirac, on some foreign trip to an African country, finds himself at the traditional banquet where finger bowls are placed to the side of each guest, because the food that evening is rather messy to eat. So far, so good. Everyone dips their fingers daintily and regularly into the finger bowls. It is only at the end of the meal, when Chirac's African host drinks the contents of his finger bowl, that Chirac realizes with alarm that he is going to have to do the same, because the rest of the African delegation have in the meantime followed suit. So down the President's throat the dirty liquid goes, like a bitter medicine, while the President tries hard to pretend he is sipping his country's best Bordeaux.

On the whole, we managed to avoid stomach disasters: in the first year Tiriac did fall ill, and in the second I did, but luckily not too badly in either case. Over the years, my stomach has managed to become immune to most bugs, but

I am also very careful and avoid eating salads and drinking the local water unless I am absolutely sure it is safe to do so.

After we'd finished playing tennis for the day, we would almost always seek out the local cinema and go and see whatever English language film was on. One evening, we were sitting in the circle, quietly watching the action on screen, when I suddenly felt something run across my feet. I leapt out of my seat, just as I saw a long tail disappearing under one of the nearby seats.

'A rat, a rat!' I screamed at Ion.

'What are you talking about, a rat?' he replied, exasperated.

'There, look! Look!' I pointed in terror at this large hairy animal watching us carefully as it gnawed away at something nearby.

'You're right. Shit, let's get out of here.'

And we ran out of the cinema, as fast as our legs could carry us.

In India, Tiriac and I used to play singles, doubles, mixed, anything, because they gave us a little bit more money every time we played an extra event. One day, I partnered a turban-wearing, eighteen-year-old Indian player called Jasjit Singh for a men's doubles. After the match, he asked me if I could play with his mum, in mixed doubles. I did a quick mental calculation and figured she must be about thirty-six or thirty-seven.

'How good's your mum?'

'She's number 2 in India,' he replied.

'OK,' I said. Then I saw her shuffling onto court, a vision in a wonderful pink sari. 'What's happening, can you run? Will your sari be OK?' I asked, worried.

'Oh yes, no problem, no problem, no problem,' she replied, smiling calmly.

But it was a problem, a problem, a problem, because I was the only one who ran that day. I don't know what she was number 2 of, but it can't have been of India. I swear she didn't run once for the ball and, sure enough, her sari stayed firmly on.

In another mixed doubles match, this time a final, Tiriac was on the other side of the net. I had broken the strings on all my rackets by this stage of the week, and, in those days, there were no stringers at tournaments. There was not much you could do in such a situation, other than ask to borrow someone else's racket. So Tiriac lent me his last spare racket. At one point, he broke a couple of strings on his own racket and asked me for his last good racket back. So I took his broken racket and proceeded to beat him with it. He was not amused. Things got worse when, in the men's final, later that day, I borrowed a terrible Indian racket – it did have strings but it was a really odd shape – and beat him again. Then he really was mad with me.

Along with Egypt and Italy, India remains one of the countries that I remember with most affection. Not only did we enjoy the hospitality of the people when we played there, but we also managed to get a sense of what those countries were like beyond just the tennis. Normally, when I played tournaments, I was so busy playing singles, doubles, and mixed doubles that I had no time or energy to go visiting the sights. But I spent so many weeks in these countries in the early years that I felt I actually had time to get to know them a bit.

Our Davis Cup encounter with France in 1966 led to another lucky development in my career. The referee for the tie was Signor Martini, who was high up in the Italian Tennis Federation. As with the Musketeers René Lacoste and Toto Brugnon, I obviously impressed him enough for him to recommend me to his Federation, and this secured me an invitation the following year to come and play a series of tournaments in southern Italy plus, best of all, the Italian Open at the famous Foro Italico in May. This was fantastic for me and, for the next few years, I spent April and May playing in places such as Catania and Palermo in Sicily, Reggio Calabria and Naples, before heading up to Rome. The Sicilians and the southern Italians really adopted Tiriac and me, because we quickly picked up the language. We made a good friend in Sicily, who owned an orange plantation, and he used to invite us over for dinner every night and bring us basketfuls of oranges.

The rest of the time, Tiriac and I would often buy pizza and eat it on the nearest beach before heading back to whichever low-cost hotel we were staying in that week. As anyone who has been to Italy knows, the country is full of these pizza shops where you can buy pizza by the weight. There are only four flavours, and the pizzas themselves are incredibly cheap but totally delicious if you are ravenously hungry and have little money.

In Rome, we stayed with a guy who became a close friend, Francesco d'Alessio. His father was very rich and owned racehorses. He even named a couple after Tiriac and me in the end, though I don't think my horse could run much because he never won a race in his life. Francesco used to take us out to Trastevere, the old and bohemian part of Rome near the Vatican. In typical Italian fashion, we always seemed to be about twenty noisy people for dinner – tennis players, friends of his, anyone he picked up along the way. Most of the time, I had no idea who half of them were and where they came from, but we always had a great time. At the end of the evening, we would simply call for '*il conto*', divide it up, and go our separate ways until maybe the next evening.

On other occasions, Tiriac and I would take a bus up to the Via Veneto, the most glamorous street in Rome at the time. We'd first of all go to the cinema, then we'd sit at Doney's café, the best café to be seen at, and ogle the girls. We didn't chat any up because we still had no money. No fame, no money, no action, as far as the girls were concerned. They simply weren't interested.

In the spring of 1967, Ion and I returned to Bucharest for a Davis Cup tie against Spain. We were in Lugano, Switzerland the week before and we must have overspent our allowance, because we no longer had enough money for the plane trip back. So we took the train instead. This was no ordinary journey, though. It took something like twenty-eight hours, involved God knows how many changes in God knows how many countries, and sitting on backside-numbing wooden benches for most of the trip. We managed not to let anyone into our compartment, and we took it in turns to sleep, three hours each, in the luggage net above our heads.

When I eventually staggered off the train in Bucharest, I was not in the best shape to pit myself against Manolo Santana, the player who, along with Roy Emerson, was one of my all-time idols. He was the number 1 clay-courter at the time, a winner of the French and US Opens, the reigning Wimbledon champion, and the guy who really invented the topspin lob, which I was later to make one of my trademark shots. Manolo could lob on both sides, so, after watching him practise it and even getting to hit with him for a bit (it was unusual to be asked to practise with an opponent), I went away and practised it myself for hours and hours, because no matter who you are you only learn to do those shots by practising them really hard. I still assumed I was going to get wiped off court, so I thought I don't care,

I'm just going to try to copy exactly what he does. If he drop-shots me, I'll drop-shot him back; if he lobs, I'll lob.

So the match starts. I break him first game. 'Jesus, good start,' I thought. Next thing I know, I've stretched out an easy 6–0 3–0 lead. The crowd are going wild because this is the best clay-court player in the world and I've got him totally bewildered. The Spanish captain, Jaime Bartroli, turns round to his players: 'Have you ever seen this fucking guy play?' They all shake their heads. Mystery. Manolo was playing with Tretorn rackets, which he was testing because he was trying to sign up with them, but in his bag he still had his old Slazenger ones. I can tell you, after that he switched pretty quickly back to Slazenger ones and finished me off in four sets.

We eventually lost the tie 3–2 (Tiriac and I won our doubles and I beat Gisbert in one of the singles). At the traditional post-match dinner, I made sure I went up to Santana and said: 'You know where I learned that shot? Watching you. And practising.' He laughed and very kindly signed his photo for me '*para un futuro campion del tennis*'. I still have it to this day. It meant a lot to me that a player of his reputation should be so nice to me. At tournaments afterwards, he would always smile, say 'hello', chat to me, and this is an attitude that I always tried to adopt with young players when I became successful, and I hope I carried it through.

Although we were technically amateur sportsmen, there was still a gap between the sort of money I was subsisting on and what the top amateurs, such as Santana and Newcombe, were making. It was commonly accepted that they would be paid appearance money for every tournament and, in those days, they could easily make $500–$1,000 per week – good money, in other words. The player restaurants at grand slam events such as Wimbledon were the best places for tournament directors to get together 'informally' with players and secure what was really under-the-table money. The game's governing body, the International Lawn Tennis Federation (ILTF), turned a blind eye, and everyone was happy with what was clearly a very hypocritical situation.

At that time, I was never in the category of those paid large appearance fees, but Ion, by 1967, did manage to get some tournaments to pay us small amounts to turn up and play. Otherwise, the only payment I received was from my Federation, who gave me a weekly allowance to cover my expenses and my hotel accommodation. They would also pay for flights and for me to play in the Davis Cup. They insisted that Tiriac and I practised for a week before the actual week of the tie, so every Davis Cup tie took up two weeks of our schedule. The various ties added up to ten to fourteen weeks a year, because we usually reached the later rounds of the competition. Tiriac and I took the view that this was a small price to pay for total freedom to travel the rest of the time. Later on, when we both turned pro, our Federation's only requirement in terms of prize money was that we played the Davis Cup for free. We were allowed to keep all the rest of our income – a huge favour for a Communist country to grant to two of its sportsmen.

The following year, 1968, brought earth-shattering changes, not just to various parts of Europe but also to the world of tennis. Czechoslovakia tried to distance itself from the Soviet Union that spring, and all of us who came from Communist countries watched developments carefully. Nicolae Ceauşescu, who had become president of the State Council in Romania the year before, was determined to pursue an anti-Soviet policy from the start, so he resisted the USSR's pressure to support them militarily, which of course made him very popular in the West.

Tennis, meanwhile, had increasingly developed two parallel worlds, the amateur and the professional. Great players such as Laver, Rosewall and Emerson had established their reputation on the former tour and then turned pro to improve their bank balance. Finally, in 1968, those who ran the game, including people such as Herman David, the Chairman of the All England Club, decided that this crazy situation had gone on long enough and they announced that some previously amateur tournaments would be open to all. This allowed us to play each other in some tournaments at least and to measure, truly, who were the best players in the world. It was another couple of years, however, before the distinction between amateur and professional players finally ended.

The first open major, the French Open, was in May '68. At the same time, there was chaos in the streets of Paris, and the whole country ground to a halt as it fell victim to a general strike and to student and workers' demonstrations. Public transport no longer worked, airports were closed, and in Paris the streets were piled high with litter bags, because the dustmen were on strike as well. The tournament organizers were determined that the French Open should still go ahead, so they were forced to lay on coaches to come and get us in Belgium. As a result, the crowds that year were huge, probably because people were not at work, and the atmosphere was like that of a happy siege, if such a thing can exist. It was made all the better because players were at long last reunited with those who had turned pro some years before, so for many it was like finding long-lost friends. I loved the way so many of them played – Laver, Rosewall, Gonzales – but my favourite was still Emerson. He served and volleyed on every point, and he was also having fun and still winning. I used to think, why aren't I winning, because I'm joking as well?

One evening, Tiriac and I had gone to a bar near our hotel. Because it was close to the Bois de Boulogne, an area used a lot by prostitutes, most of the girls in there were actually on the game (by then, I had worked out why they were continually going up and down the stairs). We got talking to one who told us her life story, and, by the end of the evening, I felt so guilty about not paying for her services that I emptied my pockets, gave her the money I had on me, and gave her the tracksuit top I was wearing. Tiriac thought I was completely crazy, but she had a kid at home, she was a young girl, and business was obviously not good in those troubled times, so I figured maybe this could allow her to buy some food for her baby. Maybe I was naïve and she just went and spent all the money on herself, but that's what I'm like. I'm very trusting and a bit of a soft touch, which, of course, has sometimes counted against me.

That year, Tiriac and I reached the semifinal of the men's doubles at Roland Garros, where we were beaten in four sets by the legendary Laver and Emerson. So, on the whole, we were pleased with our first tournament with the pros, even though I had lost in the 2nd round of the singles to the Australian Dick Crealy.

We got ready to move on to Lugano, full of hope for the summer months ahead. That night, however, I started to feel a sharp pain in one side of my lower back, and by the morning I was writhing and moaning in agony. As I was still sharing a bed with Tiriac, he eventually got fed up and began to kick and shove me to stay quiet, because he thought, in his semi-comatose state of sleep, that I was having some bad dreams. It was only when I woke him up completely with my screams that he realized something was seriously wrong. He immediately called a doctor, who told me I had developed a kidney stone and confirmed that, until it passed, I would continue to be in agony. Great. He gave me some strong painkillers, which helped. The stone obviously dislodged itself later that day into another part of my kidney, and I was able to breathe again. Still shaken from the ordeal and worried about the doctor's prediction that my problem would return and probably need an operation at some stage, I set off with Ion for Switzerland.

For the first few days, I seemed OK, but then, the night before my quarterfinal against the Indian Mukerjea, the pain started again. It felt as if I had a knife in me. Kidney stones are known to give pain that is excruciating and, apparently, worse than many women experience in childbirth. I was barely conscious, such was the agony. If Ion had not been there, I honestly don't know what I would have done. It was clear that I needed to be repatriated to Romania very quickly. Ion had to stay behind because he was still in the tournament (which he went on to win), so he arranged for a doctor to come at once while he set to work organizing my journey back. The only way – and to this day I don't know how I managed – was for me to take a train to Zurich, fly from Zurich to Budapest, wait six hours, change planes, and finally fly on to Bucharest, arriving at midnight. I thought I was going to die. I do remember, though, that the doctor had given me a massive painkilling injection before I left Lugano and that I was swallowing painkillers during the whole of the journey as if they were M&Ms.

As soon as I arrived home, I was admitted to a military hospital and operated on at once. But although I felt relief no longer to be doubled up in pain, I was soon very depressed to realize that I was going to be out of action for weeks, if not months. I spent a month recovering in hospital from what, in those days, was quite a complicated and serious operation. I lost so much weight in the three months I was off that, at

65 kg, I really looked like a skeleton by the time I re-emerged fully on the circuit late that autumn. In the meantime, I had missed the whole of the summer, including Wimbledon and the US Open – which I had still not played – and was worried that I would find it difficult to get back to the level I had reached.

To cheer myself up while I was convalescing and practising, I started driving around Bucharest in my new car, a green Fiat 125 that I had bought the year before in Germany (cheaper than buying it in Italy). I was so proud of it that I used to drive around town whenever I could, even though for the first year or so I did not actually have my licence. Well, I figured the best way to learn was to practise. Of course, one day I got caught, so I went straight to pass my test and get a licence.

The year 1969 was another breakthrough one for me. After my traditional visit to India, where I won three tournaments, I headed to the USA for my first trip to the other side of the pond. My first stop was Philadelphia, where Ed and Marilyn Fernberger had run a big tournament for years, at the Spectrum Stadium. They had this huge ten-bedroom house where they put up a lot of the players, like Newcombe, Roche and all the Australians – plus me. Marilyn had told me to take a cab from the airport to her house. That was fine, but what she didn't know was that I had no money and I was arriving at one in the morning. The house itself turned out to be miles from the airport, so the cab fare was really expensive, something like $7. So here we were, the cab driver and I, crawling around the neighbourhood looking for this house in the middle of the night. On his wing mirror, the cab driver had this huge light that faced sideways and that allowed him to look at the door numbers, like a sort of searchlight. I remember being impressed by what I took to be a clever American invention, because normally when you're looking for a house number in the dark, the car's headlights are pointing straight ahead and you can't see a thing. Eventually we found where the Fernbergers lived. It was 2 a.m. by now, and I woke up the entire household. I then had to explain in bad English that I had no money for the cab fare. 'Here, give him $10,' said Marilyn generously, whilst I, of course, felt like keeping the $3 change. It was an embarrassing start to my stay.

After Philadelphia, I had been signed by Bill Riordan, who organized one of the first pro tours in the USA and who was in direct competition with Jack Kramer, who ran one of the others. Bill looked after me in those early years; he was like an agent but also a friend. He put me up in his house in Salisbury, Maryland and lent me an old car to drive around the first week, until, that is, the engine caught fire one day outside the stadium. Firemen had to rush to put out the flames, while I was standing there helplessly, worrying about who would pay for all this. I have to say that, although cosmopolitan Washington DC was not far away, the good people of Salisbury clearly thought I was a real oddity and were fascinated by this Communist alien who had landed among them. They asked me all sorts of questions. What was life in Budapest really like (like many people, they were convinced the Hungarian capital was in fact in Romania), did we have electricity, cars, that sort of thing. Were we still in the Middle Ages, in other words. I always answered politely and even showed them that I could use a knife and fork. Still, the people were very nice, and the tournament was well organized, so I could not complain.

I was still technically amateur at the time, as far as the Romanian Tennis Federation were concerned, so I was not formally earning prize money. Instead Bill paid me a guaranteed weekly sum, about $50 a week, if I remember rightly, and reimbursed my expenses on top. Later, I would receive as much as $250, as Bill worked out that not only did I entertain the crowds but I would also sign for another pro tour, Lamar Hunt's World Championship Tennis (WCT), if he did not take good care of me.

This was a limbo period for the sport, because, whilst many tournaments were now open, the Davis Cup was still reserved for amateurs. As this was what my Federation cared most about, I myself was not allowed to turn fully professional until a couple of years later, when the Davis Cup finally became open.

Bill's tournaments took me to a few more small American towns on my introductory tour of the USA, towns like Macon, Georgia, deep in the south of the country, and Omaha, Nebraska, where Tiriac and I, in another of his crazy money-saving schemes that lasted a week, slept in a $1-a-night mobile home. Other than noticing that the food portions were pretty big, and the cars and the people even bigger, I did not have too much time to make comparisons between the American and European way of life. I was living and breathing tennis, to the exclusion of almost everything else.

Even when it came to girls, although I was now able to chat them up and get them into bed pretty easily, I have to say that, until I got beaten in the singles, and often even the doubles, I was a good boy. But once I was out of a tournament, assuming I did not win it, which was still often the case, I went out looking for girls. Tennis is a sport where there is no shortage of girls willing to sleep with a player, just for the sheer hell of it. They're tennis groupies. Many of the girls at that time were not interested in anything more than being able to tell their friends what they had done.

I honestly don't think they planned for anything more than that. The notion of kiss-and-tell to the newspapers certainly did not exist, nor, thank God, did the idea of using the media to extract money from a man if she became pregnant. Usually, the most they might want was to hang around with you for the week, or maybe travel around with you for a little, not that I ever allowed the latter. When you visit a different beach every week, why take a bucketful of sand with you from the previous week? This was the late Sixties, and sex was on tap. For those who could get it, sex with no strings attached was quite common. For tennis players, let's just say it was the norm.

So, having finally got rid of my inhibitions a couple of years before, and now that I was earning a little bit and had more confidence, I would usually find myself a girl before the week was out. If I was staying in someone's house, such as the house of a volunteer at the tournament, it could be a bit tricky to smuggle the girl in and out, though sometimes they had a suitably willing and attractive daughter so I didn't need to worry.

The last tournament on that winter American tour of 1969 took me to Colombia, and the coastal town of Barranquilla. Colombia was not the drug capital of the world in those days, and good players used to turn up for this event. My week in Colombia was one of my most successful so far, and I won the tournament, even though it was the windiest place I have every played in. I beat two highly rated players, first Mark Cox, then my old adversary Jan Kodes in the five-set final. That gave me a huge boost of confidence, because I realized that I was able to keep up with the top guys. As I headed back to Europe, I felt I had taken another step up in terms of the level I had reached.

Most of the matches back then, both singles and doubles,

were played as best of five sets, unlike now where they are mostly best of three, other than in grand slam tournaments. Also, tournaments usually had men's and women's draws, because the women had not yet developed their own separate tour (this happened in the early Seventies). In any given week, I would play singles and doubles as best of five sets, plus mixed doubles. That is why, when I am asked if I practised a lot during tournaments, I answer that, once I started passing a few rounds, I did a minimal amount of practice – usually about half an hour a day – because I got all the practice I needed by simply playing matches. The doubles were my practice sessions. Fortunately, Tiriac recognized this and let me do as I wanted most of the time. By contrast, Guillermo Vilas, who Tiriac coached and managed in the Seventies, had the capacity to work like a mad dog (and, I should add, was happy to practise for hours every day). My game would have been neutered if I had been on a similar treadmill. I needed to stay fresh mentally in order to play my game that relied on inventiveness, instinct, and speed. Slogging away on a practice court for hours before a match would not have been the way to make me perform at my best.

That said, I remember one year, at Queen's Club, when I was challenged by Roy Emerson, who loved to stay superfit.

'Come on, Ilie, I'm going to jump the net, twenty-five to thirty times with both feet. Can you do that?'

'Sure, that's boring,' I reply dismissively.

'No, come on, try.'

So I start to jump. I quickly get to twenty-five, thirty. Then I just carry on. Fifty, sixty, seventy, no problem. Emerson's just staring at me, really surprised. After jumping it one hundred times, I announce: 'I'm bored, can I stop now?'

He got the point. I suppose I was just lucky that I was

both naturally fit and did not need to practise much once I reached a certain level.

Also, I was very sensible when it came to smoking and drinking. I have never smoked in my life, and I never drank alcohol until I was well into my twenties. I would always drink Coca-Cola, Orangina, or Fanta. I still do. My first alcoholic drink was beer, which I'm afraid to say I liked very much from the moment I drank it, and I do now drink a bit of red wine. But that's it. I'm very careful about how much alcohol I drink.

This was sometimes a problem when we went out with the Aussies, especially John Newcombe and Tony Roche, who Tiriac and I got on very well with. In Paris in 1969, the traditional players' party was held in Montmartre, and the one area where I could not keep up with John and Tony was drink. They really liked the beers, non-stop beers. They never got drunk, they just had this huge capacity for drinking them. That night, I had to stay until 4 a.m., until they'd finished drinking. Looking back, I'm not sure why I didn't just get up and leave, but maybe I was still too shy or needed to share the cab fare back to the hotel. I just remember having to wait hours for them to finally call it a day with the beers before we all headed home.

My relationship with Tiriac remained incredibly close. Usually, wherever he went, I went too. The only difference now was that I was getting results in singles and doubles, whereas his were mainly in doubles. But he was still an enormous influence on me, even though in many ways he is very different from me. It reminds me of the film *The Odd Couple*, with Jack Lemmon and Walther Matthau, because we were such a contrast, both in terms of physique and character. For example, Tiriac stays cool always, he doesn't show his emotions, and his temper doesn't flare up like mine. I have seen him upset on court, but he never reacts like me. He never loses control. Of course, we'd argue on court and off, but never badly, and, in the beginning, he was right because he knew much more than I did. I like to have fun and have never had to force myself to work at my game, whereas he has worked incredibly hard for everything that he has achieved. He has an incredibly dry sense of humour, though, and he stays very deadpan when he makes a joke, not like me. I'll tell a joke and then roar with laughter at it myself.

Tiriac also knew about business, because he is very shrewd and streetwise, though totally honest and generous. He'd talk to people to get the right contracts for me, at a time when I had no sponsors. He got me my contract with Dunlop for my rackets and negotiated appearance money for us in the early days. He was in advance of his time. He was one of the first people to see that tennis was about to become a business, it was going to become more than a sport, so he started to represent players and, later on, to promote tournaments. Despite his limited tennis talents, Ion became a major figure in tennis through his intelligence and foresight.

In other areas of my life, he also influenced me. As soon as we had a bit of money, he taught me to stay in the best hotels and eat in the best restaurants. I remember distinctly the first time I stayed in a good hotel. It was the Cavendish Hotel in Jermyn Street, London, opposite Tramp's nightclub, during our Davis Cup semifinal against Great Britain in summer '69. 'This is the life', I thought, 'I wouldn't mind more of this.' We weren't throwing money away, we just wanted to live a normal life, like the other good players. Tiriac was like a best friend, an older brother, a confidant, a father figure, all those things – in fact, my relationship with him was like a marriage without the sex, and I owe him a lot.

My results were steadily improving, partly because I was no longer just playing on clay but also on the faster hard courts around the world. They suited me well, because I was fast. I was starting to hit with more power, to serve-volley when required, whilst still drop-shotting and lobbing my opponents. I reached the 3rd round at Wimbledon, beating one of the top young Americans, Tom Gorman, on the way, so I was quietly working my way up, not the rankings because they still did not exist but the unofficial list of leading players.

The real advantage of winning a few matches at Wimbledon was that I now felt I had a better idea of how to play grass-court tennis by the time the Romanian team lined up next to Great Britain to play our Davis Cup semifinal on court 1, in mid-August 1969. Britain were favoured to win, simply because, in Mark Cox and Graham Stilwell, they had two experienced grass-court players. A lot depended on how Cox would play and, fortunately for us, he blew it.

He got really nervous. He collapsed against Tiriac in the first match, losing in straight sets. Afterwards, some people thought that Ion's habit of varying the number of times he bounced the ball before serving may have distracted Cox, because he could never tell when Ion was about to serve. Who knows? Stilwell beat Tiriac in straight sets two days later, so it can't have been that bad. My match against Stilwell did not go in my favour, and I lost it in four sets. The score was 1–1 after the first day. Everything to play for, as they say.

The next day's doubles were crucial, and Ion and I were really on form. Whilst Tiriac created openings, I was jumping around the net like a mountain goat, sending angled volleys to all corners of the court, and we both lobbed the British pair the whole time. We were confident, and we worked well as a team, whereas our opponents Cox and Stilwell, being left-handers, were both left-court players with Stilwell having to play on the right. They did not work together well, and we beat them without too much trouble in four sets.

The final day was very tense. With a huge crowd filling every seat on court 1, the result was in doubt until the very end, because Graham Stilwell played inspired tennis to cut through Ion in straight sets. It was all down to me and Cox. I have played so many Davis Cup rubbers, and so often had to score all three points to secure a team win, that I am used to this sort of situation. This doesn't mean that I don't get nervous each time, because I do. But, on this occasion, I think Mark was even more nervous than me. He started well, winning the 1st set 6–3, but after that I calmed down while he got edgy, and I won the next three sets 6–1, 6–4, 6–4. We had done it.

Our captain, Gheorghe Cobzuc, ran onto court and planted a big kiss on my lips to congratulate me (I could have done without that). We had become the first Balkan country, the first Communist country, ever to reach the final of the Davis Cup. This was a huge deal for us. We knew that we would be heroes back home, and that the papers would be full of our exploits.

I now had two really big things to look forward to: firstly, I was finally going to play the US Open at Forest Hills for the first time in my life – and I was very excited about that – and, secondly, the Davis Cup final (or Challenge Round, as it was then called) would take place in Cleveland, Ohio, against the holders, the USA, in September, just five weeks later. I felt

I was continuing to fulfil the promise that I had shown, I was proving to people that I could get results, and the world was really starting to notice me. I was on a steep learning curve, and I was loving every minute.

CHAPTER FOUR

1969–1971

That night, I picked up a girl who admitted that she had a dog with her, and the dog had to come too. 'OK, the dog can come,' I said, dubiously.

I had seen enough American films to have a picture of New York in my head, but nothing I had imagined prepared me for the real thing when I crossed over Brooklyn Bridge and arrived in Manhattan. The incredible skyscrapers, the complete mix of people there, the buzz about the city. I loved it from the start and have always felt very comfortable there. So I was not overawed when I first went to the West Side Tennis Club, Forest Hills, the venue for the 1969 US Open. In fact, the club was very sedate and traditional, and not at all like today's Flushing Meadow venue for the tournament, which is as crazy and noisy as any tournament I know.

The US Open was played on grass in those days (as was the Australian Open), but the courts at Forest Hills were very different from Wimbledon's carpet-like lawns. For a start, the American courts had a lot of bad bounces, but they were also much softer, which meant that, when you played a drop shot, it really sank. This favoured my game and was one of the reasons that I beat Stan Smith, who was already a highly regarded player, on my way to the quarterfinals, where it took Ken Rosewall to stop my progress. The tournament was memorable, because Rod Laver completed his second Grand Slam, winning all four majors in the same year. Don Budge, before the War, is the only other player ever to have done the Grand Slam, so Laver's achievement was unbelievable, and I am sure it will never be equalled.

Soon after, we arrived in Cleveland, Ohio, for the Davis Cup final, the Challenge Round. Why Cleveland? Because, we were told, it had the biggest community of Romanians in the USA. Sure enough, we went to a lot of parties with our expatriate comrades, other Romanians came over especially, and the Romanian ambassador even flew down from Washington for the matches. The stadium itself was next to a school, so I remember finding it difficult to practise with the noise of hundreds of children, who came round to watch the whole time.

What was even less fine was the court. It was meant to be cement, like the majority of courts in the States, but this one had been covered with a sort of shiny paint. It was so shiny, in fact, that you could barely see the ball. When it rained, which it did quite a lot, preventing practice, it became really slippery. It was also a court that was even faster than grass, and this definitely favoured the Americans.

During the tie itself, we had to put up with left-wing and anti-Vietnam demonstrators, who regularly tried to interrupt play. Although they were kept away from us as much as possible, some still managed to get through, shouting from the stands and displaying banners with slogans such as: 'Tennis for the rich, tenements for the poor' and 'Long live Ho Chi Minh, Long live the Vietcong'.

The tie was much closer than the score suggested. On day

one, Arthur Ashe beat me in three close sets, 6–2, 15–13, 7–5 (tie-breaks had not yet been invented). My defeat was partly as a result of the US coach, Denis Ralston, having watched me beat Smith at Forest Hills and having then given Ashe a detailed picture of my game. Then, Ion did everything he could to gain an advantage in his match against Smith. He managed to lead by two sets to one, but eventually went down in five sets. That meant we were 0–2 down.

The doubles the next day was crucial. Ion and I had never yet lost a Davis Cup doubles match, but then neither had the experienced American pair Smith and Bob Lutz, so there was a lot at stake. Unfortunately for us, our opponents were too good that day. Although the match was closer than the score indicates, it was all over in straight sets, 8–6 6–1 11–9. The Americans had gone 3–0 up in rubbers and so had retained the Davis Cup. All we could do in the third day's matches was to salvage some honour.

I was desperate to get at least one point for my country and fought as hard as I could in my match against Smith. I stretched out a two sets to love lead, but Smith was equally desperate to avenge his Forest Hills defeat, so he fought back to two sets all. The final set was long and hard. Four times I had match point, four times Smith managed to save it. Finally, he reached match point himself, and seconds later had won the set 11–9, to take the rubber. I walked off court, bitterly disappointed.

The length of my match against Smith meant that Tiriac's match against Ashe, the last in the tie and an academic match in any case, began late in the afternoon and had to be halted when Ashe was on the verge of winning in the 4th set. The reason was that we had all been invited to meet President Nixon at the White House at ten o'clock sharp the following morning, and we absolutely had to catch our plane that evening. There would have been no question of postponing the meeting, because Ceauşescu was beginning to establish closer relations with America and I think Nixon had just been to Romania the month before. So it was politically important for us to go.

We all lined up on the lawn outside the White House, alongside the American team, and Nixon made his way along the line, shaking our hands. I remember he kept one hand in his pocket the whole time, which looked strange, as if he was hiding something in there. All the Americans were being very formal: 'Hello, Mr President', and all that, but when it came to Arthur's turn he just said: 'Hi, how are you.' Arthur was not going to be overawed. I suspect it had something to do with Nixon being a Republican and Arthur a Democrat.

As for me, of course I was excited to meet Nixon and to go to the White House, but I was not tongue-tied. Not that there was an opportunity to say much, other than 'hello'. I do remember that, as a souvenir, Nixon gave us each a golf ball with his face on it.

As 1969 came to a close, I returned to Bucharest to rest. I had played a record thirty-one tournaments (winning eight singles and six doubles titles), plus six rounds of Davis Cup, with each tie taking two weeks including the ten days' practice we gave ourselves. This was a huge increase on what had gone on the two previous years, when I'd played only twenty tournaments, fewer Davis Cup ties, and won only three titles each year. That meant that in 1969 I had played more than forty weeks of tennis. I had hardly been home, and now I needed badly to reconnect with my family and friends. Home, by now, was a small apartment given to me by the army, which housed only military personnel. But it suited my needs perfectly and allowed me to come and go, at all hours of the day and night, without having to tip-toe past my parents' bedroom.

At the start of the new decade, I set off more confident about the future after the good results of the previous year. In February 1970, I won the US Indoor Championships in Salisbury, Maryland, before moving back to Europe for my traditional southern Italian circuit of tournaments, where I won yet more titles. So I was full of anticipation when I arrived in Rome for the Italian Open at the end of April. Built by Mussolini and adorned with fascist-style marble statues of dubious taste, the Foro Italico is one of the most memorable stadiums on the circuit. It also has a great atmosphere, because the Italians are noisy supporters – they are noisy people anyway, like Romanians. As long as I was not playing one of their compatriots, or in the middle of one of my scenes, they always cheered for me.

I have never been the sort of player to predict boastfully that I am going to beat a guy. But I felt good all week, so I was not surprised to get through to the last four without too much difficulty. There, I got past the tough Yugoslav Nikki Pilic in five sets, and it was my fellow East-European Jan Kodes who awaited me in the final. Kodes went on to win at Roland Garros in Paris a few weeks later, but this time it was I who came out on top, beating him in four sets: 6–3, 1–6, 6–3, 8–6. I was exhausted but exhilarated. The Italian Open was the next biggest tournament after the four majors, so for me to win it was another confirmation that I was now among the best.

After the final, I had to go straight back on court with Tiriac to play our doubles final. He would always watch my singles matches, because he wanted to see what sort of mood I was in for the doubles, which were usually played later in the day. If I was tired, even if I'd won, he'd have to cajole me into playing: 'Come on, do it for me, it's important to win the doubles.' For him, his main earnings were now coming from the doubles, so sometimes he really had to force me onto court. Once I started playing, I was usually OK. But after the singles final that year I was so exhausted and happy that we lost the 1st set of the doubles 6–0 to the Aussies Bowrey and Davidson before I had time to wake up and recover my senses. It took us five long sets finally to get the better of them, and by the end of the day I had played a total of nine sets. Importantly, though, I had won two big titles.

This called for a big celebration. Off I went with Ion to the Via Veneto, where we met up with the Italian player Nicola Pietrangeli and various friends of his. First of all, we all had dinner at one of our favourite restaurants, the nearby Taverna Flavia, run by a guy called Mimmo. He always came to see us play and would scream encouragement: 'Come on, I give you nice food, you have to win.'

We then all moved on to the Jackie O nightclub, the only place to be seen in those Dolce Vita days in Rome. The club is still there, tucked away behind the Excelsior Hotel. Nicola got us in, because he was a member. A winner of successive French Opens in '59 and '60, Nicola was a giant of the game, and, at thirty-five, had just played his last Italian Open. He had an aura about him that made him a superstar in Italy – and still does. He's like his friend, Claudia Cardinale, who I subsequently met a few times. They were both born in Tunis of Italian fathers. Nicola's mother, though, is from Russia, and he happens to share the same birthday, the same year, as my brother, Constantin. Nicola knew everyone, and, as the years went by, we would hang out more and more together, and he would introduce me to many of the well-known friends that he seemed to accumulate around the world.

By the end of a very long night, I had, of course, found a

beautiful girl to take back to my hotel. It wouldn't have been a big celebration otherwise, would it? I had met her in the nightclub, and she said she was an actress. It wasn't until a few days later, when she left a message for me when I was already at my next tournament, that I discovered she also had some fancy title, I think a contessa. I hadn't yet realized that in Italy there are thousands of people with these meaningless titles. Anyway, I was curious, so I called her back and, by the following evening, she had joined me in Naples.

Picture the scene: the romantic bay of Naples, candle-lit dinners, a lot of exercise during the day, followed by more night-time action. Well, it was a bit like that, except that, however beautiful she was, and however much I liked her, I was a bit worried that this was going in a direction that I wasn't quite ready to follow. When she mentioned that we might spend some time that summer at her parents' estate in Tuscany, I thought briefly about saying 'yes'. But when she let slip that her parents would also be there, I admitted: 'I'm afraid, *amore mio,* that I have another tournament to go to, and I am very busy this summer, so that will be difficult.'

So on I moved, to the next town and the next girl. Actually, I did stay in touch with her on and off for about a year, but it was certainly never a proper, serious relationship. I really didn't need one of those, to be honest. All my attention was on my tennis, and the women were just to have fun with, nothing more. I never broke any hearts, though, because I never promised anything. I never kept a girlfriend long enough for her to think that something more long-term might develop. That's the secret, I think. Usually, it was more a question of coming up to a girl – because I liked to be the one to choose, I didn't like it when they ran after me – and I'd ask them out to dinner, and after that it was easy. Then, other times, I'd make all that effort, invite them to the tournament and then nothing would happen. I didn't have any particular chat-up lines, although I sometimes found it worked quite well if I said: 'My problem starts if you say "yes" to me. Then I don't know what to do to you. I get nervous.' But it wasn't a regular line, just something that, in the right situation, would make them laugh and keep them interested.

At Roland Garros in 1970, I found myself seeded number 1 in both the singles and the doubles. I was really proud about that, and I guess it was the reward for having had such a good spring. I reached the quarterfinals in the singles, where I was beaten by the tough American Cliff Richey, despite Richey suffering from cramp in his hand at one stage.

In doubles, Ion and I landed our first major title – it turned out to be Ion's one and only – when we beat two more Americans, Arthur Ashe and Charlie Pasarell in the final. This was great for both of us, and for me it was yet another step up the ladder. People sometimes think that winning this sort of title brings total happiness, and that sportsmen should be able to express the depth of their emotion at such moments. Actually, at that time, what I really thought was: 'Yes, this is good but it doesn't blow my mind. I need to keep going.' Of course I was happy, but that's quite a hard feeling to describe. As winning was something that I was getting used to, winning the doubles title at Roland Garros gave me more the feeling that it was a step in the right direction.

I saw that I was finally catching up all the time I had lost by not playing junior tennis and not joining the circuit properly until I was nearly twenty. The idea, though, that I might one day become number 1 in the world, or that I might win a grand slam title, was not something I was consciously working up to. As for the majors, I thought I could maybe win one, Roland Garros being the most obvious one, because the other three were on grass and I did not think I could win one of those. But I didn't know for sure that it was going to happen. After all, so many guys have that ambition too, and yet they never manage to win a major. So I feel lucky that I did.

I was always happy just to play tennis. Tennis for me was like the theatre, a performance. '*Ce n'est pas du cinéma*', as the French say, meaning that something is not superficial but has to be taken more seriously. Even if I lose, I'm happy if I feel I have given a performance. Of course, I want to win. It's not that I'm content to be second; I'm not. But winning has never been the highest priority. Life is more important, and it was also more important to be myself. Probably if I had been different – although I don't think of myself as different, I'm just me – I might have won more titles. But I never thought like that and I really don't think I could ever have changed, because for me it was very important to play the way I was feeling. Maybe it made for ugly scenes sometimes, but for me it was the only way I could play.

Speaking of temper, why have I not yet talked about it? In truth, although I had a temper as a child, it was not getting me into trouble at this stage of my career, maybe because I was doing better and better, and there was not yet any pressure on me. Also, I was not yet a big name. Although I was winning titles, until Rome they had not been in big tournaments, so nobody was paying any attention to me. If I lost unseeded, 1st or 2nd round, they might say there's some guy on court 9 complaining, but that's it. When I was number 1 seed, playing in a quarterfinal on Centre Court, then they noticed. Finally, there were no rules then about fines. It was up to the tournament what they decided to do with any player who misbehaved. The Code of Conduct that was drawn up to fix penalties for bad behaviour did not come in until the end of 1975, so I still had a few clear years of freedom ahead of me. That's why I wasn't yet hitting the headlines for my temper.

Wimbledon was also a good tournament for me that year. Seeded number 8, I had victories over Pasarell and Richey (avenging my Roland Garros defeat of a few weeks earlier). The American Clark Graebner – who I used to call Superman because of his first name and his Clark Kent-like glasses – finally saw me off in the 4th round. Meanwhile, Ion and I, despite being unseeded, made it through to the semis of the doubles, where the Aussies Rosewall and Stolle beat us in five close sets.

It was in the mixed doubles, however, that I won my second title in a major. Having played with a few different partners over the years, I finally settled on the tiny but powerful American Rosie Casals. Of Hispanic origin, she was a niece of the famous cellist Pablo Casals, and she, too, used her strings to great effect. I immediately got on well with her, and we had great fun that first year together, cutting through the draw, beating the number 2 seeds Bob Hewitt and Billie-Jean King along the way.

I remember the mixed doubles final, because, as is often the case at Wimbledon, the rain had caused delays in the doubles and mixed doubles programme. So, on finals day, we found ourselves playing our semi and final back-to-back on Centre Court, after the men's singles final, which had been an emotional match, because Ken Rosewall had for the third time failed to win the title. He had gone down this time in five sets to the holder, John Newcombe. What was more incredible was that Rosewall's previous two attempts had been in 1954, against the Czech Drobny and 1956 against Hoad – sixteen and fourteen years before!

After Rosie and I had beaten Judy Dalton and Frew McMillan, the number 3 seeds, in the semifinals, we were told to stay on Centre Court and await our opponents for the final, the Russian pair Alexander Metreveli and Olga Morozova. I knew them both well, of course: Alex I had known ever since I had first played him in a junior tournament in Estonia, and Olga I used to tease the whole time, because she's got a good sense of humour: 'Hey, Olga, it's OK, I spoke to your government, and they give you permission to smile', I used to joke to her. Anyway, that day my Russian comrades didn't have too much to laugh about because Rosie and I beat them in three sets 6–3, 4–6, 9–7.

When it was our turn to climb up into the Royal Box to be presented with our trophy by the Duke and Duchess of Kent, I didn't really know who exactly they were. I did know they were royal, so I dutifully bowed to them, but what I was really happy about was having one more important title. The mixed doubles may seem unimportant to the public, but for those of us who played them – and in those days most of the top players did – it mattered very much, and we were really pleased to have won.

I earned £250 for winning the mixed doubles title at Wimbledon that summer in 1970, £200 for being a semi-finalist in the doubles, and £220 for getting to the 4th round of the singles, £670 in total. My prize to myself for doing so well was to buy myself my second car – a beautiful black and silver Ford Capri. Because my driving licence did not yet permit me to drive abroad, I had to get Tiriac to drive it all the way back to Bucharest from Wimbledon after the tournament. Not surprisingly, he wasn't too pleased. Actually, it may have looked beautiful, but it was not a good car and kept breaking down.

Once, though, I was coming home at two in the morning

from a party and found myself speeding round the Arc of Triumph that we have in Bucharest (an almost identical version of the one in Paris) when I suddenly saw this little group of people flagging me down. So I stopped, because I could tell they were dressed like Westerners, and I figured they needed help. Sure enough, they explained they'd come from a party but couldn't find their way home. 'Get in', I said and in they clambered, pushing to one side all my tennis rackets and shoes that were lying on the back. 'Tennis player?' asked one of them. 'Yes, and you?' 'Actors'. It turned out I had just picked up the French actor Jean-Paul Belmondo and two other well-known French actors, Pierre Brasseur (the father of Claude) and Marlène Jobert, who were in Romania shooting a film. They, meanwhile, hadn't a clue who I was. 'Where do you want me to take you?' 'Another bar?' said Belmondo hopefully. I laughed: 'No, no, they're all closed now.' 'Then back to the Athenée Palace' (it's now the Hilton). So that's where I left them. At that time, Belmondo was going out with Ursula Andress, and I remember she was coming out to Bucharest every week to see him. A few nights later, a friend of mine who knew him quite well invited me to a party where all the actors would be. They instantly recognized me: 'Ah, the guy who gave us a lift!' So that's how I first met Belmondo who became a good friend. He is a huge tennis fan, and for years he attended Roland Garros every day in his private courtside box. One year, during a doubles match, I ran so hard to retrieve a ball that I ended up in his box. He always brought his little dog with him, so I took the dog back onto court with me, tied him to the umpire's chair and played a couple of points with this dog jumping and yapping away like crazy. Everybody thought that was very funny except, obviously, the dog.

That summer, I discovered that German girls are among

the most relaxed and open when it comes to sex. I was playing a tournament in Munich and found myself chatting to a nice-looking blonde girl one evening. We were reaching the point where something either happens or it doesn't, but, instead of leading her out into the night, I discovered that she wanted her friend to join us as well, her friend being a girl. I had to do some pretty fast thinking: did I want to try three in a bed or not? Was I still shy about that sort of thing or was I losing my inhibitions? I weighed up the pros and cons, and decided to say 'no'. It's just not my sort of thing. Still, I was bit more careful with German girls after that.

Actually, I'm dead straight when it comes to sex, and I'm not into anything that deviates from a normal one-man one-woman encounter. It's like sex in a car. We've all seen the movies, and it seems like a great idea at the time, but, believe me, when you've played a long match, sex in a small place is not good. I remember trying it once – and we're not talking about a car the size of a Mini, here, but a reasonably big American car – but I got cramp in one leg. I know, not very impressive for the girl. There I was, supposedly the great athlete, suddenly seizing up at the crucial moment. 'Huh, so much for a performance,' she must have thought. 'He was good on the court, what happened to him now? He's dead.' I just about got through, but afterwards, as I recovered, I thought: 'I must remember never to do that again after a long match.'

Similarly, the Spanish girl who decided she wanted to have sex on the hotel balcony – it was enclosed, I should explain – to see if those on the street below might hear, came closest to my limit of what I was prepared to do with a girl in public. It might seem like fun at the time, but I hate hearing other people having sex (sometimes thin hotel walls give you no choice), so I can't stand the idea of others hearing me.

So really sex is best when you can spread yourselves out, you can both relax, and nobody can see or hear you. Mostly, I was still a good boy, and I'd wait until I was at least out of the singles before going to look for a girl. Sometimes, though, Tiriac would get annoyed because I'd ignored him and gone out, even though we had a doubles match the next day. He never actually locked me in for the night – despite rumours that he did – because he knew that this would not have stopped me disappearing through the window and out into the street. But I knew he found me quite difficult to control by this stage. The thing was, if I did sleep with a woman during a tournament – and I'm not talking about my wife, later on, where the situation was obviously different – I would always be conscious that I could not give 100 per cent. It's scary to say, now, but I could not go full speed ahead with sex, because I was afraid I might not play as well as I could the next day. So I would always hold something back, I would not go on all night, much as I might want to, so that I did not exhaust myself completely. I'd call them '*mon amour*' or 'darling' (most women understand those words and, that way, it doesn't matter if you forget their name), but I'd also say: 'I have a match tomorrow' (even if I didn't) 'so it would be very nice if you could leave.' I never threw them out but I would try to come up with an excuse that wasn't too painful. Those were the ones I didn't want to spend the night with. Of course, the good-looking ones sometimes left before I wanted them to. That also happens, so it works both ways. But I'm afraid to say that, for me, quite a lot of sex in those days was like taking a daily shower: you take one, it feels nice, then you forget it.

By the end of the Sixties, Romania was one of the most advanced Eastern bloc countries. We all had enough to eat, thanks to our agriculture, and everybody had a job and somewhere to live. But around this time, Ceauşescu embarked on his massive industrialization project for the country, and Bucharest started to become a building site. Bucharest had always had a reputation for being beautiful. It was called the Paris of the east because of its wide tree-lined avenues that resembled those of the French capital and also its Parisian-style pale stone buildings with their grey, slate roofs. We even have a theatre that is modelled inside on the Paris Opera House, with a sweeping double staircase and a frescoed ceiling inside the auditorium. But Ceauşescu did not care about all this. He was desperate to build factories, oil refineries, chemical plants, anything to get us away from the agricultural country we were. So he started to pull people off the land in order to build high-rise blocks of flats. Then he put people in those apartments to build the next lot of apartments, and so on. Finally he put people in the apartments who would work in the factories. This building work finished in the late Eighties, by which time there was nobody left on the land, and we suffered once again from massive food shortages. But, by the Seventies, whole areas where there had once been little houses were starting to be pulled down, and big grey apartment blocks were put in their place.

Although I spent very little time at home, I knew that I was well off compared to many of my friends, although quite a lot of them were other sportsmen, especially soccer players, who lived a reasonably privileged life as well. I was still in my small apartment, though. I did not have three cars lined up outside my home (I had given my green Fiat to a friend), and I was not throwing lavish parties every night. If we went out, yes, I would pay for everyone but I have always thought that was normal. But when my friends insisted on paying their bit, or invited me round to their home, I would happily accept as well. I didn't want my new life to make a difference. So I tried hard – and still do – to minimize the effect that my wealth had on those around me.

My parents were very simple people, so this helped. They would never ask me to buy things on my travels for them, other than small things maybe, like decent whisky and shaving foam for my father, or coffee and Toblerone chocolate for my mother. In 1970, things had not yet got very bad in Romania, and I was not yet earning the sort of money that I would later on, so the gap in wealth between me and those around me was easier to smooth over.

What was less easy to smooth over were the cracks in my relationship with Tiriac. Inevitably, as I became more successful, I gained confidence and turned to him much less for help and advice. I started to stand on my own two feet. I got my own friends, and I also liked to go out with women. We did still socialize a lot together, though, because we were part of a whole group of players who would play against each other during the day and then go out together for a meal in the evening. Sometimes, we would all then go on to a nightclub or bar.

There were two groups on the tour: the Romanians, Italians, French, and Spanish in one – the Latins, really – and the Anglo-Saxons and Americans in the other. Curiously, the Australians were with us. Maybe because they too liked to have a good time. Then, later, Borg came along, as did Vilas and other South Americans. We'd play each other, beat each other, and that evening we'd all be eating together. None of this happens today. Each player is an island, surrounded by his 'team', his coach, his masseur, his psychologist, his stringer, his girlfriend. You name it, they're all there to protect him from, God forbid, some contact with another player.

Tiriac and I would still be together a lot, day and night (though we were no longer sharing a room), but I had distanced myself from him. I needed him less. Sometimes, he tried to stop this happening by attempting to control me, by telling me to play in a particular way, or to do a particular thing. I would just go and do the opposite, just to annoy him, because, as countless umpires and referees have discovered over the years, I have never liked being told what to do. Eventually he realized what I was doing, so he would tell me to do the opposite of what he *really* wanted me to do, knowing that I would then do the opposite, which would be what he had wanted me to do in the first place. A complicated way of controlling somebody, I think. I did not realize he was doing it at the time, but I discovered later when he told other people.

One of the last occasions when he influenced me strongly was in spring 1971. I was due to defend my title in Rome, but Ion called the director there and told him that we weren't going to play because I wanted to have a guarantee on top of any prize money I might earn. The guy said that was not possible, they were not giving any guarantees. So we went to Madrid instead, and they paid me a lot of money to play.

At the end of that week, we both found ourselves in the final and it happened to be the day of his birthday, 9 May. So the night before the final, he suggested we both go out to dinner.

'Ilie, come on, you're much better than me', he starts, 'tomorrow, just give me a couple of games, you know, then that'll be OK. I have the money anyway, so I'll be happy. Just don't kill me.'

So I say: 'OK, I won't wipe you off court.'

The next day, the 1st set goes 6–2 to Tiriac. I say to myself maybe I'm being a little bit too nice. So I try harder. The next set goes 2–2, 3–3, 4–4, 5–5 – and he ends up beating me in straight sets. So much for his birthday treat. We then go out to dinner again, and I say to him:

'Hey, what happened, I know it's your birthday but I cannot be *that* nice.'

He looks me straight in the eyes and replies: 'Nastase, that just shows how stupid you are.'

I was shocked: 'You're right, I am stupid because I let you win.'

'That's a lesson I'm teaching you now,' he continues. 'Not to be nice to anyone, not your friends, your brother, your sister, your parents.'

'Yes, but why are you telling me that now, after the defeat? Why don't you tell me that before the match? Then I could learn the lesson and win as well?'

'Yes, but this way, that will teach you,' he says.

And he was right. I had paid a high price for the week. I might have won $10,000 or whatever for playing the tournament, more than the winner's cheque actually was, but I hadn't won the title. And I hadn't played in Rome either, which is where I had really wanted to play. I never let him influence me like that again.

Fortunately, this did not affect my form, and a month later I began a run of results that took me all the way to my first major singles final, at the 1971 French Open. On the basis of having won the big clay-court tournaments of Monte Carlo and Nice in April, I was seeded 3, behind Ashe at 2, and Kodes, the holder of the title, at 1.

The tournament began well. I was winning easily and having fun, helping to judge the Miss Roland Garros contest, along with fellow player and friend Pierre Barthès, and going to the players' party that was held that year at the Paris Lido.

Then, in the quarterfinals, I came up against Stan Smith, the number 6 seed. Stan might not count clay as his best surface, but he was such a determined competitor that I knew I had to play well to beat him. The match started in fading daylight at 7.40 p.m., and by 8.30, the floodlights, which they used at Roland Garros in those days, were on. Within fifteen minutes, though, having adapted to them, we were taken off court. Smith must have been relieved, because, after just an hour's play, I was already leading 6–1, 6–3.

The next morning, under sunny skies, he woke up, won the 3rd set 6–3 and went a break up in the 4th. It's getting a bit tight for comfort, I thought. There's no way I want this to go into a 5th set, with him having won two sets that day. I got the break back with three winning shots, including a backhand topspin lob that landed plum on the line. At 4–4, and serving, Stan had a point to go up 5–4. Instead, I hit a cross-court passing shot that helped me to break him again and, one game later, I won the set 6–4 and the match.

This win gave me a lot of confidence in the semis against another American, Frank Froehling, who played with a big topspin forehand, because of his unorthodox grip for the time. This style was very unusual for an American. Still, Froehling had managed to beat his compatriots Arthur Ashe and Marty Riessen on the way, so he was having a good run. Our semifinal was a strange match in which I won the first eight games very easily, to lead 6–0, 2–0, then Froehling had a spell when he won seven straight games to equalise at one set all. I don't remember playing less well during the 2nd set, but Froehling, who was a player who blew hot and cold, was just making every shot. Sometimes that happens, and there's not much you can do other than hope things change before you lose the match. In my case, they did, but I had to play really well, chase lots of drop shots, which Froehling liked to hit, and make lots of running passing shots to win in four sets. I was now through to the biggest match of my career so far and had a chance to win my first major.

The night before the final, I just had room service with Tiriac. We tried not to talk too much about the match – I'd played Jan Kodes, my opponent, so many times, there was no point trying to talk tactics – and I went to bed. I tried not to think too much about the importance of the day ahead. This was my routine before big matches, and it never really changed over the years. The only thing I liked to do was wash my socks out and wear the same pair as I had used in the semis. It wasn't so much superstition as knowing that they were comfortable and, psychologically, that was always important. I never used the same shirt or shorts but, for some reason, I used to like to use the same socks and – even more inexplicably – the same sweat band. Don't ask me why.

On the day of the final it was raining off and on. I had woken up with swollen eyes, and it was the first time I started to have an allergic reaction to pollen. I felt good, though, and arrived at the club about an hour before the match. I managed to practise for ten minutes, just enough to warm up, then went back to the dressing room to get a quick massage, to keep the muscles warm.

The final itself was close and tense right up to the end, 2 hours 40 minutes later. Both of us were playing well, which always makes for a good match, and I went a break up in the 1st set, after a wrong-footed Kodes was sent sprawling to the ground. I helped wipe him down with a towel, which made the spectators laugh. Jan never gave up though – that's one of his strengths – and he broke, saving two set points at 4–5. At 6–7, I was serving to stay in the set when, on the first point, I contested a line call against me.

This was enough to break my concentration and lose me the game and the set.

Of course, it's easy to say that I should have stopped muttering about the line call, but I really felt it was an error. I did not want to disrupt Kodes so I did play on quite quickly, but my rhythm was broken and I lost the 2nd set 6–2 in half an hour.

The score and length of the 3rd set was an exact replica of the second, except that it was me who won it this time. In those days, players went off for a fifteen-minute break between the 3rd and 4th sets, and it was always psychologically important whether you were leading or losing by two sets to one. The break could also interrupt the impetus of a player who was playing well in the 3rd, so it was a big part of the mental battle that is always played out on a tennis court.

When we came back on for the 4th, I immediately went 2–0 and 3–1 up. We were both playing some really classic clay-court tennis, with lots of drop shots, passing shots, angled volleys, and, especially, lots of running. I remember we were playing with Tretorn balls, which were very soft, and because of the dampness of the weather they were very heavy and difficult to play with. The crowd were loving the match, and I was not so wrapped up in it that I did not notice some points where we got standing ovations. Kodes, though, stuck at his task and, after breaking me back to level at 3–3, he reached 6–5. I then had to serve to stay in the match. I reached 40–15 easily enough, but the game slipped away as Kodes strung together a series of winning shots. The match was over, and Kodes's coach, Pavel Korda, jumped onto court to plant a kiss full on his mouth, just as Gheorghe Cobzuc had done to me two years earlier in the Davis Cup.

Of course, I was disappointed that I had not won. I

certainly thought I could beat Kodes after my good results that spring. But I also knew I had played well, I had given a lot of pleasure to the crowd, and I felt for a first major final it had gone well and that I had other chances ahead of me. You can never be sure, but I was sufficiently confident of myself, by this stage in my career, to think that I would not be one of those players who only ever reached one big final, never to be heard of again.

I was therefore surprised not to do better at Wimbledon, where I was beaten in the 2nd round by Frenchman Georges Goven, who could at best be described as a bit of a journeyman pro. That night, in an attempt to drown my sorrows, I picked up a girl and was just fixing up to take her back to my hotel when she admitted that she had a dog with her, and the dog had to come too. 'OK, the dog can come,' I said, dubiously. I just wanted him to stay quietly in the bathroom. No chance. He was in the bathroom all right but he barked through the whole thing, because I'd insisted on closing the door to stop him jumping onto the bed. Eventually, he went to sleep, so I couldn't use the bathroom. Not good but it was only when he decided to do his business at three in the morning that things really became a nightmare. There I was, mopping up the smelly mess in the middle of the night, half naked, wondering whether I had paid a rather high price for getting laid. All I can say is that I didn't spend long with the woman the next morning.

In early October 1971, Romania reached the Challenge Round of the Davis Cup, just two years after our previous final. This was the last time the Challenge Round was played, when the holders of the Cup would simply go through to the final the following year. After that, they would have to fight their way through earlier rounds, like everybody else.

On the way to the final we had beaten India in New Delhi

during what must have been the monsoon season. In any case, I have never seen so much rain in my life. The tie itself lasted about six days, instead of the usual three, and they had nothing but rags to cover the courts, which of course were not much use. Then they would spend hours just mopping up.

In the final, we were again due to meet the USA, this time in Charlotte, North Carolina. Surprisingly, our opponents decided to lay a clay court for the encounter. It was an American clay court, which looks like grey-green shale and is not as slow as the continental version. But, still, it was clay. Some people thought the Americans were crazy, because this certainly gave us more of a chance. Also surprisingly, Frank Froehling, who had been out in the cold just a few months before, got picked, because he'd shown what a fighter he was and had got good results that summer. Dependable Stan Smith was the other singles player and Stan teamed up with the up-and-coming Eric Van Dillen for the doubles.

Although we knew we had a better chance than in 1969, the Americans still had a massive advantage playing at home. The Davis Cup produces results that often bear little relation to tournament play. Although we won two rubbers (Ion and I won the doubles, and I beat Froehling in the fifth match), we still lost 3–2 because Smith beat both Ion and me. Froehling justified his selection by beating Tiriac on the first day, after coming back from two sets to love down in a really long, tense five-set match spread over two days.

We were getting huge coverage in the Romanian press by this stage in our careers, and it would make out my results were the best in the world. Communist media did not like to criticize its sporting heroes, not like now in Romania where they are as bad as any Western press in building up idols and knocking them down again. Even later on, when I was doing bad things on court, the papers would write about them in a way that covered up what had gone on, so they might say I had been disqualified but never why. They tried to hide the truth from the people, even though it was never a problem for me to say what had really happened.

Sportul, our national sports daily, belonged to the Ministry for Education and Sport. It was a state paper and was always putting me on the front page, especially when it came to the all-important Davis Cup. So we were very aware of the impact this defeat would have, which is why, this time, we were more disappointed to lose than in 1969, when nothing much had been expected of us. Fortunately, the '71 final had also been played in America, which prevented the terrible pressure on us that came from playing at home – pressure that we would experience twelve months later when we reached our third Davis Cup final, against the Americans yet again, but had to play it in Bucharest.

I don't know if it was the dog in the bedroom incident earlier that summer or simply the fact that I was getting so used to picking up girls almost whenever I wanted. Either way, I think subconsciously I might have been getting less satisfied every time the chase was successful. I was now twenty-five and had never actually had a long-term, serious girlfriend, so it was not surprising, looking back, that things suddenly changed. And fast.

CHAPTER FIVE

1971–1972

We were passing each other nervously on our way to and from the bathroom until eventually they called us into the little anteroom just before we walked out onto Centre Court.

My US Open tournament in 1971 got off to a bad start, when I was beaten in the 3rd round of the singles by the Aussie Bob 'Nailbags' Carmichael (so-called because he used to be a carpenter before joining the tour). In the doubles, though, I did better, and by the end of the first week Tiriac and I were through to the quarterfinals to play Bob Hewitt and Frew McMillan, one of tennis's all-time great doubles teams. We were scheduled on the Grandstand Court, near the main stadium.

The match got under way to a half-empty gallery. Down by the courtside, however, were three spectators who were cheering and clapping for us so hard that I thought they must be Romanian. One was a teenage girl, one was, I assumed, her mother, and the third was an unbelievably beautiful young woman, with shoulder-length dark hair and huge brown eyes. I tried hard to concentrate on the match, rather than on her, but we still lost quite easily and, before I knew it, she was gone.

Later that day, I was back on court with Rosie Casals to play a mixed doubles match. I spotted the young daughter and her mother at once – they were courtside again. This time, the stands were full, and it took me a few more minutes during the warm-up, with only one eye on the ball, to pick out the young woman who was now sitting about twenty rows up at the top of the stadium. Determined not to let her out of my sight this time, I asked a friend of mine to get a note to her saying that, when the match was over, could she possibly wait because Mr Nastase would like to meet her.

As soon as the match was over (we won, by the way), I was over like a flash, in case she decided to make a run for it. She spoke French, which I barely did, and, although I spoke broken English, hers was terrible. Somehow, though, we just about managed to talk long enough for her to tell me she was called Dominique Grazia, she was twenty-one, she lived in Brussels with her French father and her Belgian mother, and she was in New York for a week's holiday. Soon, her mother arrived with her younger daughter, Nathalie, and I asked Madame Grazia if I could possibly take Dominique out to dinner that evening. 'No, no,' she replied with charm and tact in perfect English, 'it is I who would like to invite you to dinner with the three of us.' I knew enough about manners not to insist, and later that evening we all met up at a French restaurant called l'Escargot, near their hotel off Madison Avenue.

I remember her mother doing most of the talking, while I tried to answer the questions that she fired at me. Dominique, like me, was quite shy, so she listened but did not say very much. As for Nathalie, who was fourteen, she was tongue-tied with happiness. I discovered she was such a big fan of mine that she kept detailed scrapbooks about me at home; and the reason they were in New York in the first place was because she had been promised a trip to see me play after getting good school exam results that year. Dominique had simply tagged along for the shopping and sightseeing. She admitted she had no interest in tennis at all, and none in me either. Well, at least I knew.

At the end of the evening, I asked Madame Grazia if I could take Dominique out the following evening on her own, and I must I have behaved OK during dinner because she graciously accepted. So the next night we went out for dinner, then on to the Hippopotamus discotheque, one of the best in Manhattan at the time. I remember several players were also there, including Arthur Ashe. Although I don't like to dance – I get very self-conscious and think everyone is looking at me – I forced myself so that I could at last get a bit closer to Dominique.

She told me she had had a very strict and sheltered upbringing and had not been allowed to date boys until she turned eighteen. Then, she got engaged to the first boy she went out with – who was barely older than her – and stayed with him for two years until she had called it off the previous year. A rather different path from the one I had taken these last few years, I thought. Although we kissed, nothing more happened that night. For the rest of the week, I never once took her back to my hotel – I'm sure her mother would not have allowed it. I either had dinner with her, or the four of us would dine out or meet up at the tennis club when I was playing.

By the time they were due to leave New York, I was through to the mixed doubles semifinals and frantically trying to work out a way of seeing Dominique after the tournament, because I knew I was in love with her. I decided there was only one thing for it: I told Rosie Casals that I was going to have to pull out of our match and follow Dominique back to Brussels. Rosie, understandably, got mad at me, screaming that this was typical of me, chasing women as usual. It did no good; I changed my flights and hopped on the plane with the three of them. Madame Grazia had obviously warned her husband that there was a change of plan and that Dominique had a certain Ilie Nastase in tow with her, because he was not at all surprised to see me when he came to meet us at the airport.

There was no way I would be allowed to stay with them, so I slept at the nearby Hilton Hotel and spent my days at their home, which was an enormous house built in the Twenties, with huge grounds and a tennis court. Nathalie took dozens of photographs of my few days with them – she probably felt as if she had died and gone to heaven – and I continued to get to know Dominique. However, with my reputation preceding me – which she knew all about, thanks to her sister – I resisted trying to get her back to the hotel and decided to take things slowly, because no woman had ever had this effect on me. I remember I had on a pale aubergine-coloured suit that I thought was quite nice (this was the Seventies), but, as a mark of how much I was already under her spell, Dominique managed to explain that she wasn't too keen on it and to suggest which clothes of mine she preferred.

When I had first met Dominique I had no idea what sort of family she came from, but I quickly learned all about their past. Her maternal great-grandfather had become very wealthy through various business projects, including building the Cairo metro, and had been made the First Baron Empain. As a result, Dominique's mother was the Baronne Empain, the half-sister of the current baron, who in 1975 was kidnapped and had his little finger famously sawn off to force the payment of a ransom. The baron also headed up the Schneider industrial group, a huge company based in France that makes all types of electrical goods. Dominique's father was also an industrialist whose family came from Italy originally, and she had three older brothers – Daniel, Bernard, and Jean – as well as her sister Nathalie.

After three days, it was time for me to jet off again, back to the USA, for the Pacific Southwest tournament in Los Angeles. For the first time ever, I wanted a woman to accompany me on tour, but ironically she was not able nor willing to do so. This was partly because her parents would never have allowed their daughter's reputation to be compromised in this way by a strange Romanian they barely knew and partly because Dominique herself was a bit scared by the idea of travelling with me. She resisted me every time I asked her if she wanted to accompany me to a tournament. So the Davis Cup final in Charlotte came and went, the Embassy British Indoors in London came and went (I beat both Newcombe and Laver on my way to the title), and we continued our relationship by speaking on the phone a lot and me hopping over to Brussels for a day or two whenever I had a spare gap in my schedule, which was not often. Very frustrating.

Eventually, I invited her to a tournament in Stockholm in November, and she said her parents would let her come, as long as they accompanied her. What a choice! 'No problem, sure, come with your parents,' I heard myself say enthusiastically. So, after making sure my room was well away from theirs, I arranged for them to stay in the same hotel. Surprise, surprise, I was so happy and relaxed that week that I won the tournament. I also finally made love to Dominique after weeks of waiting, and realized that I was serious about the relationship and wanted her to start travelling with me as soon as possible. I couldn't believe what had happened to me in the space of a few weeks, but it was not just my usual impetuousness that made me act like this. I had been around long enough to know that this was very special and that I was very much in love.

Unfortunately, when we went our separate ways again at the end of the week, Dominique had other ideas. She felt things were starting to get too serious too quickly and that, unlike me, it was time to put the brakes on. She also wanted to explore life a bit before getting into yet another big relationship. I had really hoped she would join me in Paris where I'd be playing in the end-of-year Masters tournament. Instead, she told me during yet another of our long phone conversations that she thought it would be better if we had a bit of a break from each other. In fact, she had decided to improve her English and join her brother Jean in Cambridge for an indeterminate amount of time. Stunned, I did manage to point out the obvious, that she could improve her English on the tour as well, but that was clearly not the main reason. She wanted to cool things down before we got much more involved. The problem with my life was that it was all or nothing. I could not date women like everybody else, seeing them once or twice a week. It was either a case of travel with me or see me once every three months. Not very good for developing a relationship.

So I had no choice but to agree to her request and went off to Paris on my own. Just to show her what she was missing, I made sure I won the tournament. This was a really big win for me, because the Masters gathered together the eight top-ranking men from the fourteen Grand Prix series of tournaments held during the year. We all had to play each other in a round-robin format, and I played so well that week that I ended up winning every single match, beating players such as Stan Smith and Jan Kodes (who that year had won the US Open and French Open, respectively) on my way to the £6,000 first prize. I had also come second in the Grand Prix rankings of points accumulated during the fourteen tournaments, and this qualified me for a $17,000 share of the $150,000 bonus pool. The end of the year, for tennis, had brought me a lot of success and money. It was personally that I was now hurting.

After a rather sad Christmas with my family in Bucharest, I set off again for the USA in the new year, winning tournaments in Baltimore and Omaha. I did not speak to Dominique for weeks because the whole separation had been her idea, and I did not want to annoy her by phoning the whole time. I figured she'd either fall in love with an Englishman or she'd come to her senses and realize what an amazing guy I was!

After a great spring, when I retained my clay-court titles in Nice and Monte Carlo and won in Madrid, I was feeling confident for the French Open in May. Unfortunately, I had a bad tournament: within two days, I had lost to the young Roman Adriano Panatta in the 1st round of the singles. Adriano was already a good player, but as last year's finalist I would have been expected to beat him, so I was not pleased to go out in this way. In the doubles, Tiriac and I also lost in the 2nd round to the Belgians Mignot and Holmbergen, hardly a top-class combination, so I was feeling down about my results when I returned to my hotel that evening. There, I was immediately handed an urgent telegram. 'Bravo for your brilliant defeat', it said, teasingly. It was from Dominique, just when I thought I would never see her again. I called her straight away in Brussels, where she was now living again and invited her to Paris. To my surprise, she accepted at once, and within twenty-four hours I was waiting impatiently at the Gare du Nord for her train to pull into the station. This time, her parents did not accompany her. At long last, we were alone.

By the end of a wonderful week, I had decided I wanted to spend my life with her, so one evening we went out to a really nice restaurant in the Latin Quarter. I started telling her how much I had missed her and was she planning to stay for a while. 'Yes', was the answer, 'I think so.' I didn't quite go down on bended knee – luckily, as it turned out – but when I did finally ask her to marry me, she just said: 'No'. Nicely, but firmly, 'No'. She wasn't ready yet. Fine, I thought, no problem, I'll just keep trying. And over the next couple of weeks, I asked her twice more. I'm someone who is very tactile, very romantic, so each time I set it up so that the atmosphere was right, the conversation was right, she couldn't possibly refuse me. But, however hard I tried, still the answer was 'No', she wasn't ready yet. OK, forget it, I thought, I'll just wait. Maybe after Wimbledon.

No sooner had she returned, though, than she was off again, this time on a long-planned family holiday to Sorrento, in Italy, for the whole two weeks of Wimbledon. I tried to persuade her to skip it and stay with me in London, but her family was very traditional about these things, and the holiday was not something she could miss. So again I waved her off, reluctantly, and flew over to London.

At Wimbledon, I was seeded number 2, behind Stan Smith at number 1. One journalist said I was too high but I didn't care, even though he was probably right because I had never yet got past the 4th round. In the end, though, compared to Stan – or 'Godzilla' as I always used to call him because of his 1.9 m height and enormous reach – I had a harder path through to the final, because I had to beat some good grass-court players on the way. In fact, it's better to have a tough draw and to have to beat good players on the way, because then you feel you deserve to win the tournament and you are full of confidence. If you haven't had to beat anyone much, you don't know what you are capable of when you finally get to a big or tough match.

My first test came in the 2nd round when I faced Clark Graebner, who I had had a few on-court arguments with in the past (he had a temper, like me). He had also beaten me at Wimbledon in 1969 and 1970. This time, I beat him easily enough in four sets, and we never exchanged a word. This was a good win for me so early in the tournament, although I must have been so excited at beating him that I did not bother to lock away the £45 I had kept in my racket cover, and when I got back from having a bath I discovered it had been stolen. This, added to the $300 I had had stolen from Roland Garros the previous month, and in a similar way, made changing in the locker rooms of Paris and London an expensive privilege.

After getting past the German Jurgen Fassbender in straight sets in the next round, I faced Tom Gorman, from the USA, in the 4th round. Tom was my pigeon: in the twenty-one matches we played, I beat him eighteen times, so I was confident. The match was scheduled on Centre Court, and I knew that a win here would take me into the second week of the tournament for the first time ever. I had already noticed that the British public definitely fell into two camps when it came to supporting me. Some of them obviously liked me, particularly the girls and the women, but others definitely hated me. In my behaviour, I represented all that was un-British: I did not have a stiff upper lip, I hadn't been to the right school, and I dared to question authority. In that match with Gorman, I remember one military-looking man, with dark glasses (resembling a member of Russia's secret police), clapping one of my double faults for a very long time. Still, he didn't get any satisfaction, because I beat Tom in four sets.

After this win, I could see the draw was looking good for me. I had Jimmy Connors in the next round, and either Spain's Manuel Orantes or the Aussie Colin Dibley in the semis. At the time, I was beating them all a lot. I thought if I could pass these guys, I could make it to the final and win it. Even better, the press weren't yet taking much notice of me.

In the quarterfinals I played the nineteen-year-old Connors on Centre Court. He, too, was a crowd favourite, but Jimmy, who was later to become one of my best friends on the circuit, was playing his first Wimbledon. He was so pumped up for this match that he was spraying his shots all over the place and trying to hit harder and harder. I, meanwhile, was playing my usual touch game, which Jimmy found very difficult, because he hated it when he wasn't given pace to hit against, as Ashe understood when he beat him in their notorious 1975 Wimbledon final. Everything I did seemed to work for me that day, and I beat Connors easily 6–4, 6–4, 6–1.

By the time I reached the semis, the press was waking up to my chances, especially because, out of the four semi-finalists, only Stan had a track record on grass. The other two, Jan Kodes and Manuel Orantes, were like me relatively inexperienced. I was drawn against Manuel, who was the 3rd seed and who had beaten me on our previous encounter indoors in Washington. I, however, was playing much better than him on fast courts, like cement and grass.

This time, despite my initial nerves, I was playing so well that I shot off to a quick 3–0 lead before Manuel had time to work out where he was. I just tried to stay the way I normally am on court, talking to myself, walking around a lot, playing my usual non-percentage tennis. I won the first two sets 6–3, 6–4, and at 5–4 in the 3rd I reached match point with a service ace winner. At that stage, I remember trying hard to concentrate on staying in the point, letting him take the chances, and not to think about the importance of where we had got to in the match. I missed the first serve. My second went in, and Manuel advanced to the net. I whipped up a high ball to his forehand side, and he put the volley into the net. I had won, I was through to the final, and I threw my racket high into the air, knowing that I was the first Romanian ever to appear in a men's singles final at Wimbledon. I never thought it would have been possible. The crowd cheered loudly, I remembered to bow to the Royal Box, and I left the court a happy man.

Then the press and television went crazy. Everybody wanted to interview me: female journalists wanted to talk to me about my private life, and tennis journalists about my chances against Smith in the final. The media made a big thing of the fact that I was a lieutenant in the Romanian army, while Smith was just a corporal. Eventually, I got back to my hotel and called Dominique on the phone. Out in Italy, they were not able to see any of the tennis, so she had no idea how I was getting on. I did not want her to come over for the final, because I knew myself well enough to realize that this would disrupt my preparations and break my concentration, which has always been fragile at the best of times. So we decided we would just stay in touch by phone. I also managed to call Bucharest and speak to my parents, who wished me luck but who were also firmly staying put at home, although I knew the TV there would show the match.

Luckily, I was not completely on my own. Ion had gone

back to Romania after losing in the singles, because we were not playing doubles together that year, but I still had an Italian friend with me, Michele Brunetti. He was a lawyer from Ancona, who had also refereed an India–Romania Davis Cup tie the year before, and he was staying at my hotel, the Adelphi, in Queen's Gate, Kensington.

The final in those days was played on the Saturday, and, the night before, I remember going to bed late and watching TV because I could not sleep, then waking up in the early hours and playing the match through in my head, working out what I was going to do. In my version, of course, I ended up winning.

When Saturday dawned, it was pouring with rain. It was one of those days where it looks as if the rain will never stop. I heard afterwards that Stan, who is a fervent Presbyterian, went to church. I went for a run with Michele, right up to Speaker's Corner in Hyde Park. There, we sat on a bench and listened to some guys ranting away until some people started to recognize me. Then, as I was not really in a mood for talking, we ran back to the hotel and called Wimbledon. They said don't come down, it's not scheduled to stop raining. So I ordered up tea and toast, and munched my way through that, though I was not really hungry. I also spoke to Dominique a few times that afternoon to tell her what was going on, but I had to stay ready to go at a moment's notice if the weather changed, so all I could do was watch TV and hang around the hotel. Eventually, at about 5 p.m., it was clear the weather was not going to change, and the club called me to say that the final was postponed to the next day, the first time in Wimbledon history that it would be played on a Sunday.

I remember the journalists calling me at once to ask if I was going to go to the traditional post-Wimbledon ball, where the two singles winners have to open the dancing. Billie-Jean King had won that year, and, as things stood, Stan and I were both going to be dancing with her – or neither. I just said that I was not going to go unless I was ordered to, in which case, like a good soldier, I would do as I was told. Stan ended up going – he must have liked dancing more than I did – and I decided to go the movies, instead, to see a horror film. I thought that would take my mind off things.

I had another sleepless night. The next morning, though, when I got up at about eight o'clock, the weather was dry. I remember having coffee and toast for breakfast and just swallowing it mechanically, as quickly as possible. It's like going to an exam, it doesn't matter how good you are, how well prepared you think you are, you never know what's going to happen, so you are always nervous. My stomach was churning, because there was no pretending this was not an important match. However happy I was to have got this far, I knew I was capable of beating Smith and winning my first-ever major title.

I arrived at the All England Club at about eleven o'clock and arranged a practice court immediately. Fred Perry was there (I was sponsored by his clothing company at the time), and he had been supporting me throughout the two weeks. Fred was one of those past champions that I liked and admired very much, so his encouragement meant a lot to me. I ate a sandwich and a banana, and hung around the players' restaurant with Michele, talking to anyone else who was around. The mixed doubles was still behind schedule as well, so some of the players were there too.

Then, around 1.15 p.m., I went out onto court 4, the one that's nearest the Royal entrance and the changing-room entrance, and had a practice with Bjorn Borg, who was only sixteen at the time. He was in the boys' final, which he won against Britain's Buster Mottram. Fred liked Bjorn's game as well as mine, so it was he who suggested I hit with him, and I think that was probably the first time I had ever seen Bjorn play. We practised for twenty minutes, just enough to warm up but not to break into a sweat.

I then went straight back to the main changing room while Bjorn went to the juniors' one, under court 2. I changed my shirt and waited another five minutes, because by now it was about 1.50 p.m. By this stage of the tournament, the main changing room was empty, and no one other than players was allowed in. So there was just me and Stan and silence. We were passing each other nervously on our way to and from the bathroom until eventually they called us into the little anteroom just before we walked out onto Centre Court. Players wait here until everyone is seated in the Royal Box, and then they can quickly walk out onto the court without the royal family having to wait. As we entered the room, I remember being told that the British Prime Minister, Harold Wilson, was also in the Royal Box that day. The anteroom itself is tiny. It only measures about two metres square and contains literally a couple of chairs. I was sitting almost knee to knee with my opponent, and I could almost smell him. Once I started to win matches, though, I got to like this bare little room. It's part of the excitement of going out to play on the most famous court in the world. But of course, the pressure was there that day, and I cannot say that I was not nervous at 2 p.m., when we were finally led out onto Centre Court by Leo, the little locker-room attendant who carried our bags and rackets on finals day.

That's the tough bit, when you first go out in front of the people on Centre Court. The door is opened, and you can hear a buzz of noise. At that stage, you can't see the crowd because you're walking out behind the screen, but some of them have seen you, so they start to clap. Then, once everybody sees you emerge onto court, they all start to clap and cheer very loudly, and the noise hits you hard in the face.

The warm-up period is the worst part, because you are still emotional and nervous. You're trying to concentrate on what you're doing, but your body is shaking and your mind is jumping around. That only really stops when you start the match, and even then you never know how long it will be until you calm down completely.

Finally, after a three-day wait for Stan and me, the umpire said: 'Play', and we were ready to start. Despite any nerves we might have felt, we both played well from the start. My backhand passing shots down the line were sneaking through the tiniest gaps, I was matching Stan for power, and I was retrieving everything. He, in return, was producing more touch and finesse shots than I had ever seen him play and was returning serve and volleying well. The 1st set went with serve until the ninth game when, after getting six break points, I finally managed to break Stan's serve to win it 6–4.

In the 2nd and 3rd sets, I broke serve first but was broken back each time. I also began to get really annoyed that my rackets were strung too tight and this was affecting my game and my concentration. Earlier that week, I had borrowed a racket from Panatta and I'd loved it. So when he'd left the tournament, he lent me the racket. Unfortunately, I had broken the strings during my semifinal against Orantes, on the Thursday, and in those days, there weren't stringers on site, even at Wimbledon, so I'd had to go to a shop in Wimbledon to re-string this racket. It wasn't until I started the final that I decided I didn't like the way it had been strung. I was obsessive about racket-string tension, and I admit it may all have been in my head, but for me it wasn't done the way I liked it. Even before the match, I was worried about this and I'd got Michele to step on the strings to loosen them up. So this preyed on my mind throughout the match.

By the time I had lost the advantage of the breaks and both of those sets, I had gone through every single one of my rackets and had ranted so much to Michele that he eventually left his seat in the players' enclosure in an effort to get me to calm down and concentrate. At the change of ends, there were no chairs then, so we stood next to each other at the umpire's chair drinking our water. Stan, though, was his usual reserved self. His rackets and towels stayed in a tidy pile, whilst mine were scattered messily around. On court, his only sign of tension was to run the palm of his hand constantly over his straw-like hair in an effort to flatten it. Michele's disappearance seemed to work, because I broke Stan when we were 4–4 in the 4th set. I then had to serve for the set to equalize the match at two sets all. Despite Stan saving two set points on my service game, I finally won it 6–4. Now we were into a 5th set. I stopped worrying about the rackets and got down to business.

Games went with serve until, serving at 2–2, Stan had to save three break points, one with a surprising backhand drop shot, after the game had gone to seven deuces. I still felt I could win, even though Stan was playing well, because I was playing well too. Most of the points were being won with winners, rather than lost with errors. We moved on to 4–4. Suddenly, Stan was 0–30 down on his serve. I had him at the net, and I hit a forehand passing shot down the line. Stan lunged at it, the tip of his racket just reaching the ball, and he hit a winning stop volley off the wood. Luck, no doubt about it. If he'd lost that point, he would have been 0–40 down, I might well have broken him and served for the match. Anything could have happened. But the final – as all close matches do – rested on just one or two points and on luck. And this time, it had gone against me.

After Stan made that shot, he won the game, and I suddenly found myself saving a couple of match points in the very next game. I tried to stay relaxed, to breathe deeply, but it was all very tight. This was the first Wimbledon final since the Second World War to get to 5–5 in a 5th set. On my next service game, serving at 5–6 – and serving to stay in the match is definitely harder – I got to 40–0 before Stan produced some winning service returns, and I double-faulted. Suddenly I had a third match point against me. I won that with a high forehand volley winner. But again Stan came back. Soon I faced a fourth match point. This time I was at the net and had an easy high backhand volley. Normally, I would have put it away, no problem. But I just underplayed this one, and it hit the tape and fell into the net. After two hours forty-five minutes, I had lost the match by the smallest of margins. Stan hurled his racket high up in the air and leapt over the net to console me. I remember, as we hugged, I remember that he ruffled my hair, which was nice, and said: 'Bad luck'. Although during the match I had hated him, or rather his game, because he was tall and catching everything, when he won I could not hate him. I cannot hate somebody just because they have beaten me. Also, I respected Stan. He was a good player, had been the runner-up the year before, and was the US Open champion, so he was a deserving winner.

Still, the prize-giving ceremony was terrible. I had to watch as Stan strode up and held the trophy aloft in triumph, while I just sat slumped on a courtside box waiting for my turn to receive my medal. In those days, the runner-up came on after the winner and only had a small medal to collect. I do remember, though, getting a bigger cheer than Stan when I went up to shake the Duke of Kent's hand, which was nice, but I would have swapped that with the trophy and getting no cheer at all. The Duke said something along the lines of: 'Hard luck, it was a tough match for you. Maybe you'll come back next year and win it.' He's a nice man and, I think, from many years of watching the tennis, he understands and appreciates the game. His wife does as well, and she's always been very kind to me.

Stan eventually left the court, and I went off briefly to change my shirt. I then had to come straight back on, because I was still in the mixed doubles semifinals with Rosie Casals. When she arrived, she was very gentle and encouraging to me. Because our match against Clark Graebner and Billie-Jean King, the number 3 seeds, was tight, she asked me a few times whether I wanted to quit. 'Do you want to forget about it? I don't mind.' But actually that was good, because I felt I had a responsibility. It was not fair to her for me not to try, even though I was upset at losing the singles. So we won that match 9–8, 7–5, and I was then given a fifteen-minute break before the mixed doubles final – my second final of the day.

We played the number 1 seeds, Kim Warwick and Evonne Goolagong. I tried hard in that match, which we won 6–4, 6–4. It was a consolation for losing the singles, and I was relieved to end the day with a win and a trophy.

By the time I had finished, it was about 8.30 in the evening, I had been on court for more than six hours, had played three matches and nine sets, and I was completely exhausted. In fact, I was so exhausted that I was no longer upset about the singles. When I got back to the locker room, it was eerie because it was almost empty: Stan was just about to leave, his friend Donald Dell, the American player who later became a highly successful lawyer and agent, was still there with some champagne. Then there was me and Warwick. I took a quick shower and came out to meet Michele, who was waiting to take me to dinner in an Italian restaurant called Ponte Vecchio, near the Old Brompton Road, which a lot of players used to go to in those days.

By the time we got there, it was about ten o'clock, the restaurant was full, and everybody, of course, was coming up to me to say: 'Bad luck, bad luck', which kept reminding me of my loss when all I wanted to do was forget it. The next day, when I woke up, it hurt even more, because once again everybody I saw said they were sorry I hadn't won. Michele had gone back to Italy, Dominique was still away, and I had to go off to Baastad in Sweden by myself, so I remember feeling very alone that day.

One week later, I was slowly starting to get over the loss. I told myself that I had not expected to get to the final of such a big grass-court tournament, that I had played well, and that the match had been decided on a couple of lucky shots, so I should be proud to have done so well. I did not know, of course, that I would never win Wimbledon. Although I was disappointed to have lost, I was no longer devastated, because I really felt happy to have got so far.

The following week, Dominique came out to Dusseldorf, where I was playing, and that helped as well. One day, we were being driven to a television studio where I was going to be interviewed – about Wimbledon, yet again – when Dominique suddenly turned to me, interrupted my ramblings mid-sentence, and, with a big smile on her face, asked: 'Listen, Ilie, why don't we get married?' I was so stunned I started to laugh. I mean, I must have asked her at least three or four times, and she'd said: 'No'. And now, here she was, asking what I should have been asking. Of course I said: 'Yes', at once, in case she changed her mind. In fact, she told me later that she'd been thinking about asking me for a few days, because I hadn't shown any signs of proposing to her again and she was beginning to worry that she'd missed her chance. Women!

We called her parents at once, just to make sure they were OK about the idea. After all, I wasn't exactly an obvious choice for a son-in-law, given their background, but her mother had always adored me, so I thought I was pretty safe. Sure enough, they gave us their blessing. In fact, a few weeks later, it was with my future mother-in-law that I went to choose the engagement ring, because I wanted it to be a surprise and I knew that she would help me choose something Dominique would like. We found a ring that had an enormous rectangular sapphire with two diamonds on each side, and I proudly presented it to Dominique, who thought it was very beautiful. So the summer went by, with Dominique jetting between Brussels, where the preparations for our December wedding got quickly underway, and whichever city I was playing in that week.

My Wimbledon final had changed players' perception of me. Before, they had seen me mainly as a clay-court player. Now, even guys like Newcombe and Laver wanted to practise with me, play doubles with me. There was definitely more respect than before, and that was a good feeling.

As for the general public, they started to recognize me a lot more. I was different anyway from the other players. People came to watch me because I was from a strange country and was crazier than the other guys, playing differently from them and talking to everybody. But off court, walking around, people would now recognize me too. I would be asked for autographs wherever I went, in airports, in restaurants, in planes. People weren't rude to me – yet – and, even if I was eating a meal or was busy, I was always happy to sign autographs. I still am. After all, even if I've got my mouth full because I'm having dinner, I've still got a free hand to sign and it only takes a second. I'm not sure why that is, but it's just my nature.

Unlike some players, I like that aspect of success, I like being recognized, I like to talk to people. I know, especially when kids ask for autographs, how much it means to them, so I never refuse them and I'm always very patient. I remember being one of those kids myself who thought soccer players were great, and I still treasured my signed photo from Santana, so I think it's normal to do this in return when you are asked for your own autograph. Nowadays, kids still come and ask for my autograph, but often it's on behalf of their parents who are too scared to ask! They think I might live up to my Nasty nickname after all.

I arrived at Forest Hills, that year of 1972, full of confidence after winning the Canadian Open the week before. I was seeded 4, behind Smith the defending champion, then Rosewall and Laver, so not a bad group of players. In fact the tournament that year was the first major where all players were reunited or were not in dispute with one or other of the bodies or tours that ran the game at the time. The ILTF ran the game, in theory, in the shape of the Grand Prix circuit of tournaments, but the WCT tour, run by Lamar Hunt, also had a lot of power and this was not to the ILTF's liking. As a result, some of the past majors had suffered from not having the WCT pros (of which I was not one) in the draw. The US Open finally brought that to an end, when both groups managed to arrive at a reasonable peace, and this meant that this was the strongest major draw in years.

I remember being in a hurry to beat my 1st round opponent, the Venezuelan Velasco (score 6–0, 6–2, 6–0), because I had to rush off to meet Dominique at the airport that afternoon as she had flown in from Brussels. My 2nd round match against Roger Taylor was much tougher, and it all came down to a 5th set tie-break. This was the third year that tie-breaks had been used, and at Forest Hills they played a sudden death, a nine-point version where the first player to get to five points won. This, together with the terrible grass courts where bad bounces were the norm, meant that the whole thing became a complete lottery. I won that tie-break 5–1, but it had been a narrow escape, especially since I had initially led the match by two sets to love, only to let Taylor draw back level to two sets all.

After that major scare, my path through to the final of the US Open was a lot easier. In successive rounds, I beat a lefthander from France, Patrice Dominguez, the South African doubles specialist Bob Hewitt, then Fred Stolle, who had earlier got rid of Newcombe in my half of the draw, and, finally, Tom Gorman, against who I had a very good record. I was feeling good, and thanks to Dominique I was very happy and relaxed.

In the final, I was due to meet Arthur Ashe, who had won the title back in '68 and who, as a player, possessed both power and finesse. As usual, the night before a big final, I had room service, watched a bit of TV, then went to bed. I avoided talking about the match itself. I still washed my socks, but by now I was able to wear new outfits for every match. The all-white rule had been abandoned at Forest Hills that year, so I picked out a pale blue Fred Perry shirt and white shorts. I loved being able to do that. No more daily shirt washing. For the rest of my career, I would always play my singles matches in a new outfit and would use the older clothes for the doubles or the practice. Later on, when I signed with Adidas, in 1975, I used to have enormous boxes of clothes in my house in France, one box for shirts, one for shorts, one for shoes, and so on. I think I was the first player to start that. The sponsors didn't care, because they knew I always looked good. That made a change from my mismatched clothing at the start of my career.

The morning of the final, I was nervous, even though I tried not to show Dominique, who was herself trying to cover up how tense she was. I don't think we ate much at breakfast that day. The grass courts favoured my game, and their softness made my drop shots bounce very low, like in water, as Ashe said afterwards. I didn't think that I was going to win, but I knew I could. I was thinking that getting to the final was not enough, but I knew this match was going to be difficult, because this was on grass and I was playing Ashe who was good on grass. If I had been playing him on clay, it would have been peanuts for me. I was quick, and I remember getting some unbelievable balls back.

I recall one point in particular: at Forest Hills the Centre Court was actually three courts side by side. The one you played the final on was the middle one. This meant you could run wide on both sides. On this particular point, Arthur came to the net and played a cross-court volley onto my backhand but so far away that I had to run onto the next court to get it. I ran into the doubles lines on that court, hit the ball round the net (which you're allowed to do), and put it in the corner. Perfect. I did that because I knew intuitively he was going to hit it there, so I started running in advance, ten metres onto the other court. That point stuck in my memory because it was so fantastic, and it gave me and the crowd such pleasure.

I was very nervous at the start of the final and lost the 1st set 6–3. I clawed back the next by the same score, then lost a tie-break in the 3rd set. I'd also had some bad line calls by then – not to mention some terrible bounces – so I was agitated and complaining to the linesmen. I think I'd whipped my towel at the umpire and thrown a ball towards him as well, just to help matters. So the entire crowd was against me – except my fiancée and any racist members of the public who didn't want Arthur to win – and they were booing and shouting at me. I was not looking good. Things got worse when Ashe managed to break me in the 4th set to go 4–2 up. Two sets to one up, break up, on grass, where it's much harder to break serve: the match was almost his. Then, and that's why tennis is the most incredible mind sport – boxing without the punches, I always say – Ashe suddenly started looking beatable. He made a few errors, and his first serves weren't going in quite as well. It looked as if he was getting a bit nervous. I got my game and my concentration together. Urged on by Dominique, who was sitting at one end of the court, and spurred on by having 15,000 people against me (because in a bloody-minded way, that could sometimes work in my favour), I broke back by going for my shots and stringing together some topspin passing shots that whistled past Ashe on several occasions. Two games later, I had broken him again and levelled at two sets all.

Still the match was not over. Ashe broke me at the start of the 5th set but, instead of crumbling, I immediately broke him back. I felt strong, mentally and physically, and carried on playing in the same risky way I always do, but at that stage everything was working. I broke him again to lead 4–2, then, keeping my nerve, finally took the set 6–3 and the US Open title with it. At the end, I remember jumping around like a madman for something like five minutes, because I was so unbelievably happy to have won. I never thought I could win such a big tournament on grass because I still didn't feel comfortable on the stuff, so to win against somebody as good as Arthur, and in such a tight match, that felt great. It also felt like justice was done, after Wimbledon. That's what it was: vindication.

There was no time to enjoy the success, though. On I went. First to Seattle, where I won the tournament, then Los Angeles for the Pacific Southwest, where I was pleased to lose in the 3rd round. Having won the last four tournaments in a row, including a major, I had played every single day, singles, doubles and sometimes mixed, for the last four-and-a-half weeks. I was beyond exhaustion – I was drained. So I returned to Brussels for a few days' rest because the next event was the big one, the Davis Cup final against the USA in Bucharest.

In Brussels, I did not touch a racket for a week. I slept and tried to relax and to think about other things apart from what lay ahead a few days later. But I was still tense when I finally arrived in Bucharest on the Monday before the tie that was due to start on the Friday. Tiriac immediately said he was going to kill me, because he thought I should have arrived the week before to practise. He said I was not taking it seriously – when in fact he knew very well I would give my right arm to win the tie – but my relationship with Ion had got even worse over the summer. We were no longer playing doubles together, and we were barely speaking. So I started to practise hard, several hours a day and, because I've got quite soft hands, I got this enormous blister, all over the palm of my hand, all open. I always get blisters if I don't play for a few days, but this one was really bad, so Tiriac got mad again, except this time he told the press, not me. If he'd said it to my face, it would have been OK, but he said it behind my back, which upset me a lot and made me feel even worse.

To complete the disastrous preparations, some stupid Communist guy from our Federation decided to put us all in a hotel. They said it was to develop team spirit and to protect us (from what?). The Americans had asked for a lot of police protection, because this was just a couple of weeks after the massacre of Israeli athletes at the Munich Olympics and Harold Solomon, who was on the US team, was Jewish. Fair enough. But us? Anyway, our Federation made a big deal out of that and locked us up in the unfortunately-named Triumph Hotel. As well as having round-the-clock police protection and a guard on our floor of the hotel, they also took away my car and stopped me from leaving the hotel, except to go to the club to practise. It was the first time somebody was controlling me totally, and, coming from winning the US Open just before, that made me really mad. What annoyed me most was that Ion said nothing, because if we had both refused to cooperate they would have had to abandon the plan. But for some reason, he thought it was a good idea. So Dominique, who had accompanied me to Bucharest with her mother and sister, was obliged to stay at the nearby Intercontinental Hotel, with the American team, ironically. We could only communicate by phone or when I saw her briefly at the club. Though I did once manage to smuggle her into the hotel, under pain of immediate execution, so that we could have sex, because I was going out of my mind with tension by then.

If I'd had her with me the whole time, I might have been more relaxed throughout. Probably they thought we'll keep him on his own, then he'll be unbelievable, like a lion. That's bullshit. I knew what was good for me, what I needed to do to perform. It's like the idea of boxers and other sportsmen being kept away from their wives before a big match. That's stupid as well. Personally, I never had a rule about not having sex before a match. Sometimes I was up for it, then I'd win a match and think: 'That was great, I have to do the same thing next time.' But the next time I'd lose, so in the end I just took the view if we both felt like it then fine, if not then it wasn't going to affect the result either way.

Having been locked away for the week definitely did not help my mood as I began the first rubber against Smith. Because I had just won the US Open, everybody just assumed I would win both my singles and my doubles. Easy as that. The Davis Cup, which meant more to Romania than any majors I might win, would be ours. In fact, the pressure on me was so terrible that I could hardly play. I felt sick and definitely performed less well than I should. After a close 1st set which went to Smith, despite me serving for it at 9–8, I collapsed in the next two sets, going down in straight sets 11–9, 6–2, 6–3.

Tiriac then excelled himself in all areas of his game, including gamesmanship, I have to say, to beat Gorman in five sets, after coming back from two sets to love. The crowd was wild, the atmosphere was crazy, but at least we were still in with a chance when we began our doubles the next day. I still felt it was all down to me, and, because of my loss against Smith, I felt even more pressure, if that's possible. The American pair, Smith and Van Dillen, however, were playing with a confidence that we did not expect, and the straight sets score of 6–2, 6–0, 6–3 gives some idea of what a total nightmare the match was for us. The crowd couldn't believe what they were seeing and were almost stunned into silence. If ever I wanted to dig a hole and disappear from view during a match, this was probably it.

The final day had Ion playing first against Smith. Only a miracle could save us, because, although I knew Tiriac would pull out all the tricks, as he said himself, he was still 'the best player in the world who can't play tennis.' Sure enough, Ion did everything he could, including stalling, complaining about line calls, disrupting Smith's flow. But nothing could be done. He clung on for five sets, but eventually had to concede victory. The Americans had won the Davis Cup, and Romania had lost its best and last chance.

There was still my final rubber to play against Gorman. As I came onto court, I remember being upset that the crowd was chanting Tiriac's name, not mine. Although (maybe because) the match counted for nothing, I played really well and beat Tom in four sets. Obviously, this was hardly any consolation for my feeling of complete devastation. I felt I had let the entire country down, and it was clear that the people did too. The crowd during the three days were like a soccer crowd. They couldn't understand why I was not winning or that I could have a bad match. They had come to support me, and, as far as they were concerned, that alone should have been enough to make me win. In fact, I always played my best matches outside Romania. Inside, there was just too much expectation, and the hopes of a whole country were too much for me to bear.

After the presentation ceremony, there were speeches, most of which were meaningless for me. I remember, amongst others, the son of Dwight Davis, the founder of the Davis Cup, thanking the good people of, yes, Budapest for their hospitality. So much for the general knowledge of the Americans. But Ion really did a good thing: he grabbed the microphone and said that if Romania was here today it was because of me, not because of him. I'd got all the points in so many ties that the people should realize that and thank me for it. I really appreciated his words because I could not have said anything myself.

It didn't stop some people crucifying me after the final, accusing me of not trying and not caring. That upset me very much, and I flew out to Barcelona for the Spanish Open, feeling tired, depressed, and vulnerable. Dominique, through this whole time, told me not to worry, not to take any notice of these people attacking me because those who knew me well understood what sort of pressure I had been under and that I had been trying for every single point. But even she admitted that she was shocked to hear the reaction in Romania. There is no doubt in my mind that losing that final remains the saddest and most traumatic experience of my entire tennis career, worse than either of my Wimbledon final losses. In fact, winning the Davis Cup for my country meant so much to me that, if I was able to exchange my US Open title for the Davis Cup, you know what I would do? Take the Davis Cup. Every time.

CHAPTER SIX

1972–1973

Henri Cochet, one of the Musketeers, handed me the trophy, and at that stage I did feel very happy. I had wanted to win that tournament since I was a kid.

After the trauma of the Davis Cup, it felt good to be back playing normal tournaments again. I reached the semifinals in Barcelona and also played in Paris, Stockholm, and London, where I won the 1972 Dewar Cup. I took the opportunity there to dress up in a kilt, telling the Scotsman John Dewar: 'You can call me Lord Nastase now.'

Then it was back to Barcelona for the end-of-year Masters tournament, where I would be defending the title I had won in Paris the year before. Barcelona is not a good city if you like going to bed early. Nothing seems to happen before ten o'clock at night, and that included the tennis, so we found ourselves regularly playing into the early hours of the morning.

This time, the top eight players who had qualified from the Grand Prix circuit of now twenty-two tournaments were split into two groups of four, who would play each other in a round-robin format. The top two from each group would then go through to the semifinals. After some good results in the previous weeks, plus a week's recuperation in Brussels staying with my future in-laws, I had recovered my confidence and my energy, so I easily won my three round-robin matches against Tom Gorman, Manuel Orantes, and Bob Hewitt in straight sets. My semifinal opponent, Jimmy Connors, did not fare any better than them, and I found myself in the final against either Gorman (who had come second in my group, so had got through to the semis) or Godzilla, Stan Smith. Again. Obviously, I preferred to play Gorman, but as their match went on late into the night I went to bed not knowing the result, figuring that it didn't make any difference to me anyway. I knew both their games so well that I would adapt mine to whoever was the winner. That said, I'd played Tom already ten times that year and won nine of our matches, whereas I had lost all four of my matches against Stan.

Surprisingly, I got to sleep pretty fast that night, but I would have slept better if I hadn't been woken in the early hours by Tom himself, Jimmy, and my friend the journalist Richard Evans, who is now the *Sunday Times* tennis correspondent but for a long time ran the ATP offices in Monte Carlo. Tom thought I'd like to know I was playing him the next day. Surprised at the news that he'd beaten Smith and annoyed at having been woken, I didn't notice, as I slammed the door in their faces, that they were all trying to stop laughing as they delivered the news. Late the next morning, when I eventually emerged, I saw the schedule in the hotel lobby. It took a few moments for the news to sink in. It wasn't Tom I was playing but Godzilla. Then it all came back to me: those bastards had played a trick on me the night before. Actually, it was Tom who was mainly responsible because he was a big joker, like me. What had happened was he was match point up against Stan, but because he had injured his back, in true sportsman's fashion, he had defaulted to allow Stan to go through. Nowadays, players wouldn't do that. They'd get the trainer to come onto court fifteen times and then try to make it through to the final. For me, if you're hurt you default, otherwise you keep playing. So I think Gorman was right to do what he did – though not to trick me afterwards.

The final began, and I raced ahead to a two sets to love lead, 6–3, 6–2. Smith, though, had no plans to lose so quickly, and he grabbed the next two sets by the same score. My future father-in-law, watching from the stands, began to shrink visibly and turn white as nerves overcame him, and this turned out to be the last time he ever had the courage to watch me play. As for Dominique, she was getting used to the ordeal by now.

I had this habit of always squeezing the ball before serving it. On this occasion, a strange thing happened: I was squeezing the balls and thought they felt really soft, even the new ones. Then we found out after four sets that the ball boys were amusing themselves by sticking drawing pins in them. So in the 5th set we were playing with proper balls, at last, and they were flying everywhere. It was completely different from the first four sets, but I held on firmly. I was determined not to let Smith beat me yet again, and I managed to win the final set 6–3.

For the second year running, I was the Master. The psychological benefit of winning the tournament and against Smith in particular, after everything he had put me through that year, was enormous. Although I had won £6,000 for the week, the money was not important. On top of that, I had also qualified for the Masters by coming top of the 1972 Grand Prix circuit, with more points than any other player.

This was a double that no one had yet achieved, and it had earned me a bonus of £21,000 and taken my earnings that year to more than £100,000. This was a vast sum for me, considering what I had been earning just five years before, and it made me the highest earning player that year. I had had an extraordinary year of great ups and terrible downs, I had played thirty-two tournaments plus six rounds of Davis Cup, won twelve singles titles, including a major, and nine doubles. Yet again, I was completely exhausted, nervously and physically.

There were still no official rankings, but many felt I could be called the number 1 player in the world. Even those who did not, agreed that I was difficult to ignore, for better or for worse, and that I had made the sort of impact on the sport that contributed to its growing popularity worldwide. Tennis was no longer the aristocratic game of gentlemen. It was going global, and the crazy guy from Romania was playing a big part in the shake-up.

Although I was making a lot of money, particularly for a tennis player, I was not consciously chasing the dollars. I have always taken the view that, if you have success, the money takes care of itself. You don't need to go looking for it. After I had won the 1970 Italian Open, contracts had begun to come in; not big ones but more than I had had until then. One of my first sponsorship deals was with Nike shoes, in 1969, for $5,000 all up. I also wore Fred Perry clothes at the time and was playing with my beloved Dunlop Maxply rackets. By the end of 1972, I had switched to Tacchini for clothing, for $5,000 per year, which was still a small amount, considering the profile I had in the game.

The money meant that, by the end of '72 I was no longer checking the price automatically on everything I bought, but I was still very conscious of the value of money. Whenever

I returned to Bucharest, I was embarrassed to show how much money I had compared to those around me. I was like a child who has lots of toys but who doesn't want to get them out because the others will want them too, and they know they cannot buy them. So it's true that I wasn't comfortable with the situation. My parents appreciated that, and in fact my father and sisters still worked (they were all employed by the BNR bank), because they did not want to depend on me, even though of course I was happy to help them out whenever I could. My mother, meanwhile, insisted on looking after the house I had just bought, refusing all my pleas for her to get in help. But that was good because it meant that my relationship with them has never changed, and I always remained a normal person. As a result, I didn't change my personality or the way I thought of others who did not have money, and I still treated everybody just the same.

In fact, the house was one of only two obvious luxuries I had bought myself that year. The first one had been a fantastic little Lancia Delta sports car (replacing the hopeless Capri), which I had gone to collect myself at the Ferrari headquarters in Maranello. It was bright yellow, with a midnight blue bonnet and my name written in small letters along the side. I loved it. It just used to take off when my foot touched the accelerator, and because in those days there weren't many cars in Bucharest, and no speed limits, I used to have such fun driving it around.

Buying my house was not really a luxury. It was a necessity. I had been living in my small army flat until the summer of that year, and now that I was engaged I had to find somewhere nicer to live. First of all, I had to get special dispensation from the Romanian government to be able to own property, since this was not allowed under a Communist

One of the earliest photos of me. Roland Garros, 1966, during the Romania v France Davis Cup tie. René Lacoste had kindly donated the brand new kit and I'd just been given four new Slazenger rackets. Fantastic.

ABOVE: Bucharest, 1967. A clean-shaven Ion Tiriac watches me dive for the ball during our Davis Cup tie against Spain.

RIGHT: Captain Nastase in 1972. I'm now a Colonel in the Romanian Army. No, really!

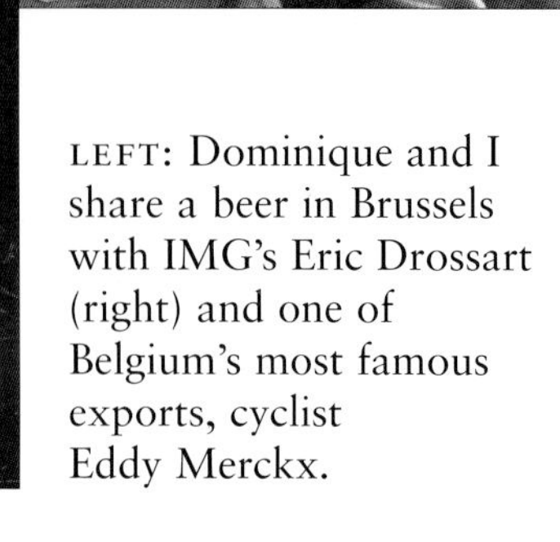

LEFT: Dominique and I share a beer in Brussels with IMG's Eric Drossart (right) and one of Belgium's most famous exports, cyclist Eddy Merckx.

ABOVE: The US and Romanian Davis Cup teams line up with President Nixon outside the White House in 1969. I am two to the left of Nixon.

ABOVE: Collecting my Lancia Delta sports car from the Ferrari headquarters in Maranello, 1972.

LEFT: Dominique, with her sister Nathalie, in Courchevel. It was 15-year-old Nathalie who had brought us together.

LEFT: One week after the civil ceremony, Dominique and I marry in church in Bazoches, France. Her family owned the nearby chateau.

BELOW: Following our civil marriage in December 1972, Dominique's parents enjoy hosting the reception at their large home in central Brussels.

BELOW: Arthur Ashe and I catching up with Johann Cruyff, one of my soccer idols, when he was playing for Barcelona.

Watching the ball closely during my 1972 Wimbledon final against Stan Smith.

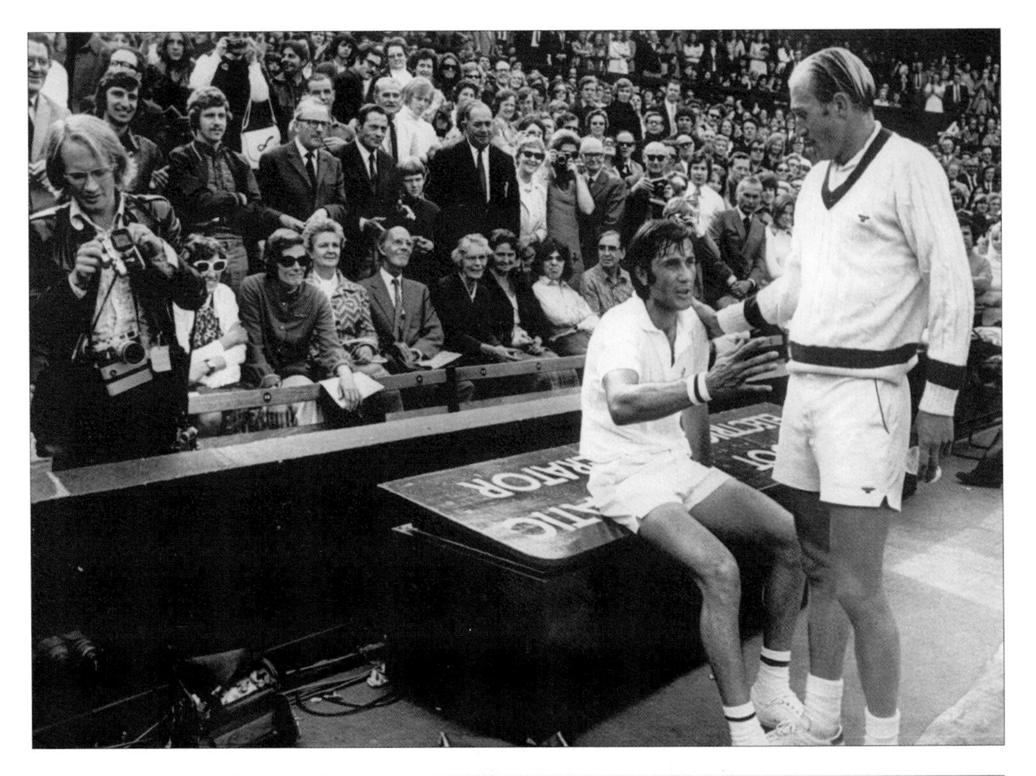

ABOVE: Stan Smith consoles me after I had narrowly lost our epic Wimbledon final in 1972.

ABOVE: Rosie Casals' dress infringes Wimbledon's all-white rule. I try to hide the offending design but she is ordered to change outfit.

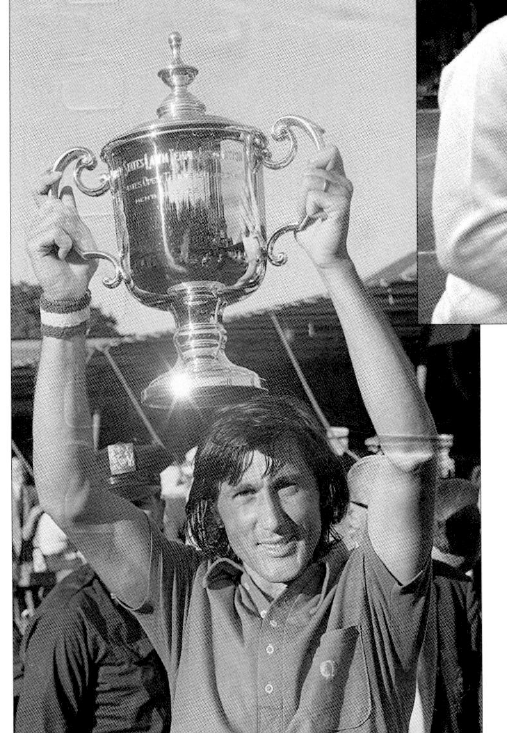

LEFT: September 1972, Forest Hills, New York. I win the US Open, my first grand slam title, beating Arthur Ashe in five sets.

Wimbledon 1973, boycott year. The shock of the tournament: I have just lost in the 4th round to US college graduate Sandy Mayer.

About to play a lob against Nikki Pilic, during our one-sided French Open final in 1973.

Happy after winning the French Open at Roland Garros in 1973. To the left is Henri Cochet, one of the legendary Musketeers.

Getting my own back against the snappers. I walk off court backwards following my 1976 Wimbledon semifinal win against Raul Ramirez.

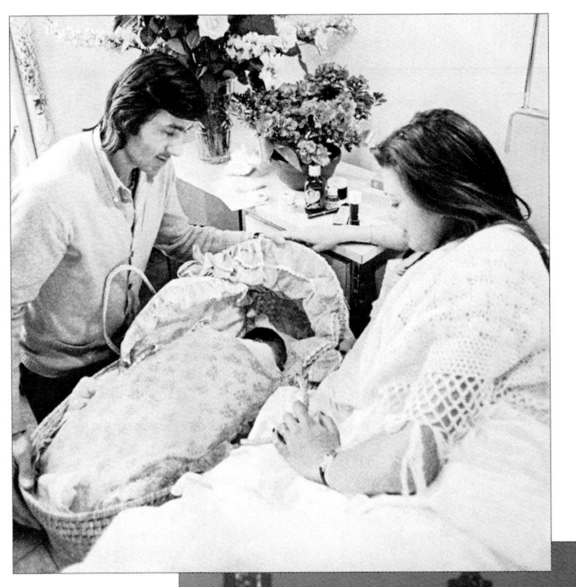

Admiring one-day-old Nathalie, born at Paris' American Hospital in March 1975.

My daughter Nathalie's baptism in Bazoches' tiny village church. Her aunt and godmother Nathalie stands next to Dominique.

On the *Johnny Carson Show* in 1977 to launch Adidas' Ilie Nastase tennis shoes which I wear on set.

regime. I had asked a friend of mine to look around, and he took me to this street where he'd seen a possible house. We got out of the car, and he pointed out a house.

'Do you like it?'

'Sure, I like it'. For me, compared to my apartment, it looked great.

'It's OK, we're going to see the one opposite. It's even better.'

I had a look round it, but I thought he was joking because the house was bigger than the first one and seemed too good to be true.

'You want it?' he asked.

'Yes, but you're sure I can?'

'Yes, I'm sure.'

'OK, then I sign right away.'

And that, in my typically impetuous manner, is how I bought the house that I still live in today, more than thirty years later. What I did not know was that Ion had also had a look round it and had made the mistake of delaying his decision, so he wasn't pleased when he discovered I'd nipped in and bought it from right under his moustache.

Still, now he lives in a huge house that he rents from the government. It used to belong to the prime minister and it's so enormous that, whenever I go there, I go: 'Mmm, nice offices.' He always says it's the last time he's going to invite me and tells his security guards: 'Don't give him anything to drink, just make him sit there.'

My house was perfect. It did not need anything doing to it, and my parents had a self-contained flat at garden level, while I had the rooms above. It also meant that, when Dominique finally came to Bucharest as my bride in December, she had somewhere nice to stay.

Straight after the Barcelona Masters, we headed back to

Brussels to get ready for the first of the two marriage ceremonies five days later. My government had had to give me special dispensation for this as well, because normally Romanians would not have been allowed to marry someone from the West. Once that had been granted, Dominique, and especially her mother, had gone into wedding overdrive during the autumn. I had no idea what had been planned. They had sensibly kept me well out of the preparations, but I did know there were to be two marriage ceremonies. The first, a civil ceremony, where you go to the town hall to be married by the mayor, was to be in Brussels on 7 December, and the second, a week later, a religious ceremony at their other home south of Paris.

Dominique arranged for me to have a suit made in Brussels for the civil ceremony, and I bought a Louis Feraud black velvet suit for the church service. For the civil ceremony, Dominique wore a very stylish emerald-green dress and jacket, which made her look really stunning. Afterwards, we all went back to the family house and had a sit-down lunch for about 150 people. I remember the Grazia's dining room was so big that we managed to seat all the guests around the huge U-shaped table. Two of my sisters, Gigi and Ana, were there for this and the church ceremony a week later, but, sadly, for various reasons, including my father's increasing heart problem, my parents and other siblings were not able to attend the two weddings. Ion had been invited but he did not come, and because of the state of our relationship I didn't want to go into the reasons why. So my best man was the French tennis player Pierre Barthès, who I was very friendly with and whose Canadian wife, Caroline, Dominique also got on well with.

After the civil ceremony, we all decamped to France for the church ceremony, which was an equally big affair. What

I had not realized until I got engaged to Dominique was quite how rich her family was. As well as the big house in Brussels, they also owned a beautiful château in Burgundy, dating back to Louis XIV. Set in enormous grounds, it was reached by a long tree-lined avenue and was surrounded by a moat and a drawbridge. The family also owned so much land beyond the château that half the nearby village of Bazoches-sur-le-Betz belonged to them – that's a lot of real estate, as they say in America. The good thing about them, though, was that they kept very low-key about it, and Dominique had never told me anything, so I was surprised, to say the least, the first time I saw the château that autumn. The village church that we got married in was tiny and beautiful – it could only seat about 100. It was just next door to the château grounds, so we were able to walk to it on the day itself.

We spent the week rehearsing the ceremony. I hate that sort of thing, but I was nervous about forgetting the words or getting them wrong. There was also the impossibly complicated seating plan to organize for the 100 or so guests, most of who had not been to the Belgian part of the wedding. I had a few friends from Romania and a few tennis friends, but the vast majority of guests were from the Grazia's side.

The night before the marriage, Madame Grazia insisted I sleep in a different room from Dominique – in fact in a totally different wing of the château, over the courtyard from my future wife – in case I might be tempted to tiptoe over in the night. I thought that was a bit crazy, given we'd been living together for the past six months. I know there's a superstition that it brings bad luck to share the same room the night before, but, hey, that didn't do much good to us, did it?

The day of the wedding was sunny but freezing, so we both arrived at the church shaking with nerves and cold. The press and television cameras were there – I'm told we even made the BBC's evening news – and there were a lot of people milling excitedly about in the village square outside the church. Dominique was wearing a fantastic dress that she had had made in Brussels, and on top of which she wore an ermine jacket that had belonged to her mother. She looked very beautiful, and I have to say we really enjoyed our wedding. The sit-down lunch back at the château was different from the one in Brussels. We were seated at small tables dotted throughout the various rooms, including the baronial-style hall, the drawing room, the billiard room, and the hunting room, where they had all the hunting trophies up on the wall. Like a lot of French people from the country, the Grazia men liked to go hunting, though I made a point of never accompanying them because I hate it. The five-course lunch included seafood, cheeses from the region, and lots of good Burgundy wines. We did not go hungry. By early evening, it was time to leave and we went off to Paris to spend our first night in L'Hôtel in the rue des Beaux Arts, in the Latin Quarter. It's in the historic place where Oscar Wilde spent his last days, and it was a really romantic way to start our marriage.

Unfortunately, the next day was less romantic. We took the plane to Bucharest, but because of the fog it got diverted to Sofia in Bulgaria instead. We then had to take the train all the way across to Romania, and in mid-December, in eastern Europe, you do not want to be standing around a station platform waiting for a train to pull in. It was absolutely freezing, at least −10°C, and the train itself took hours to reach Bucharest, by which time we were cold, hungry, and exhausted. Still, we were welcomed by a huge party of friends and family who had turned out to greet us, and that warmed us up quickly.

I took Dominique to my new house to meet my family properly for the first time. She'd met my parents briefly during the terrible Davis Cup final in October, but now she was able to get to know them better. She had made a big effort to learn Romanian so that she could communicate with them, as they spoke no other language other than a bit of Russian. We spent Christmas there, but I had also arranged that we stay for a few days in a small cottage up in the Transylvanian mountains, just the two of us. She loved discovering the country, going for walks in the snow, seeing the grave of Dracul (the alleged Dracula), and stopping off in little restaurants where, as soon as we walked in, they would start to serenade us with traditional folk music. It was all great.

After a couple of weeks, we flew off for our real honeymoon in Acapulco, in Mexico. For the next two weeks, we stayed in a fantastic hotel and got some sun and heat, and spent the days lazing around the pool. Although the hotel had tennis courts, I barely touched a racket. Maybe once, with an old American guy who was staying at the same hotel.

By the start of the 1973 season, I was relaxed, calm, and ready to play. My first tournament was in Omaha, Nebraska, and in mid-January it was −25°C and snowy. All the players were lily white after the winter, and I remember arriving full of energy and enthusiasm and dark brown after two weeks in the sun, joking: 'I'm not playing with you guys until you get a tan'. I won the singles, without practice and after not having played for about six weeks. Two weeks later, I won again in Calgary. Maybe I should get married every year, I thought. It was true, I felt more settled, I had someone to have dinner with every night, to keep me company, especially if I'd lost or was worried about the next day's match. I guess I'd never really had that before, except with Ion.

After the winter in the USA, the tour moved back to Europe for the spring clay-court season, which I have always loved. Clearly love was in the air, because I embarked on my most incredible run of victories that saw me win, from 2 April through to 23 June 1973, seven of the eight tournaments I entered, including another major, the French Open. My only slip-up was in the British Hard Court Championships in Bournemouth, where I nonetheless reached the final. I had won in Monte Carlo for the third successive year, beating a sixteen-year-old Borg this time, and I was getting to know Princess Grace, who always gave out the trophy, pretty well by now. I had also won in Barcelona, Madrid, and Florence.

I arrived in Paris at the end of May as the clear favourite to win the French Open. Newcombe always used to say about Roland Garros: 'The greatest thing about the French is that it's so bloody hard to win.' Two weeks of long matches on clay means that it certainly sorts out those who are fit from those who aren't. That year, though, I was hot, and I stormed through all my opponents in easy, straight-sets wins. The only guy who came close to taking a set off me was Roger Taylor, who had a set point against me in the quarters, but even he was despatched 6–0, 6–2, 7–6. And guess who I met in the semis? My old friend Tom Gorman. Poor Tom, he was sent back to the locker room 6–3, 6–4, 6–1. I think I was just so confident that all my shots, however risky, were working. It was rare that it happened so much and for so long, but I wasn't complaining: I was through to my second French Open final. This time, after '71, I felt I couldn't leave without winning, and because I already had the US Open I had a lot of confidence. And when I was confident, I felt I could do anything. I was unbeatable, I was on a roll.

All the while, I was also progressing through the men's doubles draw with the twenty-one-year-old Jimmy Connors. My manager, Bill Riordan, had suggested I play with Jimmy during the Riordan series of tournaments that winter, and, although I was still playing a bit with Tiriac and others, I thought I owed it to Riordan to agree. Jimmy and I reached the doubles final at Roland Garros, and were due to meet the number 1 seeds Newcombe and Okker.

The tournament that year was severely disrupted by rain. Our doubles final, which was played the day before the men's singles final, was due to follow the women's final, between Margaret Court and the eighteen-year-old newcomer Chris Evert, playing in her first ever French Open. While they played a long three-set match, we were hanging around, waiting to play. Then suddenly the organizers said: 'OK, you move to court 5 at the back.' So everybody goes whoosh to that court. It was so small we could hardly hit our lobs – because Connors and I, we liked to play a lot of lobs – and there were people hanging out of trees, trying to watch the match. After nearly three hours, Court had won her match on Centre Court, and the organizers wanted us to move back there. But it was too late, we were well into our match, which in the end we only just lost in five close sets. Afterwards, a lot of people told me I was crazy to try so hard in the doubles, given that I had the singles final the next day, but I'm like that. Once I was on court, I played hard and wanted to win. It didn't matter whether it was singles, doubles, or mixed.

It was raining on the day that should have been the postponed French Open final, a Monday. Just like Wimbledon, I thought. If I had been on my own, I would have been a mass of nerves by now, but this time I had Dominique plus her mother and sister who had come over from Brussels to support me and keep my mind off things. I was lucky also because my friend Pierre Barthès had access to an indoor clay court in Paris, so I went there to practise for an hour or two each day. That, together with being in the men's doubles final, meant that I had a good preparation and stayed match tight.

My opponent, the unseeded Nikki Pilic, was a player against who I had a good record, but he was playing well, and as this was a final anything could happen. I was never like some players, Connors in particular, who would say: 'I'm going to win that final tomorrow, I'm going to kill this guy.' I'd say: 'I'll try and I'll see.' Everybody thought I would win that year, because I had been playing so well, and of course that just added pressure on me. But there was something about Pilic's game that suited me: he had a big forehand, a big serve, and I knew if I kept to his backhand then I could beat him. Also, I'd played him a lot over the years in singles and doubles, so I knew pretty much what to do, I didn't need to do the sort of video analysis some of these players do nowadays.

The day of the final, in the end, was a Tuesday. It was the only time, before or since, that the tournament has finished so late, so I was making a habit of historic, late finals. That morning, I forced down some fruit, a bit of tea, and a croissant that I couldn't even finish and decided to go early to Roland Garros. We were staying at the Sofitel St Jacques in Montparnasse, which was the players' hotel, and it was quite far from the club, so, because I was nervous, I wanted to get there quickly. I remember sitting in the back of the courtesy car, and I couldn't understand why everybody was driving so slowly. Of course they weren't. This was Paris, after all, where everybody drives like a maniac – it was just that I was desperate to arrive. I hung around the players' restaurant, drinking Orangina and munching Dextrose tablets to keep my energy levels up. I used to get through a lot of them on days like that, when I couldn't face eating anything. Then, about half an hour before the match, I had a practice on one of the side courts nearest to the changing rooms before jumping back to the dressing room, changing my shirt, and waiting to go on court.

In those days, the changing rooms at Roland Garros were immediately to the right of the main presidential entrance. The men's were on one side of a long corridor, and the ladies' were on the other. Now, they are set below ground and are unbelievably luxurious, a mixture of dark, shiny wooden floors and lockers that contrast with the modern pale green leather armchairs in the players' rest area. It's a typically French blend of old and new, and it's very stylish. Even the lights switch on automatically as you approach. Off the main locker area is the shower area, where there must be about twenty cubicles, then a massage room, which has half a dozen beds, where players can get treated by the army of masseurs that travel all the year round with them. It also contains an enormous freezer for all those ice packs that the players are constantly strapping to various parts of their bodies.

In contrast, when I played my final in 1973, the changing rooms consisted of a few benches next to the lockers and a couple of beds in a massage room with two guys to treat you, and no freezer. We were constantly queuing up for a massage, for the bathroom, or for one of the half a dozen showers available, particularly in the early stages of the tournament, when the locker room was really busy. Now, despite its size, it's still busy but with all the hangers-on.

We'd grab a bench to sit on or would perch on one of the massage tables if it was free while we waited to go on court, but usually we would just come an hour before our match, hit for maybe ten minutes, get a massage, then go down onto the court. Also, at that time, we were playing singles, doubles, mixed, so we were on and off court all day and had less time to hang around, definitely. Mind you, Paris was the major where we ate the best. Rome was not bad, but Paris was better, so when we did hang around, at least it was a pleasure.

When Pilic and I were finally called to walk down the wooden steps that led from the locker room to the Centre Court – I remember the stairs were very squeaky from the shiny polish – I was very nervous. But that was good. You have to be nervous to play, you just don't want it to last too long. The sun was shining, finally, after ten days of rain, but the wind was swirling around. I got off to a bad start, playing tentatively, and lost the first three games. The packed stadium was anticipating an exciting final. Could the hot favourite be upset by the unlikely finalist? Unluckily for them, they did not get what they had hoped for, because after my initial nerves I hit a couple of winning passing shots, came up to the net, and began to play more aggressively. I levelled at 3–3 and even gave Nikki a point after a linesman's error, just to prove the point that my arguments with umpires were not done to steal points from opponents but because I genuinely thought there had been a big mistake. I then ran away with the 1st set 6–3 after thirty-three minutes.

The 2nd set started with Pilic breaking my serve at once. Maybe he was hitting back? Unfortunately for him, I broke him straight back and raced off to a 5–1 lead before Nikki salvaged a couple of games. I closed out 6–3 with a love service game after thirty-five minutes. The 3rd set was even worse for Pilic. I tangled him up with a mix of drop shots, lobs, passing shots cross court or down the line – my backhand was working especially well that day – and my legs carried me effortlessly to all corners of the court. Pilic in fact did not reach game point during the entire set, and twenty minutes later I had won the 1973 French Open, without dropping a set, a feat that I later learned had never been achieved. I felt incredibly proud but, unlike my victory dance at Forest Hills the year before, I didn't leap for joy when I won. I simply shook Nikki's hand and patted him on the back, satisfied with my win but almost embarrassed by the score of 6–3, 6–3, 6–0. I think it was the most one-sided final ever – certainly for ages – and it had hardly been a contest. The whole thing had felt too easy: majors, and particularly Roland Garros, are meant to be won with sweat, if not blood and tears, and I had not shed much of the first and none of the others.

Afterwards Henri Cochet, one of the Musketeers, handed me the trophy, and at that stage I did feel very happy. I had wanted to win that tournament since I was a kid. Growing up on clay, the tournament you hear the most about is not Wimbledon, it's the French Open and also, to a lesser extent, the Italian Open. The big one, though, was definitely the French, and for me not to have won it would have been a big failure on my part and a big regret.

Nowadays, after the presentation ceremony, the winner would have to come straight off court and into the press room for an endless round of press and television interviews, whereas then the journalists just followed me into the changing rooms and spoke to me there while I was getting showered and changed. It was much more informal.

Nor were there, thank God, the on-court speeches that the

players now have to give and which I usually find excruciating to listen to. One of the few exceptions was Justine Henin-Hardenne's very moving speech after winning the French Open in 2003, when she talked about her mother looking down on her from her place in heaven. Otherwise, though, they are usually an embarrassment. First of all, the players both have to remember to thank the sponsors. We know who the sponsors are, they're all over the bloody court! At the US Open, the men have to thank Heineken, which is bad enough when most of them obviously don't drink the stuff. But the women, they have to thank Tampax. No, that's not a joke, it's true.

The winner then has to come out with something stupid like: 'I have to congratulate my opponent, who played really well'. As if the opponent believes that! The opponent should be back in the dressing room. He's lost the match, he doesn't want to hang around, waiting for his turn to make some insincere speech. When you've lost, what can you say? 'Jesus, you can see I lost, I'm not happy. Goodbye.' The whole thing is ridiculous. They should just have some champagne for the winner, like in Formula 1, let the loser get off court and forget about those stupid speeches.

Dominique and her family were waiting for me at the players' restaurant afterwards, and I had a celebratory beer, my first for ages, and – I remember it to this day – a huge *baguette jambon/fromage*. I was starving after having eaten virtually nothing all day. I then returned the trophy – they give the winners miniature replicas to keep. People came up to congratulate me, including, I remember, a young Romanian called Gunther Bosch, who was coaching juniors at the time and who subsequently discovered Boris Becker. Before long, the Grazias returned to Brussels, and Dominique and I went back to our hotel to pack and to have a quiet dinner and early night. The next morning we were on a 7 a.m. flight to Rome for the Italian Open, which for once was being played after the French and which was already underway. The celebrations would have to wait.

In Rome, I went straight on court the day I arrived. Still on a high from Paris, I tore through my first four matches in straight sets, with the loss of only eleven games in total, including my quarterfinal match against Kodes. Then, I was up against Paolo Bertolucci of Italy in the semis. Bertolucci was a beautiful touch player, but his love of pasta, combined with his naturally stocky build, prevented him getting the best out of his game. Still, he was playing in front of a home crowd, and they wanted to see him beat the favourite. I remember the atmosphere was already whipped up, because there was a soccer match against Brazil at the nearby Stadio Olimpico, and thousands of wild soccer fans had somehow got into the tennis without tickets, so there were police all around. The crowd was going crazy at me. I was arguing about certain calls that I thought were blatantly in Bertolucci's favour and, by the time we were called off at two sets all because it was getting dark, I had had coins, Coke cans, and at the end a glass bottle thrown at me. That one I put coolly in my pocket, because I wanted to show the ILTF what had happened. The whole thing was out of control, and police ended up on court. I didn't have a problem with Bertolucci, that's for sure. When we got back to the locker room, some guy who claimed to be the father of a ball boy attacked me – who knows why – and had to be pulled off me. The next morning, the atmosphere had cooled, thank God, and I finished poor Bertolucci off 6–0 in front of three people.

An hour later, I was back on court to play Orantes in the final. That was incredible, it was all over in sixty-five minutes. I left him one game in each set, and it was the most one-sided important final I have ever played. I was embarrassed for him, because Manolo was a good player on clay. I think he got nervous, whereas I'd had a warm-up that morning against Bertolucci, so I was all over him. But I also think that, after the French, I believed I could beat anybody, at least on clay.

My victory did merit a celebration: winning the double of the Italian and the French back to back has always been a real physical feat of endurance and not many players have achieved it, certainly not with the loss of only two sets. So we all went out with Nicola Pietrangeli to Mimmo's restaurant. Because it was hot and there were so many people in our party, Mimmo laid out one long table outside and we spent the evening eating, making a lot of noise, and having a lot of fun.

Then it was over to England and the pre-Wimbledon tournament at the Queen's Club in west London. By the time I arrived, I realized that the row that had been simmering in Rome was on the point of exploding. This involved Nikki Pilic's fight with his Federation: he had made himself unavailable for a Davis Cup match earlier that year and had gone off and played a tournament instead, making himself thousands of dollars in the process. The Yugoslavs wanted to suspend him for disobeying them. I happened to think he was wrong, because I thought that to play Davis Cup was the least we could do, those of us from Eastern bloc countries, in return for the freedom we were given to travel as we pleased and make as much money as we could. The only thing I was expected to do, and I did it happily, was turn up for every tie and play for free. Because I wasn't in agreement with Pilic, I had not paid too much attention to the dispute that had actually started in Paris.

The problem was that, the autumn before, the tennis

players had formed a union, the Association of Tennis Professionals (ATP), which was supposed to defend the players' rights, mainly against the game's governing body, the ILTF, which for years had ordered the players about to suit its needs. Pilic had been suspended by the ILTF for one month, shortly before Roland Garros, although his appeal allowed him to play there and in Rome. The whole issue was a test case, especially as the ATP felt that the European players, in particular those from Eastern bloc countries, had up until then been at the beck and call of their national associations.

Ironically, I had only recently joined the ATP and paid my $500 dues. I was nonetheless expected to follow them when, at Queen's Club, they called their members to strike and boycott the Wimbledon Championships the week after. The executive director of the ATP, the American ex-Wimbledon champion Jack Kramer, was immediately condemned by the British press, who thought he was largely responsible for the situation, and he was forced to resign as a BBC commentator. The majority of players, however, signed up to the ATP's call for strike action, and they all started to jump on me and put pressure on me to do the same.

It didn't help that I was suddenly the favourite to win. I think if I had been a bad player, nobody would have cared if I played or not. But, boy, did they care! Players were cutting me dead in the club, one or two suggested I fake an injury at the last minute, or even 'throw' my 1st round match. I had threats night and day during the whole week of Queen's. I could hardly sleep, I did not know what to do, because, in the meantime, my Federation had called me to order me to play.

I wanted to win Wimbledon, of course. When I decided to play it was not because I thought I would win, because actually I was very tired by then. I'd been playing solidly for nine weeks, and I badly needed a break. But for my Federation there was absolutely no question of me not playing, and, unlike players from the West who did not have this problem, I knew that if I disobeyed their orders the sanctions could be ferocious. I wasn't prepared to put that to the test. My parents and family were still in Romania, I wanted to be able to keep my passport, come and go as I pleased, and play Davis Cup. I had too much to lose by joining the boycott and the other players did not seem to realize that.

It was a time of terrible stress. The papers were obsessed about what I and Roger Taylor, the other high-profile ATP member who ended up playing, would do. Dominique and I became front page news. Ironically, my opponent at the final of Queen's was Taylor. During that final, as a mark of how tense I must have been, I fell and my back seized up completely. I think the crowd thought I was having a joke as I lay there, unable to move. Eventually, an old man came down from the stands and massaged my back to loosen it up. One of my muscles had gone into a spasm, and for the next week – until I got beaten by Sandy Mayer half way through Wimbledon – the back continued to give me problems.

Straight after the Queen's final, two days before the start of Wimbledon, I was summoned before the disciplinary committee of the ATP, chaired by Stan Smith of all people, to justify my decision to play The Championships. It was like a court appearance. I was informed of my rights, which included legal representation, the support of any witnesses, and the opportunity to appeal against their verdict. It was incredibly humiliating. I explained that, the day before, I had been handed another message, this time from President Ceauşescu himself (who had never called me personally before or since), ordering me to play, and that there was nothing I could do. This had no effect, and I was subsequently fined $5,000 and labelled a traitor to the cause. For some weeks afterwards, I was ignored by certain players who felt strongly that I should have made a stand. My view was and still is that these people had the luxury and freedom to choose whether to take a stand. I did not.

The one who upset me most was Ion. He had been hovering in the changing rooms even on the first day's play at Wimbledon, trying to get through on the phone to our Federation so that I could tell them I was not playing. He put unbelievable pressure on me, saying he was not playing, so I did not need to either. But the situation with him was very different: he did not have my high profile in Romania, he was at the end of his career, he did not have much close family, nor a wife in the West. He could afford to take a gamble, whereas I could not. My refusal to obey him was the final nail in the coffin for our relationship. From that moment, not a word passed between us for well over a year. Even to this day, he still admits he wanted to kill me for what I did at Wimbledon.

The first Monday of The Championships finally arrived and, as the previous year's finalist, I opened play at 2 p.m., an honour normally reserved for the defending champion, in this case Stan Smith, who was on strike. This was a very bittersweet situation for me, especially after coming so close to winning the previous year, so I was very nervous when I walked out onto Centre Court.

The crowd, though, were fantastic, and they gave me a standing ovation. I was very touched by that, and it is one of the reasons why I always love coming back to Wimbledon. I feel I am very loved there, whatever bad things I may have done in the past. I think they have always had a soft spot for me, because not only did I make them laugh and do crazy things, I also played good tennis and won their doubles and mixed doubles titles. That year, 1973, was when English schoolgirls and young women really started to follow me in big numbers, screaming out my name, running onto court at the end of matches, and chasing after me for my autograph. That too made me realize that I was popular, and I have to say I always enjoyed being mobbed and screamed at – what man wouldn't, let's face it. After my years when women never gave me a second glance, it felt good to be desired by so many, even though most of them were too young for me.

I was disappointed that the All England Club never once thanked me for saving their tournament. They were desperate for me to play, it was quite clear, but never once, either before, during, or after the whole affair did anyone thank me. That remains one of the worst things that happened to me in my tennis career. Not so much getting beaten but not being thanked by Wimbledon. I got fined by the ATP – more than the prize money I won that year – and Wimbledon never offered to pay the fine. Obviously it wasn't the money that was the point; I could afford to pay, although $5,000 was a lot in those days. But I thought the gesture of offering would have been nice.

By the time I walked out onto court 2 to face American inter-collegiate champion Sandy Mayer in the 4th round, I was not in good shape mentally or physically. That court is disliked by all the players anyway, because it's so noisy and there have been a lot of memorable upsets there over the years. Mine was one of them. I was just lifeless on the day, I couldn't get going. I wasn't even nervous or able to get mad, and for me that's catastrophic. It was all over in four sets. Afterwards, I remember some of the screaming girls who had been mobbing me all week – along with their new discovery Borg, I was their number 1 idol – were in tears and running onto court to hug me. I patted a few of them on the head, but I was just resigned, not angry. I felt totally drained. My fifty-two match-winning streak had finally come to end in the most traumatic and public of ways. Yet, in a funny sort of way, it was a relief to be out.

Four hours later, Jimmy Connors and I were back on the very same court to play our doubles, and we even went all the way that year to win that title. Compensation of sorts, I suppose. By then, the tournament was running late – again – and I was forced to scratch from the mixed doubles, where Rosie Casals and I were through to the quarterfinals, because I had a long-standing agreement to open the new tennis club of my friend Pierre Barthès, down in Cap d'Agde, in the south of France. As well as being my best man six months before, he had stayed on at Roland Garros to practise with me before my final, so I felt strongly that I owed it to him not to pull out. I offered Wimbledon the possibility of me finding a way of doing a quick day-return, but there simply wasn't time.

Wimbledon 1973 was as emotional a tournament as I have ever played. It ended badly for me, but I still believe that I did the right thing to play, not only for personal reasons but also for the crowds who were so supportive of me throughout. I hoped the All England Club appreciated it at the time, even though they never showed it. Maybe one day they'll let me know.

Later that summer, in August, the first ATP official ranking came out, and ironically I was their first-ever world number 1. At the time, I didn't sit there and congratulate myself. I wasn't thinking: 'Wow, this is something I have worked so hard to get, I really deserve it.' Some people said: 'Well done', but I didn't make such a big thing of it myself. It was better that I didn't go crazy and big headed about the whole thing, even though I managed to hold on to the ranking until the end of the year, which was a long time compared to now, when it sometimes changes every few weeks. But if you aim to be number 1, it puts pressure on you, whereas I never aimed at that, partly because the official rankings did not exist when I was younger. Once I was there, of course, everybody badly wanted to beat me, more than if I was 2 or 3. There was also great pressure to stay there and, when I lost, I would think: 'God, I'm going to be number 2, 3, or 100.' Luckily, at first, I wasn't thinking too much about that. As I was number 1 for forty weeks, I didn't start worrying about that until later, in '74 or '75. But, sure, you don't want to give up your number 1 place.

It's hard to get to number 2, but it's harder to get to number 1 and stay there. I can't explain what made me go from 2 to 1. It just happened. It's like the difference between winning a grand slam title and being a finalist. I'm not sure there's much difference. It's often a little luck. Look at my Wimbledon final against Smith. I could so easily have won that, and I would still have been the same player. That's why, when they say Kim Clijsters should not be ranked 1 because she has not yet won a major, I don't agree. She should be number 1 if she's consistent, like in Formula 1. That's OK with me.

I certainly didn't change the way I behaved to other players when I got to number 1. I have always talked to everybody, whether I was ranked 1 or 20. It's like when I was young: Laver, Emerson, Santana, the best players, the ones with most class, they talked to everybody. Generally, the arrogant ones are the ones who weren't number 1.

Of course, when you're the best in the world, suddenly everybody wants to be your friend, to be seen with you. That's normal, it didn't bother me. Some may have tried to take advantage of me, particularly for business stuff. I know Dominique tried to keep some away, so they'd try to catch up with me when she wasn't around, but I didn't care. I was just playing tennis, and by then I was being managed by Mark McCormack's IMG agency, which took care of all the money and business side of things. I really tried to keep out of all that and ignore a lot of what was happening around me.

What I really wanted was to play tennis, keep enjoying it, please the crowd as well, if possible, while still winning matches. That was difficult, and it ended up putting pressure on me. But for me, the pleasure part was almost more important than the rankings. Sometimes I lost matches that I enjoyed very much: not major matches, sure, but ones where I'd played shots that had given me pleasure, risky shots that I'd practised and tried out in the match. Not that I liked to lose: I hated to lose, and anybody who says they don't mind is a bullshitter. But if I enjoyed myself and pleased the crowd as well, then that was better than nothing. I think I can confidently say that neither Borg nor McEnroe ever had that attitude.

There are two types of losses in my mind. The ones where you don't expect to lose to a guy, because you usually beat him, and the ones where you're playing a rival at a big tournament and the match could go either way. The 1973 US Open, at the end of August, gave me one of the first type of losses. I lost to the Rhodesian Andrew Pattison in the 1st round, which was not a good way of defending my title. Although Pattison was a respectable player, the sort of hard-working pro who would never set the tennis world alight, I was not devastated because it was a one-off. I knew if I was going to play him ten times, I'd beat him eight, so I just had to try and forget about it. The worst losses were against a guy like Smith, where I could lose to him four times in one year. These affected me much more. Of course, I was disappointed to lose to Pattison, but I didn't lose any sleep, not in the way that I did when I used to lose to Smith. There, only time could make things better and, even then, it took a few weeks to get over losses such as the Wimbledon final of '72.

That autumn, as a reward for what we had done for tennis in our country, Ceauşescu gave me and Tiriac the highest order in our country. Called the *Meritul Muncii Clasa I* for meritory work, the main advantage of this honour was that from now on we were exempt from paying tax. I had to put on my military uniform for the ceremony. After Ceauşescu had given a speech, he came over and said: 'Son, you're a little bit too excitable, sometimes I can see you swearing in Romanian.' I replied in a slightly joking manner: 'I cannot help it, I just have a Romanian temperament.' Ceauşescu didn't look pleased. The prime minister, who was hovering, made a sign to me that I should not have answered back, I should just have agreed and then apologized. 'Go away, drop it', he gestured nervously, so I skulked off to mingle. I was really shocked by the prime minister's reaction, but I had discovered that it was obviously a crime to answer back to Ceauşescu.

I was also bugged, and a file was kept on me by the secret police. I would regularly get followed by secret agents posing as friendly expatriate Romanians who would try to befriend me. In Bucharest, during the years I had my Capri, I would get followed the whole time by the secret police, because not only was it a foreign car – in the days when they were incredibly rare – but it still had the original British number plates on. So I'd drive around and notice that I was being tailed by another car, until the moment when the agents would either get close enough to recognize me or they would see me getting out the car. Nothing escaped their notice. I knew for sure that my house was bugged, and I realized who these guys were, but that was normal for Romania at the time. That's why whenever journalists asked me about the regime, I knew I could never say anything. They'd push me to express an opinion, and all I could do was give a diplomatic answer. Of course, I was aware that things were getting worse by then, I wasn't stupid, but if I'd started to get critical I was finished. So I'd just say: 'Oh I'm just a tennis player, I don't want to get involved.' Occasionally, the journalists would end up putting words into my mouth and back home they weren't happy with that, but they never complained to me directly because if they had I would have left the country for good. So I stayed out of politics in return for not being pressurized by the government, and it was a convenient, unspoken agreement that worked for both sides.

Before the end of the Grand Prix season, I notched up two more tournament wins: the prestigious Conde de Godo Open on clay at Barcelona's Real Club de Tennis, then the Open Jean Becker at the Stade Coubertin in Paris. I therefore arrived in Boston for the end-of-year Masters, sponsored once more by Commercial Union, having yet again come top of the Grand Prix rankings, which earned me a $55,000 bonus. I began the week badly, losing my opening match in my round-robin group to Gorman, the guy I normally never lost to. I think I must have been shocked by the loss, because after that I beat Kodes and Newcombe easily, then in the semifinal – and on my first wedding anniversary – I overcame my doubles partner, Jimmy Connors. My final against Tom Okker was a straight sets win for me, so by the end of the week I had done the double for the second year running: I had won the 1973 Grand Prix rankings and the Masters tournament as well. Despite my Wimbledon trauma and my strange result at Forest Hills, I had had a great year. I had won my second major, and out of the thirty-two tournaments I had entered I had won sixteen of them in singles and thirteen in doubles. I was ranked number 1 in the world, and all along I had still managed to have a lot of fun. That's what pleased me the most.

CHAPTER SEVEN

1974–1975

I'd needed a big rush of adrenaline, a big fright, to get my game flowing. Afterwards, I remember telling the press: 'This is the second time I have concentrated in twenty-nine years.'

After a few years of regular approaches, Lamar Hunt's World Championship Tennis finally persuaded me to play on their winter circuit in 1974, rather than on Bill Riordan's. What convinced me was not so much the money, although the annual six-figure dollar amount on the table was obviously nice, but the strength of the opposition. All the top players would be there, from Newcombe and Smith through to Kodes and Borg, who, aged seventeen, won two titles on the WCT circuit that winter. I too won a couple, in Richmond, Virginia and in Washington DC, and qualified for the end-of-season play-offs in Dallas, WCT's equivalent of the Masters in December. So, overall, I felt I had had a pretty good WCT season before heading back to Europe for the spring and summer.

Within weeks, as a measure of Borg's progress, we both found ourselves in the final of the Italian Open. Me, as defending champion, him, as the new kid on the tour. When he beat me in straight sets, the world really sat up, although those of us who had been playing him for a year or so were not surprised, because he was already very good a year before when I'd beaten him in the Monte Carlo final. He had this really big topspin and an on-court attitude that was totally inscrutable. I used to call Bjorn the Martian, because whenever he came off court, if you were in the locker room, you could never tell whether he'd won or lost. He'd come in, peel off those tight Fila outfits he wore, fold them into a neat pile, and shuffle off to the showers with that rolling walk of his. He was without emotion, it seemed, whereas if I'd lost I'd tear my clothes off and stalk off to the showers leaving a mess of clothes and rackets behind me, talking and sometimes screaming at anyone within earshot.

Two weeks later, having just turned eighteen, Bjorn did the same double as I had done the year before and added the French Open to his Italian Open win. Orantes, his opponent in Paris, was two sets to love up in the final, playing unbelievably well. I remember watching the match and leaving at that stage, thinking it was all over. Next thing I knew, the Martian woke up and whipped Orantes in the last three sets 6–0, 6–1, 6–1. Incredible.

Connors had caught the attention of Sergio Tacchini during the Italian Open, and, as I spoke Italian and wore their clothes anyway, Tacchini's president Sergio Palmieri came to me and said they would like Jimmy to wear their clothes, so could I have a word with him, which I did. Jimmy played hard to get, so they asked him to name his price. The two of us had dinner together at the Cavalieri Hilton, where many of the players stayed. I went through the contract with him, but Jimmy was worried because his manager, Riordan, wasn't there and he didn't know how much to ask for. 'I was number 1 last year and I have $5,000,' I tell him. So Jimmy says to me – and I thought he was joking: '$25,000.' I tell Palmieri, who goes back to Tacchini, and they say: 'No problem'.

'You son-of-a-bitch', I tell Palmieri, 'you only give me $5,000.' So the next day, I tell Jimmy: 'It's OK', and he says: 'Fine, but I want it in cash.' So Palmieri goes off again and comes back the next day with a big suitcase full of Italian lire. Jimmy gets mad. 'Fuck, I don't want this, I'm going to have to go to a bank. Tell him I want dollars.'

So Palmieri gets him his dollars and I stay on $5,000. Of course, they were right, because within three months he'd killed Ken Rosewall in two finals to win Wimbledon and the US Open, so they got a good deal. Which was more than I did.

I made the quarterfinals at Roland Garros in '74, where I was beaten in five sets by the tiny American Harold Solomon, whose favourite surface was clay. I was not too disappointed, because it's always really tough to defend your title; and to win it again, back to back, is very unusual. Borg did it, of course, on clay and on grass, but then he's not from this planet, as we know.

To drown my sorrows after my loss, I went off to the cinema with Dominique and her mother, who was over for the tournament. We decided to see *Les Valseuses*, a film that had just come out in France and was a huge success. It launched Gérard Depardieu's career and is a story of two long-haired layabouts who get together with a girl and travel around the country pursuing hedonistic pleasures. They spend a lot of time in bed or naked with the girl. At the time, it was a shocking film, and I can't think why we went to see it with my mother-in-law, because I have never been so embarrassed in a cinema in all my life. Still, it did the trick, and by the time we came out I'd long forgotten about Harold Solomon.

We also went to the most exclusive nightclub in Paris, Castel, during Roland Garros (minus my mother-in-law, I should add) and that's where I met Mick Jagger for the first time. We got talking about tennis, which he followed quite a lot, and he talked to me a lot about cricket, which is the sport he loves the most. After about half an hour of cricket chat – and I'm pretending I know what he's on about – he suddenly bursts out laughing: 'You son-of-a-bitch, you don't know anything about cricket, do you!' Well, it's true, I didn't, but I'd also been telling him how Ion and I would play cricket every year at Wimbledon. It would be on the middle Sunday and we'd be bussed over to some ground outside London by Bob Howe, an ex-tennis player who now worked for Dunlop. All the Aussies would be there, Newcombe, Roche, as well as Bob Hewitt, the South African, and some British players. It was a proper match, against another team, they'd give us the equipment, the bats and pads, though I'm not sure about the boxes. Anyway, I didn't know much about the rules, I just knew that when I batted I had to run, but otherwise I had no idea. As for the bowling, I was very keen to learn the proper movement, and actually I think I've got quite a good action, as I demonstrated to Mick in Castel. Bob Hewitt was showing us how to hold the ball. But Tiriac just took the ball and threw it like he was throwing a tennis ball. Straight at the head. He almost killed two guys. I think he knew, but he pretended all innocently that he had no idea.

My Wimbledon that summer of '74 was no better than my French Open, because I got beaten by the heavy-hitting American Dick Stockton in the 4th round in a match that was interrupted several times by the rain. The only thing everybody remembers about that match is that at one point

I grabbed a spectator's umbrella. I wasn't trying to distract Dick, as some people thought. But it was getting to a crucial part of the match: I was down two sets to love, and the 4th set was going with serve and reaching a critical stage. It had begun to drizzle and I thought we should go off, but to dispel the tension I was feeling I thought it would be fun to play a couple of points with the umbrella in my hand. It was a completely spontaneous act and it's a classic example of, 'OK, I lost the match, but I gave people pleasure and fun', and, even thirty years on, they still remember. And that makes me really proud, as proud in fact as some of my victories. It means I left an impression on people that was not just about the tennis, not just about the arguments, it was also about the fun. Because I always felt passion out there, I never knew in advance how it was going to come out. It often came out as wanting to entertain, to move people, to talk to them. I'd try to play those crazy shots, once, twice, three times, until they worked. That's how I loved to play. The public never knew what I was going to do next, because I never compromised. I was always myself, I played how I wanted to, not how others suggested I should. But always I had to show my emotions on court.

I admit that joking for me was often a way of getting rid of nerves. It didn't mean I was not trying and that I didn't care if I won or lost. I think a lot of people didn't realize that. It would calm me down and would hopefully not show to my opponent that I was nervous. Because even when you're ahead and especially when you're about to win, you can get really nervous. Not many players will admit to that, but it's true. You can be almost afraid to win. It might show if you double-fault, then the public notices, but all players got nervous, even Borg the ice man, or Connors, who everybody said had guts. It's just they didn't show it. So for me, joking around reduced the tension, but it wasn't done with any cynical intention of putting off the other player. I needed the outlet, simple as that.

That summer, Dominique realized she was pregnant. We'd wanted children but had been told, after she came off the pill at the beginning of the year, to use condoms for a few months, while her body got back to normal. Fine, except that there was no way I was going to go into a drugstore in the States, in Richmond, Virginia, as it turned out, and ask for some. Sorry but I wasn't running the risk of everybody recognizing me – I was much too self-conscious about that sort of thing in those days – so I'm afraid I sent Dominique instead, who bought the entire contents of the shop before getting up the courage to ask for what she really wanted.

She strongly suspected she was pregnant, though, in early August when we were in Bucharest, playing a Davis Cup tie against the French. One evening, we'd invited round for dinner Philippe Chatrier, the President of their Federation and later President of the ITF, Pierre Barthès, and his teammate Patrice Dominguez, and we were eating some caviar, which is not expensive in Romania like it is in the West. Normally, Dominique would eat it by the spoonful, she loved it, but this time she turned green just looking at it. She felt really sick. As she'd been feeling like that for a few days, she thought she might be pregnant, so we went to see an old doctor who examined her in detail and said not only was she not pregnant but she had blocked fallopian tubes and would probably never conceive. We were completely stunned and devastated. She immediately flew back to Brussels, in tears, headed straight for a specialist, who promptly told her that she was fine and that in fact she was two months' pregnant. That was fantastic news. From then on, other than her being sick every day for the next two months, she felt really well and carried on travelling with me most of the time until the end of the year.

At the end of August, just before the 1974 Forest Hills, Romania met Italy in a European-zone Davis Cup final. It was played in Mestre, next to Venice, in terrible heat and humidity. Tiriac, who had not played Davis Cup in '73, decided to give the Cup one final go in '74 – he was thirty-five by now – because he thought the draw looked OK. We were still in our non-speaking period, so he played not only the earlier tie against France (where he played just doubles) but also the entire tie against Italy (where he played two singles and a doubles) without saying a word to me. Our doubles matches in those ties became notorious as we managed to spend the entire time on court without exchanging so much as a word. We spoke to our captain, sure, but not to each other. In the end, that was probably a factor behind us losing the Italy tie because, though I won both my singles, we lost the crucial doubles.

The fall-out between Tiriac and me was a subject that fascinated both players and journalists. They couldn't understand how we could go from doing everything together to no longer even speaking. They were convinced we must have had one big fight or argument, which we never did. As they wanted a good story, they made more of it than there actually was, at least as far as I was concerned. I think the problem was more Tiriac's, and he admitted later on that he should have been more understanding of me: 'Either you accept Nastase as he is, or you kill him.' But it was funny in the locker room, because people would go to him and say:

'Where is Nastase?'

And he'd go: 'Who is Nastase?'

They would come and tell me what he'd said and I'd go: 'Tell Tiriac that, whenever the ball is too wide or high for

Tiriac and he shouts "yours", Nastase is the guy who has to run. He is the guy who's always running for him.'

So that year it's true we weren't speaking, but it was necessary I think, after the intensity of the relationship that we had had. Sometimes, to create distance, you have to hurt those you have been closest to, and you end up doing it in a violent way, not on purpose, but because that's the only way to make the break. It's the same in marriages when they end. Then, after a few years, you can be friends again. That's what happened with me and Ion, because gradually, by the late Seventies, we began to talk again. Not about the past, because that was all behind us, but he started to play Davis Cup doubles again and we socialized a bit together, though it was some years before he actually went inside my house. But I think that was more to do with having lost the house to me in the first place. Now we are friends again, his son is godfather to my youngest daughter, and we all get on very well.

At the end of the year, after winning two more big clay-court titles back to back in Spain, the Melia Trophy in Madrid and the Spanish championships in Barcelona, I went off for the end-of-year Masters tournament, which this time was played on the grass of the Kooyong Stadium in Melbourne. I was attempting to win the title for the fourth year in a row. It was too far for Dominique to travel when she was six months' pregnant, so I went on my own. Flying out of Heathrow on Qantas airlines, I noticed I was wearing an orange-coloured Guy Laroche blazer that was not very different in colour to those of the air stewards. So, to pass the time, I offered them my services, whipped a little napkin over my arm and started wandering up and down the aisle, offering tea and coffee to people. I don't remember scalding anyone, but I certainly made them laugh.

I started my week well by winning all three of my round-robin matches against the moustachioed Mexican Raul Ramirez, then Harold Solomon and Manuel Orantes. My semi against Newcombe came after he'd expressed a few words on the subject of gamesmanship and what he thought my attitude towards it was. Actually, I always got on very well with John, so I'm sure he was just being his usual frank Aussie self, but the media built things up to a level he never intended. In the end, our match went off without a squeak on my part, and I beat him in straight sets.

I was through to yet another Masters final, this time against the Argentine Guillermo Vilas, who was now coached by Ion. Vilas was not expected to win because he was, like Borg, a clay-court topspin specialist who loved nothing better than to stand at the back of the court bludgeoning back ground strokes until you gave up. He was superfit. It took him more than three hours, in heat that was around 40°C, to get the better of me. He had led two sets to love, I had pulled back to two sets all, and somehow he had made the crucial break to win the final set 6–4. There is no doubt that Ion must have told him all there was to know about my game on grass, but I also have to hand it to Vilas that he played the match of his life that day. Even he was really surprised and was very modest about his victory afterwards. For me, though, I was really disappointed. I'd wanted badly to win the Masters, as it had become 'my tournament', and it would have been a great way to end my rather up-and-down year, one that had seen me win tournaments and more money than ever before, but that, inevitably after my domination of the game the previous year, had left me with a feeling of dissatisfaction.

It also meant that I started 1975 slightly anxious about my form and I did not get into a rhythm, because I only played a couple of tournaments in January and February before deciding to stop and be with Dominique for the final month before the birth. The birth was to take place at the American Hospital in Paris' western suburb of Neuilly, and we decided to stay in a hotel in the nearby Avenue Victor Hugo, in the 16th *arrondissement*. Some Armenian friends lived in the same street, so we felt safe as we spent those few weeks just going for walks, shopping, and preparing for the arrival of the baby. We'd go to local restaurants for lunch and dinner, and to the movies in the evening. Altogether, it was a very calm time that did me a lot of good.

One night in March, Dominique felt the first contractions, so we went straight to the hospital. Her mother came over from her hotel as well, and we waited anxiously for the birth. Actually, the labour progressed quite quickly and Dominique decided that she preferred to give birth on her own, with just the midwife for company – the same one who had followed her pregnancy throughout and who she trusted completely. She wisely realized that I was of a nervous disposition and that I might well not survive the experience of the birth itself, so I was sent to wait in the corridor, in typical fashion for those days, together with my mother-in-law. Just after 6 a.m., on 12 March 1975, after a sleepless night, I was told that my daughter Nathalie had been born, safe and well, weighing a heavy 3.75 kg (8 lb 4 oz) and that Dominique, too, was very well. I was close to tears as I went in to see my daughter: I was '*fou de bonheur*', as they say in French, crazy with happiness. I understood then that having children puts all other troubles into perspective, and whenever I got into trouble in later years, or had problems in my life, if I spent time with my kids everything was all right again. She was perfect, with jet-black hair and tanned skin, just like her mother. We named her Nathalie after her aunt, because she had been so important in our whole story.

A few days later, as I arrived to visit my two women, I saw that there was an unbelievable scrum of photographers, press, and camera crews outside the hospital, all surrounded by police. It was a crazy scene. 'Hey, I know, my daughter's just been born, but even so', I felt like saying, 'can't you keep calm?' They wouldn't even let me into the building, until a policeman recognized me and let me through. Then I heard that Aristotle Onassis had died that night at the same hospital.

After a week, all three of us went to stay with our Armenian friends. Dominique got the baby blues just at that time, she would start to cry for nothing, and of course I had no idea what to do about it. What was even worse was that, just eight days after Nathalie's birth, I had to fly off to play my first tournament in six weeks, and I had no choice but to leave Dominique there feeling anxious and vulnerable, with a tiny baby. That was not easy.

So it's not surprising that I was not in the best of moods when I arrived, jet-lagged and at the last minute, in Tucson, Arizona for the American Airlines Games. Somehow I battled my way through to the final, where I lost to the Australian John Alexander, despite getting loads of blisters on my hand because I hadn't played for so long. It felt odd playing again, and I was worried that I might have lost my touch. Despite beating Laver in the quarterfinals, I was not relaxed when I played Ken Rosewall, who I had never yet beaten, in the following round. I managed to beat him, but during the match not only did I lose my temper at the bad umpiring but he also lost his with me, because at one point, when I'd dropped my racket, he ended up tossing it dismissively to the side of the court. Even I could tell I'd gone way too far, because for Rosewall that was about as strong a reaction as you ever saw from him.

I stayed in close touch with Dominique, who was by now back in our flat in Brussels, and she seemed to get better. But it was still difficult for me to play with a clear head, when firstly she was no longer with me, and secondly she was at home coping with a new baby. Still, I arrived in Bournemouth in mid-May for the British Hard Court Championships in a reasonably good mood. I was defending the title I'd won the year before, in '74, and I had always enjoyed this clay-court tournament in the quiet seaside town. Captain Mike Gibson was the tournament referee. Despite occasional tensions between us, we sort of got on quite well. I would sometimes tease him by imitating his incredibly English accent, but he thought I was a bit crazy anyway, so he put up with me.

It was cold that week, and the day of my quarterfinal against France's Patrick Proisy was so grey and drizzly that, at one stage, I tried to remove a linesman's gloves to keep my hands warm. I was trying to keep the crowd happy as well by clowning around a bit, because I could see they were freezing to death.

Everything was going OK for me. In the 1st set I was leading 5–2, when Proisy saved two set points and managed to get back to 4–5. He was serving at 15–0 when I hit an angled smash that was called out by an elderly linesman. It was definitely in, so I went round the net to show him the mark and to protest, because I wanted the umpire to get off his chair and come and have a look, as they systematically did on the continent. He refused point-blank. I began to get really mad, and the crowd started to slow clap and complain. But I stood my ground. I could see the mark, the ball was clearly in, and I didn't see why I should be robbed of the point by the incompetence and stubbornness of an ageing umpire and linesman. But all the umpire, Eric Auger, would say was: 'Nastase, play on.' Suddenly, who do I see standing there, looking stern, but my friend Captain Gibson, who had turned up to call us off because it was drizzling. Instead, he asked the umpire what had happened and, when I intervened, he said:

'Nastase, I don't want your opinion. I'm giving you two minutes to play, otherwise I'm defaulting you.'

So I shot back: 'How many whiskies did you have to come to a decision like that?'

The umpire meanwhile was now saying, amid pandemonium: 'Nastase, please play on or else you will be disqualified.'

I was so mad because nobody would listen to me, it was clear the ball was in. Even Proisy said afterwards:

'Look, I'm sorry, I know the ball was in, but I couldn't help you out there.'

Anyway, within a minute, Gibson did the film directors' 'cut' sign across the throat, and the umpire disqualified me. Some in the public clapped, maybe because they were fed up with waiting. I gathered my stuff and stormed off court.

Afterwards, the umpire claimed I spat at him, which is certainly possible, but he was lucky I didn't do something else. Normally, I didn't get mad when I was winning, as I was then, but it was the complete injustice of it all that had driven me crazy, really crazy. So I was really disappointed that they defaulted me, after I'd won their tournament the year before. I'd done promotions in town beforehand for the sponsors, I'd been really helpful. It all seemed very unfair.

There was an ironic postscript to the story. That same day, Roger Taylor was also involved in a match where the umpiring was of such terrible quality that he ended up walking off court. He couldn't stand it any more. So the championship management committee realized something had to be done, because this was already headline news on the television, and it made them look really incompetent. They issued a statement putting the blame firmly on the umpires, saying that, from now on, if the players were unanimous that there had been an incorrect decision, the linesmen/umpire had to accept their decision. They added: 'If the umpire believes the decision of the linesman is open to doubt, he should signify this to the linesman, who should then allow the umpire to adjudicate. With a little more diplomacy, the events of yesterday could have been avoided.' In other words, my situation should never have been allowed to happen, and they accepted I was unfairly disqualified. From then on, in Britain, umpires got up off their backsides to have a look at marks on clay courts, like they did in the rest of Europe, and they overruled clear errors. So I guess I was vindicated, but it was too late and most of the good to come out of the story got totally lost in the next day's media reporting, which made me out to be a 100 per cent bad boy.

Dominique heard the news as she was driving down to Bournemouth having decided to come over for a couple of days. She was in tears when she arrived, and after a quiet dinner in a London hotel we immediately flew back to Brussels for a couple of days to allow me to calm down about the whole incident. Within a week, however, I was in Rome for the start of the Italian championships and my next run-in with officials. Again, not my fault. I know that some of the problems I had in tournaments were my fault – I don't deny that – but this one in Rome, coming straight after Bournemouth, was not caused by me either. I was the victim again.

I had reached the semifinal and was due to play Raul

Ramirez. Now I'd had a problem with him the summer before in the States. Ramirez was a crafty player, who I thought was always looking for opportunities to dispute points – and I wasn't the only one. So on that hot afternoon I was already tense when I was waiting to go on court, the third scheduled match that afternoon on the Centre Court. Ramirez was late. So late, in fact, that he really should have been defaulted. They'd defaulted Dick Crealy earlier in the week for being less late for a mere doubles match. At Wimbledon, I'm sure they would have scratched Ramirez by then, because the ATP rules at the time said that, if a player was more than fifteen minutes late for a match, then he would be fined and defaulted. So this was blatant favouritism.

After thirty minutes, there was still no sign of him, and I'm ranting and raving at everybody in the locker room, saying they should default him. Other players such as Pilic were saying: 'Just get dressed and go'. But Richard Evans, who was the European Director of the ATP at the time, persuaded me that I should stay and wait until Ramirez arrived. He said it would be better for me and that the crowd would riot if, after waiting all this time, it was announced that there was no match. So, because Richard is a friend of mine and I did not want to disappoint anybody, I reluctantly agreed. But my stomach was in a complete knot, and I could hardly breathe from nerves and anger. Eventually, Ramirez sweeps in, a full forty minutes late, blaming the traffic, which was bullshit because the Foro Italico is not so far from the Holiday Inn where he was staying. I think he just didn't leave on time, that's all. We rushed onto court, the crowd booed because they didn't understand, and of course Ramirez was not fair play enough to pick up the mike and explain what had happened.

I was in such a state by then that, despite a little ceremony that had been organized beforehand by the tournament to give me a medal honouring ten years of me playing the championships, I went to pieces during the match. At 6–2, 5–2 down in the five-set match, I'd had enough. I gathered up my stuff and left the court, to the boos and whistles of the crowd who still had no idea what had gone on. Of course, I got fined (Ramirez got to the final and then beat Orantes to take the title). After I came off court I had to get the doctor to prescribe me some tranquillizers before I was in a fit state to go back on court later in the afternoon for my doubles semifinal, which I won with Connors. And guess who then beat us in the final? Gottfried and Ramirez. After the singles incident, I got murdered by the press. It didn't matter that I had been in the right, and that frankly I got screwed by the tournament organizers. As far as the media were concerned, Nasty was just being his usual self and causing problems for everybody. My reputation was now firmly established, and it became harder and harder to battle against it.

After my headline-making spring, I had an unsurprisingly disappointing Roland Garros in '75, where I lost in the third round to Adriano Panatta. I was scheduled to play in Nottingham as a Wimbledon warm-up, but the director there, Tony Pickard, decided to issue a very public: 'If this fellow Nastase is not prepared to come and play the game as it should be played, then he's wasting his time turning up.' How's that for offensive? Connors almost withdrew from the tournament in support of me, but I just replied by saying: 'Who is this guy Pickard anyway? He's crazy', and stayed away, preferring to coach the French Davis Cup team instead in Paris.

This meant that I arrived at Wimbledon cold, not having

played on grass all year, and with everybody looking at how I was going to behave. I didn't think I was going to win the tournament, that's for sure, but I just hoped for the best, and that I would do well. In my first match, against the Russian Kakulia, I had a grandmother as lineswoman on one line. She kept giving me bad calls and eventually admitted that she couldn't actually see because the sun was in her eyes! At least she was honest. So I picked up her chair, put it on my head and carried it to the other end of the court ('I'll put your chair where the sun doesn't shine' was my first thought) and lined it up, just so. Then I kissed her hand, and after that I never had any more problems with her.

My 2nd round match against Sherwood Stewart was a different affair. The day had got off to a bad start, when, arriving at 11.55 a.m. with Connors, we had been barred entry by the gateman who told us pompously that nobody was allowed in before midday, he didn't care who we were. Remember that Jimmy was the defending champion here. My match was scheduled as the second match on court 1, after Jimmy's, and I was not looking forward to it. The bearded Stewart was a solid player from Goose Creek in Texas, who was comfortable on grass – he was a good doubles player with his partner Fred McNair – so, with my lack of practice, I knew anything could happen.

At two sets all, the 5th set went first in my favour, then in his. After three hours on court, he had stretched out a 4–1 lead, only for me to break him back to get back to 3–4, with me to serve. I was up 40–30, game point. I served, went to the net, and Stewart sliced a backhand down the line past me and, as far as I was concerned, out. That should have been my game and 4–4, but the linesman said nothing, and the umpire called: 'Deuce'. I could not believe my eyes or ears. The ball was a good 5 cm out, never mind that chalk flew up, as someone later said. Journalists who reported the match the next day, including the veteran Laurie Pignon from the *Daily Mail*, were all in agreement. The ball was out. I protested, more in amazement than in anger, while the crowd, who filled every available space including in the standing-room section at the top, was going berserk, shouting: 'OUT'. Stewart, when I appealed to him, turned his back on me, and the pandemonium continued for several more minutes. All along, the linesman just kept smiling, which of course made me even more mad. But there was nothing to be done, I smashed my racket in fury and frustration, and the game restarted at deuce. Naturally, I lost the next two points, and Stewart served out the next game to win the match of his life. I stormed straight off court without waiting for my opponent.

Back in the dressing room, I slumped down on one of the benches and started to cry – something I don't remember doing either before or since in my adult career – and the tears just kept coming. I think it had been a build-up of loss of confidence, of fear that I was no longer the player I was, of loneliness now that I was travelling on my own, and of a deep sense of injustice at the various incidents that had happened in just a few weeks. Suddenly, nothing was going right. I felt umpires, linesmen, and luck were all against me, and I had nothing to fight back with. I was at the end of my tether. Connors tried to console me, but I showered and dressed quickly and headed off with him, back to the Inn on the Park hotel on Park Lane, where we were staying. Later that evening, he took me to the Playboy Club to try to take my mind off things. He liked to play blackjack – I never gambled, I just watched – and he figured that, surrounded by all those bunny girls, I would feel a bit happier. But it took a lot more than that to get me over that sort of defeat, because it was symbolic of what was happening to me at that time.

Basically, throughout my career, the happier I was when I came onto court, the better I played. If I had a small problem, if I fought with somebody or with my wife beforehand, or I knew she was upset about something, it would bother me. Then, if I missed a shot, it would be easy to think: 'Jesus, why did we fight or say that?' In tennis, nothing should interfere, not even a girlfriend or a wife. When I was happy and nothing bothered me, on the court it was fantastic, and I guess that's how it had been for much of '72 and '73, the years I had my best results. In '75, with Dominique away from me for so long and the pressures mounting, I was finding it harder and harder to keep my head together on court. Then, it became a vicious circle: everybody was expecting me to do something, the umpires were trying to punish me, and that put more pressure on me and made me more likely to explode. I felt cornered.

Jimmy kept trying to find ways of making me forget the defeat, and a couple of days later, when we were playing doubles on court 2, we came up with the idea of going on court in rugby shirts. Court 2 was the best court to do that on, because it was closest to a small side exit under Centre Court that led to our changing rooms, so it was good for nipping to and from the court. That entrance also came in useful when I was chased to and from various courts by screaming girls. We got the rugby shirts from a local sports shop in Wimbledon. Jimmy wore the green jersey of Ireland, because of his Irish roots, and I wore the red shirt of Wales, not because of any Welsh ancestry but because I was a Communist, of course. The crowd loved that when we walked on court. What they didn't know was that we were also hiding bowler hats that we then put on, instead of the rugby shirts, during the warm-up. It was all done in fun, but the All England Club failed to see the harmless side to this and we got fined for the whole thing. We had infringed their all-white rule. End of story.

What's stupid is that I agree with the predominantly white rule at Wimbledon. I think it's a nice tradition, and if you look at a few years ago, when Agassi started to play in black or in denim shorts with cycling shorts underneath, you realize how horrible players can look in coloured clothing. So I think Wimbledon do a great job trying to control that. It was just a shame they didn't see the funny side of things with us.

One of the other fun things to happen at Wimbledon in '75 was the unveiling of my waxwork at Madame Tussauds. They had been making it during that year and had met me a couple of times to take detailed measurements of every part of my body – well, almost – and I had donated one of my Sergio Tacchini outfits to complete the model. Coming face to face with my image was a strange experience. It's sad that when they no longer feature you at the museum, they just melt you down: I think they should ask if you want to buy yourself, because it would be a great thing to have around the house.

Connors went through to the final of the tournament, and everybody assumed he would win against Arthur Ashe, his opponent. Jimmy's mother, Gloria, who accompanied him to every major, called me in Brussels, where I had returned after I had been knocked out of the tournament in singles and doubles, and asked if I would return to support him because I was his friend. So I came over, sat with her and the actress Susan George, his then girlfriend, in the players' box. During every change of ends, while Ashe was meditating, Jimmy was reading this letter that his grandmother had written to him but it did no good. He was losing to Ashe's clever play. So Gloria told me: 'Nasty, go down there and tell Jimmy to step into the ball.' So I borrowed a camera from a guy, went into the photographers' pit behind the umpire's chair, and told Jimmy: 'You have to step into the ball.' He just turned round and snarled: 'Fuck you.' That's exactly what he said. Probably he didn't realize it was me before he turned around, but after the match he came out of the dressing room to where I was sitting in the waiting room – he was wearing just his socks and jock strap, I remember – and he said: 'Come on, I didn't meant that.' We ended up going to dinner, because I forgave him. I could understand the situation.

After Wimbledon, I went off to the States for the hot and tiring summer season there. Things began badly at the Washington Star International when I came up against Cliff Richey in the quarterfinals. I'd had a lot of problems on court with him in the past, but never off court. He was a hard player but a nervy one: once, when he was foot-faulted, he just ripped up the line. So I knew I could talk to him, infuriate him, and make him mad. Sometimes I got too carried away and things got too close, I'd be match point down before I would beat him. So I knew that he would fall into my trap, but it didn't work against everybody. For example, there was no point messing around with the top guys like Laver, Smith, Rosewall, and, later, Borg. It didn't affect them, and they were too good anyway. I would never have beaten them if on top of having to play my best I was joking around. And I'm sure they probably thought: 'It's going to be tough to beat the son-of-a-bitch, but when I do, what satisfaction.' But some guys got affected quite easily by what I did, and I knew I got inside their head before we'd even hit a ball. But I never meant to put my opponent off.

I didn't go on court to screw them, I was on court to win. If they couldn't take what I was doing, because I was getting angry, mimicking them to tease them or having fun with the crowd, then that was their problem.

When it came to Richey, it's not that I didn't respect him. I did, because he was an unbelievable competitor. It's just that I knew I could get under his skin. He'd call me a Commie, I'd call him an animal, because his eyes were always bulging on court. Every match was a fight, and I liked it, I hate to say it. It was a challenge.

So in this particular match, I was match point down and got foot-faulted. I went berserk, argued, and flipped my shoe at the line judge. Sure, I was to blame. But I was losing, and hey, I was a bit more tense when I was about to get knocked out of a tournament. Exasperated, Richey left the court, was persuaded to return after a delay, but left again because I asked for two serves. By then, his face was bright red, and the crowd was going nuts. Eventually, after another delay, he came back but I was still arguing for my two serves because he had been off court so long, although I knew it was my fault as well. The umpire then announced I had fifteen seconds to start playing again, and the crowd started to count down loudly and enthusiastically. When they got to zero, I was defaulted. There and then. I knew I had it coming to me. Afterwards Richey said: 'Nastase has pulled that crap 49,000 times. It was time to stand up to him.' I guess he was right; he'd called my bluff and he'd won.

My difficult summer continued in August with the Canadian Open in Toronto. This time, I was due to play Orantes in the final, but I was not in good shape even before the match. I'd played five or six tournaments in a row, and I was totally exhausted. What the public doesn't understand is that some days you have an off day. You're just not feeling sharp, in the same way that somebody who works in an office does not always work flat out every day. This day in Toronto was one of them. I got to 6–6 in the 1st set, reached 3–1 in the tie-break, then a service return of mine was called out. I lost control, I accept, but I really believed I was cheated out of the point. My problem was that, once I started, I sometimes found it impossible to stop. Unlike McEnroe, who seemed to have an in-built stop button somewhere, I didn't. So I felt the linesman had cheated me out of a crucial point, and ultimately, if I lost, out of money and a title.

My protests came to nothing, the crowd turned totally against me and I just couldn't play properly after that. I was so disgusted at what had happened that I lost the next two sets, and the match 6–0, 6–1. Afterwards, total scandal. I was accused of 'throwing' the match, which to this day I insist I never did, even though it's true I was not in a frame of mind to be competitive. But the sponsors wouldn't let me come back for my doubles final until my partner Kodes insisted, and they also fined me $8,000, the equivalent of my runner-up cheque.

Sometimes it's true that I was embarrassed afterwards by what I had done, and I would apologize to the player concerned, but nobody believed my apology. For me, I never felt hate for my opponent; I wanted to be able to sleep at night. I just wanted to win, and I thought I had a right to argue for a call if I thought there had been a real mistake. I'm not saying I was always right to do so, but that's what my soul told me to do, and 98 per cent of the time I think I did the right thing.

In August 1975, a real revolution happened at the West Side Tennis Club, the venue for the US Open: the terrible grass courts were finally replaced with American clay courts. So it was not surprising that it was a European clay court specialist, Manuel Orantes, who won the singles that year, beating the holder Connors in straight sets. I had promised to be a good boy, to behave, and I did just that, beating Ramirez in a tough five-setter before falling, like many others, to Orantes in the quarterfinals. Connors and I had some consolation when we teamed up to win the men's doubles, beating Tom Okker and Marty Riessen in the final. Despite all our clowning around, we had become one of the best teams on the circuit, and this was now our second major title, after the Wimbledon one in '73.

Our desire to have fun, though, often got us into trouble, and this happened again at London's Royal Albert Hall in November, the venue for the Dewar Cup. The Royal Albert Hall is always full of people in black ties drinking champagne and eating noisily in the boxes, and in a previous year I had once run wide for a shot and ended up hopping into a box and taking a mouthful of someone's food, just for fun. This year, Connors had beaten me in the semifinals of the singles, but surprisingly had been outplayed by Eddie Dibbs in the final. He was so pissed off he didn't want to play the doubles final. So John Dewar, who was a very good friend, asked me to try to convince Jimmy to play, adding that he'd give him more money if he agreed to do so. So I said to Bob Howe, the tournament director: 'Listen, I have an idea. Get me some bow ties and a bottle of champagne'. When Connors was cooling off in the locker room I reasoned with him: 'Listen, these guys, they've paid a lot of money, it's a final. Shit, you have to play, otherwise we'll get a lot of bad press. I've got an idea, we'll have some fun.' So he agreed. We were playing the German Karl Meiler and the Pole Wojtek Fibak in the final, and they were very serious guys.

We walked on court with our tracksuits on, hiding our bow ties. Bob crouched in the pit that ran alongside the court, waiting to hand me the champagne in the ice bucket. We warmed up with our tops on and played the first game. At the change over, we took the tracksuit tops off, I got the champagne from Bob, and shook the bottle open. The people in the top circle, in the cheapest seats, cheered really loudly, but those in the expensive boxes, wearing black ties, weren't pleased, and we got some bad press the next day because some people thought we were insulting those in the boxes and not taking the match seriously. All I was trying to do was to get Jimmy to play the match, but of course nobody knew what had gone on beforehand and that they nearly didn't get a doubles final at all. It was easier to jump to conclusions and blame Nasty for yet another misdemeanour.

By the time the '75 Masters came round – to be played, this time, in the Kunglihallen in Stockholm – I had had a crazy year. Despite not playing for much of February and March, I had still played thirty-one tournaments, finished fifth in the Grand Prix ranking, won ten singles and five doubles titles, including the US Open. A couple of my singles titles had come just before the Masters itself, and this gave me much-needed confidence. However, the ATP's new Code of Conduct, written by its president Arthur Ashe, had made its first official appearance at the Swedish Indoor championships, in November. This, ironically, was to have a major effect on the outcome of my first match in the Masters against who else but Arthur himself.

As I already explained at the start of this book, I was 1–4 down in the deciding set against Arthur when I started to stall during my service game. I was being heckled really badly by a guy, and, as a way of getting rid of the tension that I was feeling at this crucial stage of the match, I had not been able to resist answering back. Arthur finally got mad with me and stormed off court, which meant he was automatically defaulted. But as I had been on the verge of being defaulted myself by the referee, the tournament decided that my disqualification should stand, while Arthur was reinstated, partly of course because of his normally perfect behaviour on court.

So, after the Ashe disaster, I had no choice but to win my two remaining matches in my round-robin group if I wanted to qualify for the semifinals. Deep down, I think I felt I didn't want to go out of the tournament that had been so good for me in previous years. Sometimes, when I had my back to the wall, when I'd got really upset, I played my best tennis and this was definitely such an occasion. I was lucky to have been given a second chance, because other times my problems on court ruined my concentration and stopped me performing well. So I behaved 100 per cent for those remaining matches and beat first Orantes, then Panatta, to earn myself a semifinal against Guillermo Vilas, who had won the Grand Prix rankings that year through consistently good play. Still behaving impeccably, I destroyed him in three straight sets, and came up against Borg in the final. Playing in front of his home crowd, poor Bjorn seemed impotent against my play, and my 6–2, 6–2, 6–1 victory in sixty-five minutes gives some idea of how easy it was for me that day. I served well, I mixed up the pace and length, and anticipated accurately everything Bjorn tried. In fact, since my Ashe match, everything had fallen into place, as if I'd needed a big rush of adrenaline, a big fright, to get my game flowing. Afterwards, I remember telling the press: 'This is the second time I have concentrated in twenty-nine years.' I never explained when the first time was. So I was the Master again, for the fourth time in five years, and after a year when my name had been in the papers not so much because of my tennis but more often because of my behaviour. It felt fantastic to have some praise again, to have beaten an in-form Borg in front of his home fans, and to realize that I was still able to produce world-beating tennis.

CHAPTER EIGHT

1976

'Hey, Leo, where are you going with all that? Are you emigrating?' He replied in his perfect British accent: 'Come on, Mr Nastase, don't joke. You have a final to play.'

I'd won the Masters at the end of 1975, but I had no idea what 1976 would bring. Unlike players such as Borg or Connors, who I think set themselves targets at the beginning of each new season, I never made plans for what I wanted to win that year. How could I? Please! I didn't even know if I could finish a tournament without being disqualified. So I would just see what happened and hope to do well.

I had done two things at the end of 1975 that would have a big impact on my year: first of all, I had signed to play Team Tennis for Hawaii Leis from the spring to the end of the summer. Although I could still play Wimbledon, I would miss Roland Garros, something that I did not discover until after I had committed myself to Hawaii, when Philippe Chatrier, President of the French Tennis Federation, decided to ban Team Tennis players from his tournament. But I had been persuaded to sign by my agents, IMG, who thought it might do me good to have a break from tournament play.

The Team Tennis courts had different coloured sections rather than lines, matches were played over one set, and shouting and heckling by the public were positively encouraged. It seemed perfect for me. Of course, Team Tennis were also offering good money, around $200,000 for the season, so that too was an incentive. I'd had a disappointing year in '75 and was coming up to my thirtieth birthday, which, for tennis, usually means your best days are behind you. I thought maybe I could not win any more big tournaments (I signed just before winning the Masters) and that, together with the fact that things with Dominique were beginning to get a bit shaky, meant that I thought it would be good to get away for three months, to let things settle down.

The other important thing I did was to change my racket, from Dunlop to Adidas, from the start of 1976. I'd already signed a six-figure ground-breaking contract with Adidas in 1975 to wear their shoes and clothes, but the switch in rackets was probably a mistake because none of them was as good as the Dunlop Maxply, even though I was working with this guy in Belgium who was making them. My Dunlops were tailor-made and the grip was round, because I held it very low down. If it had been like a normal racket, it would have slipped out of my hand, whereas a round grip moulded better to it. This allowed me to play wristy shots that I could delay until the last minute, thanks to my strong wrist, and this made my game difficult to read. Lew Hoad was the first to have a racket like this. Also, my Dunlop was very 'nervy'. It had special weighting, a thin neck, and was very flexible in the head, and that too allowed me to do things with the ball, especially when I was at full stretch. I remember going several times to the Adidas factory in Belgium, but they were never able to make the racket exactly as I wanted. So while they were trying to develop the right racket, I started to paint Wilson rackets with the Adidas stripes and lettering. In fact, when I played Wimbledon in '76, in my final against Borg, I was playing with a painted Wilson. In the end, Adidas made a racket for me that I was never as comfortable with as my Dunlop. The head was a little bit bigger, the frame and neck were thicker, and it was a bit heavier. It was like changing from a favourite Ferrari to any other make of car. Could be good but never as good. I know Tiriac says I could play with any racket, but in my head it was really important to be 100 per cent happy with the racket and the strings, as I showed during my '72 Wimbledon final. I could change my shoes and my clothing, but I should probably never have changed my racket.

I arrived in Hawaii in April after the end of the WCT season and was put up in a big suite at the top of one of the best hotels in Honolulu. Fairly quickly, though, I realized that the travel in Team Tennis was really bad. Our matches against the other teams were one-night stands. We'd go off to, say, Phoenix, Arizona, for one day, then go back to Hawaii, then off again three days later to San Diego in California for another match. Hawaii, of course, is already half way across the Pacific Ocean, so it took a few hours just to hit the mainland of America, never mind go anywhere beyond. The toll on me soon became quite heavy, especially mentally.

I also became bored. In Hawaii, we'd practise in the morning, outdoors, because it was so hot and humid, but then we had the rest of the day to ourselves. Even the matches, in the evenings, only took a couple of hours. So I was on my own a lot, with my family thousands of miles away. Things between Dominique and me had sometimes been strained the previous year, because we had been apart quite a lot in what had been a tough time for me professionally. So, in the end, of course, the inevitable happened. Although I was never close to her, I did start to see this Norwegian girl on and off. The fact that one of the British papers decided to do Dominique a favour by calling her up and informing her made no difference. She wasn't stupid. Like many women she had an instinct that things weren't right, and that, if you go away for three months, things can happen. It didn't come as news to her, and I didn't need to explain anything. To be honest, I've never been very good at sitting down and analysing where my relationships are going. I always think people usually know anyway.

Still, I flew back to Paris, during Roland Garros as it turned out, which was not easy because I hated to see others playing the tournament that I loved so much. I managed to spend a few days with Dominique and calm things down, but I had to fly almost straight back to Hawaii because Team Tennis were threatening to sue me for breach of contract. So there was no time to talk.

We were reunited in Nottingham, the week before Wimbledon, for the grass-court tournament that Tony Pickard had advised me not to play the year before. There, Dominique and I started to talk. It helped that Jimmy Connors was there with his then girlfriend, the Texan ex-Miss World Marjorie Wallace, because Dominique and her got on very well, and the four of us would regularly go out for dinner.

Before Jimmy had started seeing Marjorie, I often had to help him find a girl, then get rid of her. He'd get himself into trouble because he was trying to be too romantic, to conquer them with promises of a trip. And I was much more direct. After all, he was only trying to get laid. So I'd say to him:

'Why did you tell her you would take her to Vegas? Then you're stuck with her for seven days, and you don't even like her? Don't talk like that.' But he was very innocent. He thought you had to be in love with a girl to do something with her. You can tell his mum influenced him beyond his tennis.

Anyway, that week in Nottingham, things then started to get better again between Dominique and me, and I felt calmer than I had done for a long time. There were no problems either between Tony Pickard and me. When Jimmy and I met in the final, on the eve of Wimbledon, and it was drizzling, we both insisted on playing, just so that we did not disappoint Tony and the public who were waiting to see us. So we skidded around, at considerable risk to ourselves I have to say, before stopping at one set each and sharing the title. I was very happy that, for once, I was making headlines for being a good boy, not a bad boy.

At Wimbledon I was seeded 3, behind the holder Ashe at 1 and Connors at 2. Jimmy and I were also seeded 2 in the doubles. But I didn't have a good feeling about Wimbledon, even though I'd done well at Nottingham, because I'd only played one tournament in almost three months and was really short of match practice. Somehow, maybe because I was surrounded by Dominique and also my brother Constantin, who had come over to coach me and string my rackets, I kept very calm and concentrated. Also in my camp was a Romanian guy called Mitch, who lived in the States and who, the following year, became like a manager for me when IMG rather publicly announced, during Wimbledon, that we had parted company.

I knew the media and their ways, so I had decided this year, in consultation with my team, not to give press interviews, for the first time ever in my career. It seemed to help my tennis, even if journalists themselves were frustrated, because what I did and said always provided them with good copy.

Also helping me unofficially throughout the tournament was my old friend Fred Perry. We'd always been fans of each other, and I had incredible respect and admiration for him. He'd been there during my '72 final against Smith and had supported me throughout that tournament. This time, I knew he was usually in the BBC radio commentary box, where he worked during The Championships, so it was easy for me to glance up at him and for him to nod encouragement at me. Those little things really helped, because there's not much your team can do for you once you are out there. In fact, more often than not at other tournaments, if things were not going well, Dominique or anybody else who was supporting me would get sworn and screamed at by me, and they were helpless to reply. When she had first started travelling with me, Dominique used to get nervous because she wanted me to win. By the end, she just got nervous in case something bad happened on court. It no longer mattered to her whether I won or lost. So being in my camp was never easy.

Although Jimmy and I lost in the 2nd round of the doubles (after two, long, five-set matches), I went through each of my opponents in the singles in straight sets, unbelievably easily. I cut out the joking almost totally, and beat the two Yugoslavs Nikki Spear and Zeljko Franulovic in the first two rounds, then the Aussie Kim Warwick and the New Zealander Onny Parun before coming up against Charlie Pasarell in the quarterfinals. Pasarell, surprisingly, had never got this far at Wimbledon, despite having played that record-length match against Pancho Gonzales at Wimbledon in 1969. But he could do nothing against me that day: I was sharp in my anticipation, I changed my pace and direction of shot, I served more heavily (thanks, I have to say, to my slightly heavier racket), and I was totally concentrating. I won in straight sets again and was now in the semis, where I would meet Ramirez, the player who had given me a few problems over the last couple of years.

I had decided to take a suite of rooms at the Dorchester Hotel on Park Lane, for Dominique and me plus my brother and another room for Mitch. This cost a lot of money, but I figured it was worth it if it kept me free from worry and met all our needs. To keep me relaxed on the days I wasn't playing, I would go over the road into Hyde Park with Constantin and my friends, and we'd kick a soccer ball about. Then we'd head back to the hotel, order room service, watch TV, and go to bed early. In most ways, I was living as close to a monk's life as it was possible for me to live. Deep down, though, I suppose I knew this was probably my last big chance to win the tournament, and I knew I had to take it seriously.

Wimbledon that year was in the middle of the most incredible heat wave, and by the later stages of the tournament the courts were so hard and dry that the ball no longer skidded through, keeping low, like it usually does on grass. Instead, it often just sat up like on slow courts. So although I was progressing through the draw in straight sets by playing a serve-volley grass-court game, Bjorn Borg, in the other half, was sailing through, equally easily, whilst sticking to his usual back-of-the-court clay-court game. He would lure his opponent into the net and finish him off with his fantastic passing shots that he had plenty of time to prepare. But the press weren't paying too much attention to Bjorn at this stage, they were focusing much more on me. Would this be my year at last? Even I was beginning to dare to dream that I could win.

My semifinal against Ramirez was something I was really looking forward to. After my problems with him in Rome the year before and in Indianapolis in '74, where I'd been disqualified, I was ready to take him on. I walked on court, clutching a thermos flask full of hot sweet tea to get me through the heat of the day, and set about storming through the 1st set 6–2. Ramirez looked lost. Good. Second set, I wavered, and Ramirez began to get into the match. This sort of match is nerve-racking, and it doesn't take much to get me going, particularly as I had been keeping myself in check all tournament. So I began to get annoyed by the motorized cameras of the dozen or so photographers in the pit behind the umpire. Every time I served, I would hear them all go off at once, like machine guns, and it was driving me crazy. I pleaded with them to stop, just while I served, but they took no notice. As the set wore on, I got more and more mad with them and ended up whipping my towel at them, shouting: 'I'll break your cameras, you sons-of-bitches.' Well, something like that. Anyway, the press were really happy. Finally, they thought, he's becoming normal for him; we were afraid he was becoming normal like us. But no, he's still nuts, thank God.

After that, I got going again. I'd probably needed to get that out of my system and that bit of screaming carried me through the rest of the match, which I won in straight sets – again. I was especially glad that I'd beaten Ramirez badly. But I was not finished. As punishment to the photographers, I suddenly decided to walk off Centre Court backwards, so that they couldn't get a photograph of me coming off. Ha! That will serve them right, I thought. Of course, all it did was to make sure that the next day's papers were full of headlines and photos of me walking off backwards. I presume I hadn't needed to bow to the Royal Box on my way out, otherwise I would have had to bow backside first. Now that really would have made the front page.

The next day was a Friday, because in 1976 the men's singles final was still played on a Saturday, and I had some urgent business that had nothing to do with tennis. I had to renew my visa for the States, because on the Monday I was flying first to Hawaii, then straight on to South Carolina. Coming from Romania, I spent my life sorting out my visas: I don't think there was a single country where I didn't need one, and it became my number one chore. Other things I often had to do that were also a pain in the neck included arranging flights and accommodation, but they did not need to be done every week, and, as my career progressed, my agent at IMG, Eric Drossart, would take on some of those tasks. But the visas, only I could do, and I hated that more than anything.

So that's how I found myself, one very hot morning, on the eve of my Wimbledon final against Borg, queuing up at the American Embassy in London. I'd brought along, as usual, my two passport-sized photographs, the money, the form I'd filled in, then I just waited. At least there they gave me the visa straight away, because they'd done a special arrangement for me. Sometimes, I had to go back the next day. Often, I'd have to send a telex in advance to the embassy or consulate in question, and ask if they could give me the visa for their country in whichever city I was in, because normally you should collect it in the country you are resident in. But I was never in Romania. In the beginning, most of them would say: 'No sir, you have to get your visa in Bucharest', so I had to explain that I played tennis and that this was not possible. So we'd get round it in the end. Sometimes, though, you didn't get the visa in time, you'd arrive at the airport, and they'd say: 'OK, you can come in without the visa', but they'd take me to one side, as if I was a criminal, and ask me all sorts of questions, while the whole queue was looking at me. So the visa thing was a real problem for me.

Luckily now I have a diplomatic passport, as does my wife Amalia, so we don't have to go through this any more, although I have to say that doing things like that, arranging transport and accommodation, and negotiating my own contracts, were all good training for later. It made me realize there was a world beyond tennis and that you don't go through life with people holding your hand, sorting out things for you the whole time. I don't think today's players have to bother too much about such details of everyday life. I doubt very much whether Lleyton Hewitt or Andy Roddick has ever had to queue for a visa in their life. Now, all they have to do is play good tennis. If that's all they do and they can't win, then it means they're not good enough. With us, we were sometimes distracted by other things that affected how we played.

I'm not saying, though, that my visa application had anything to do with losing the Wimbledon final, the next day, against Borg. Bjorn played very well, and I just didn't get going. To this day, I can't explain it because I wanted to win so badly. But Bjorn had been suffering from a pulled stomach muscle for a few days and had been getting cortisone injections before every match to get him through. It had got so bad that the evening before the final, his coach, Lennart Bergelin, said publicly that Borg was not certain to play the match. So I thought that must make me the favourite, the guy's hurt, I've got the experience, so maybe I relaxed a little bit. It certainly preyed on my mind that evening and night.

We just ordered up room service, watched a bit of TV,

and I didn't sleep very well. But that was normal. The next day, I forced down some breakfast and went running in Hyde Park, sweating a little bit, kicking the soccer ball around. Then we went down to Wimbledon. I had some fruit and a sandwich but that was it, because generally when I played I wanted to be on the border of being hungry. It was the hottest Championships ever, I remember, and it was the first time the linesmen were allowed to remove their jackets and ties. For Wimbledon, that was incredible. Apparently it was 41°C on Centre Court that day.

I practised with Jimmy a bit beforehand, then went back to change my shirt and wait for the signal to go to the little anteroom. It was very silent in the changing rooms, just me and Bjorn, who had had a painkilling injection just before and was now rubbing his stomach with some magic cream. In those days, the changing rooms were pretty small and cramped. There were just wooden benches with coat hooks above them, wide, horizontal lockers for our clothes and rackets, and a few baths, rather than stand-up showers. Not the sort of place where you could avoid your opponent. I couldn't tell, though, whether Borg was nervous or not. I guess he must have been, but who knows? After all, he was called the Ice Man. I have to admit, though, that I was nervous.

I started to get changed into some new Adidas clothes as I now did before every singles match. But first of all, I put my socks and shoes on. I get dressed always in this order. Socks and shoes on first. Because I have to tie the laces so they're just right. Then I feel comfortable and I'm ready. After that, I can put the rest on. I even do that when I put on normal clothes to go out in the street. My wife Amalia says: 'Are you crazy, what's wrong with you?' When we first started seeing each other, she'd laugh and tell her girlfriends:

'This guy's crazy, he puts his socks and shoes on first, then the underwear, then the trousers and shirt. Can you believe it?' But that's always how I got dressed in tennis clothes, so I do that all the time. Of course sometimes I can't get the trouser leg over the shoes, so I have to take them off and start again.

In the end, it was time to go. We emerged from the locker room that was on the left, just inside the main entrance to the All England Club, turned left, walked up a few steps, through some wooden doors, and passed underneath Kipling's words about meeting Triumph and Disaster and treating those two impostors just the same (yeah, right). Then, just on the left, before the door that led onto Centre Court, we were told to wait in the famous little anteroom. We sat there, just Bjorn and me and Leo, the little locker-room attendant who carried all our rackets and bags. Bjorn and I had agreed before we went out which end we would take with our chairs, but that was all we had said to each other all morning. In the anteroom, we didn't exchange a word. I remember managing to joke a bit with Leo, though, to try to break the tension. 'Hey, Leo, where are you going with all that? Are you emigrating?' He replied in his perfect British accent: 'Come on, Mr Nastase, don't joke. You have a final to play.'

Then we were called onto court. We emerged to a total scrum of photographers. Even I had never seen so many, it felt like a boxing match. We both bowed when we reached the service line, and each went to our corners. Borg won the toss and elected to receive. When play started, I began well. So well, in fact, compared to Borg, that I broke him in his first service game, led 3–0, and had three break points for a 4–0 lead. Dominique, who was sitting somewhere in the stands with Jimmy Connors and Marjorie Wallace, dared to hope that everything was going to be all right, that I would realize my dream. My brother and Mitch, who were sitting in the players' enclosure, knew I still had a long way to go.

Sure enough, the Ice Man cometh. Borg woke up. He held serve, broke back, got to 3–3, and broke me again to go 5–4, after which he served out to win the 1st set. I think that, if I had won that 1st set, anything could have happened. But, with Borg one set up, he got into his stride, whereas I seemed to lose my momentum. I had served really well all through the tournament, making use of my slightly heavier racket. Now, though, my serves were neutered, and he was benefiting from the slower court and higher bounce to slug great returns at me as I made my way to the net. He also served unbelievably well, and, because of the conditions, had more time to choose on which shot he would come up to the net, so he won a lot of points at the net, something he would not normally have done. Although I was fast, Borg was a great athlete as well, so he was able to run to anything.

By the 2nd set, I had lost confidence. I began to swear and shout at my brother and Mitch out of frustration. That's exactly why Dominique had wisely decided to hide somewhere in the stands, so I could not scream at her as well. I tried staying back, I tried going up to the net, but Bjorn had an answer to everything. Before I knew it, I had lost the set 6–2.

I kept trying to get myself going in the 3rd set. I was slapping my thigh the whole time, but still Borg was better than me. I'm not the sort of player who, at the change of ends, will sit there trying to analyze the game and figure out a way of changing things. I would just change ends faster. When I was winning, on the other hand, I used to take a long time: let the other guy sit there and think about it. But now that I was losing there was no point in sitting there, going crazy.

Borg, meanwhile, was spending every change of ends putting freezing spray on his stomach muscle to numb the pain. It obviously worked. It was incredible how, having totally crushed him six months before in the Masters final, the situation had been reversed, and I was now the one who couldn't play. But that's the unpredictable side of sport. Maybe if we'd played the next day, the result would have been different, you never know. But I have to say Borg played really well that day.

He broke immediately in that 3rd set and reached 5–4. He was now serving for the title. The crowd went wild and tried to encourage me. I don't know how, but I managed to break back after saving a match point with a passing shot. I survived until 7–7 (the tie-breaks were at 8–all in those days) when I was broken again. This time, Borg reached match point, served to my backhand corner, and I returned into the net. It was all over. Borg hurled his racket into the air, as Smith had done four years before. Although I had lost, I spontaneously leapt over the net to hug and congratulate him.

After another painful presentation ceremony, we came off court to face the press. It's terrible to have to do that but that was the system. In some ways, it's better to do the post-match interviews as soon as you come off court, as they do now, rather than after you've had your shower and time to think about it, which is what I had to do. I remember some guy asking me in the press conference if I was disappointed: 'No, I'm very happy. Next stupid question.' I know the press were entitled to ask me questions, but if the guy asks me a stupid question, sorry but I'll give him a stupid answer. I was upset, of course, but I didn't hate Borg. I knew though that, two weeks short of my thirtieth birthday, I had probably missed my last big chance to win the title.

Dominique gave me a big hug when we finally met up again, but there was nothing she could say that would make things better. We just went back to the hotel to pack for the next day. She returned to our house in France to be reunited with our daughter Nathalie, while I flew off to Los Angeles, then straight on to Hawaii five hours further away. Then, four days later, it was back to Myrtle Beach in South Carolina for a big Pepsi-Cola three-day tournament with Connors, Ashe, and Orantes. I was playing Connors there in the 1st round, and was down 6–4, 4–0, because I didn't know where I was. Then it started to get very dark, and I was praying for rain. Sure enough, it poured, and the next day I beat him 6–4, 7–5 in the remaining two sets. I then won the whole tournament before heading back to Hawaii yet again. That was a horrible week. Really tough physically and mentally.

There was one good moment, though, in Myrtle Beach. Arthur was celebrating his thirty-third birthday there, on 10 July. So I thought we should try and make it a bit more fun for him. I got the tournament organizers to make a giant cream cake and to put it on a big table wrapped in a white banner. On the banner we wrote, in huge red letters: 'Happy Birthday, Arthur'. Then, unknown to everybody, Jimmy and I hid under the table. We kept very quiet as Arthur came into the room for the presentation.

'Hey, guys, what's this?' he wondered aloud. He seemed a bit surprised at what he saw. But I think Arthur could already tell something wasn't quite right.

'One, two, three, now', I gestured to Jimmy when we thought Arthur had got close enough.

'Happy Birthday, Arthur!' we shouted as we burst out from under the table.

Arthur, quick as a flash, turned round and ran as fast as

he could, while I grabbed a handful of cake and threw it at him. Too late. There was nothing for it: I grabbed another handful and smeared it over my face, while Jimmy dug in, threw some more on my shirt, then licked his fingers in satisfaction. Arthur, now safely out of danger, just stood there and laughed: 'Thanks guys, you just made my birthday!'

When I look back at that time and everybody always reminds me: 'Oh, you never won Wimbledon, don't you regret that?' I say: 'Look, I was brought up on clay'. For me, the big one to win, when I was small, was the French Open. It's like Tim Henman, or any other Englishman (I don't mean Rusedski because it's different for him), I'm sure he'd say Wimbledon. Sampras will say Wimbledon, too, because he's won it seven times. But if you'd asked him as a kid, probably he'd say the US Open. Not that I'm satisfied that I never won it or pretend I don't care. Sometimes when I'm at Wimbledon, I go: 'I wish I win this one'. But if you look at the history of the game, only two guys have won all four titles in the same year, doing the Grand Slam: Rod Laver and, before the war, Donald Budge. And only three have won all four at some stage in their career: Roy Emerson, Fred Perry, and André Agassi. And Agassi's the only one to have done it in the last thirty-five years, since the game went open. So it's really rare to have all four titles. All the other recent champions, Connors, McEnroe, and Borg, they're all missing one major on one surface. I won Forest Hills on grass and, the next year, Roland Garros on clay, the two most different surfaces. Apart from Santana, Kodes, and Borg, no clay-court player has done that. In fact, if I'd never won the French, then there really would have been something wrong, because I was born on the stuff. So sure, it would have been nicer to have won Wimbledon, but for everybody to keep saying to me I'm the most talented player never to have won is like saying McEnroe is the most talented player never to have won the French Open, or Borg the most talented never to have won the US Open.

It's only in Britain where Wimbledon means so much that I get asked this question a lot. In France or America, they don't keep going on about it. So I try not to think about not having won, and I certainly never let it destroy my life. When my children were born, definitely I wasn't thinking about never having won Wimbledon. There are more important things in life. Coming from where I did, from the conditions I started in, I don't think I can be greedy and ask for more. I'm happy with what I have done, and I have always taken the view that there's no point in regretting, in looking back.

After a few weeks more of Team Tennis, I was finally able to rejoin the main circuit. I started off well, winning the last tournament before Forest Hills, in Orange, New Jersey, by beating another of the players I'd had run-ins with, Roscoe Tanner, who Borg had beaten in the 1976 Wimbledon semis. Roscoe had this big serve but not much else, and to be honest he was an arsehole and everybody knew it. He was always waving the rule book at me, and I'd been disqualified against him at the American Airlines Games in Palm Springs earlier that year, so I was really pleased when I beat him easily in the final. Many years later, he did this incredible thing to me that, if I'd wanted to, could have got him behind bars. I understand he's now been convicted for fraud and failure to make maintenance payments to his children, so I guess it happened anyway. I got a call from this guy who'd put up money to organize a tournament with him, and he said:

'Roscoe has this contract signed by you saying you're playing this tournament.'

'What are you talking about, I don't know anything about a tournament.'

'Well', he went on, 'we have your signature. And Connors's as well.'

Roscoe had obviously forged our signatures, so that this guy would put up the money. Jimmy wanted to sue him, but I said it wasn't worth it. Just shows, though, what an idiot Roscoe is.

In the 2nd round of Forest Hills I met the methodical German Hans Pohmann, who had a face that I didn't like. The problem I had during our match was not so much with him as with the umpire. I admit I had already been arguing about line calls earlier in the match, but, at one set all, having split two tight sets, 7–6, 4–6, in our best of three-set match, Pohmann got cramp. In those days, doctors were not allowed on court to treat injured players. You either played through your injury or you quit, not like now where the trainer comes on to treat players for every minor problem. So when the umpire calls the doctor onto court, I'm not too pleased but I allow it. Then, Pohmann recovers, runs like a rabbit, we carry on a bit more in the 3rd set, then he falls to the ground, again, writhing and screaming in agony. Cramp again. Doctor comes back. I'm starting to shout at the umpire, the crowd is going nuts. Pohmann recovers again, starts to leap around again as if nothing had happened, and we carry on to the tie-break that will decide the match. Pohmann twice reaches match point, twice I save them, and then, what does he do, he gets a third dramatic attack of cramp. Unbelievably, the doctor is allowed back a third time. This has never happened before. I go completely berserk. He should be defaulted, it's like a boxer, the referee doesn't just keep counting to 100, hoping the guy's going to recover. He counts to ten, and if he can't go on too bad, that's the end. The New York crowd, of course, thought this was fantastic, they are screaming abuse at me, making so much noise, and I've gone totally crazy by now.

In the end, I managed to hold myself together just about enough to win the tie-break and the match, but at the end I didn't shake Pohmann's hand, nor the umpire's. I was mad at both of them, mad at the doctor, mad at the whole situation that I felt was completely unfair. I was also mad at Jack Kramer, from the ATP who had fined and suspended me the week before, I was mad at the tournament organizers. In fact I was mad at everybody.

Back in the locker room, I screamed at Pohmann: 'You're a bastard, you behave like a Nazi.' I went nuts at him, but the fact is I got a lot of support from the players in there, and nobody came to Pohmann's defence. Of course, I got fined ($1,000), and everybody put the blame on me because they didn't understand why I had behaved like that. Apart from one or two of the real tennis writers, who bothered to explain the situation and condemn the crowd's terrible behaviour towards me, all the other papers printed a story that was totally against me, even though I was justified in my complaints. But, as usual, the bad-boy version made better reading.

Once I'd had my shower, though, I cooled down straight away. I can't explain it myself, but even after fighting to the death on court I became more than normal off court. Half an hour later, I was completely calm. I was always like that. I could start an argument in two seconds on court, and I didn't care. I let go of everything. Then, after I finish, it's gone. Forgotten about. I'm like that in life anyway. I get very upset, for example, when somebody lies, and I know. I get really mad. But then I get over it very quickly as well.

So it's true, on court I didn't have limits. I was completely blind, whether I was right or wrong to argue about a certain point – and I accept I wasn't always right. The more stop signs I saw on court, the more I went through them. But I'm glad it was that way round, rather than behaving like that off court. Otherwise, I would maybe have given myself another five years to live. It would have been too fast to live like I was living on court. People often didn't believe I was different off court. It was like I had to prove it, make a statement. They either didn't take me seriously – and some still don't – or they thought that if they say something to me I'm going to kill them, swear at them. Because it's true, sometimes I was violent on court and said some terrible things. But I really was two different people on and off court.

A lot of players were the same on and off court, and even McEnroe himself admits that he still has a problem with his anger off court. He told me recently: 'Nasty, I cannot hold it, I have my privacy. People come to me when I'm eating and interrupt me. That makes me mad.' And maybe he's right to be like that, and I'm the one who's not, but that's how I am and I know I'll never change.

My Pohmann match gave me a fine that meant I had gone over the $3,000 total allowed for the year. I'd received other fines after other incidents, including my American Airlines disqualification in April against Tanner. Now I faced an automatic twenty-one-day suspension. As had often happened, for the rest of the tournament I was really good and well behaved, so I sailed through to the semifinal, beating Tanner on the way in a five-set match that gave me a lot of satisfaction. Waiting for me in the semis was the Martian. Borg. Once again, there was nothing I could do, I think I had run out of nervous energy by the time I got to him, and he beat me in three straight sets. Having said that, considering I had spent so long playing Team Tennis that year, I had done fantastically well in the two grand slam tournaments that I'd played: finalist at Wimbledon and semifinalist at Forest Hills.

I also ended up as number 3 in the world in the end-of-year ATP rankings, behind Connors (who won Forest Hills in the end) and Borg.

The crazy thing about the suspension system is that, although it prevented me playing Grand Prix tournaments, it did not stop me playing in exhibition matches, so my manager Mitch quickly arranged some very well-paid matches around the world against players such as Connors and Borg. So, by the time I'd finished my suspension, I had made well over $50,000 – not bad as a punishment for bad behaviour. No wonder those suspensions never put me off.

I didn't know it then, but 1976 was the last of the really good years. It went so fast, though, that I didn't enjoy it at the time. I was going from tournament to tournament – I played thirty and won nine singles and one doubles – and I thought winning like that was normal. I didn't pinch myself and think: 'Enjoy it because it won't last'. And I was never obsessed about having been number 1, because what good would it do to say: 'Hey, I was number 1', when I no longer was?

On court, although I played mainly for myself, I also played for the crowd. I liked being in front of people, to try exciting shots. The shot over the shoulder after chasing the lob, I started that one. Now they all do it, but I'd practised it like crazy, and, because of the heavy wooden rackets of the day, it was difficult to do if you didn't have a really strong but flexible wrist. So I loved to enjoy myself, and if the crowd enjoyed themselves too that was fantastic. What else was better than that? Of course, some players might say: 'I don't care about pleasing the crowd, I just want to win.' But for me it was tough, because I had to win matches too. Trying to combine enjoyment and winning, that was a constant battle for me.

With success, I also got recognized more and more, not just at tournaments but out in the street, in restaurants, everywhere I went. Although I loved being the centre of attention on court, I was still quite self-conscious off it. I stayed shy, even when I was at my peak, and never tried to take advantage of my fame. I was always embarrassed in restaurants, for example, when they would say: 'Come on, we'll give you a seat right away', even though there were a lot of people waiting. I'd get to my table and think: 'Jesus, everybody's looking.'

Another thing that happened, particularly when I was number 1 in 1973 and the Code of Conduct was not yet written, was that I could get away with a lot of crazy things in tournaments that worse players could not. My manager would say: 'OK, Nastase will come and play, he's number 1, don't fine him' (the fines were at the discretion of the organizers in those days). Later on, from '76 onwards, every time I swore, it was $250, every time I showed the finger, another $250. I was paying a lot of money out in fines, and if I hadn't been winning so much I'd be sleeping under a bridge by now. But I was good then, and everybody wanted me.

That autumn and winter of '76, I was able to spend a bit more time at home, for the first time in months. Earlier that year, we had finally moved into the country house that we had bought at the end of 1975 from the Rothschild family. Situated about 100 km south-east of Paris, between Fontainebleau and Sens in Burgundy, it was in the same village, Bazoches-sur-le-Betz, where Dominique's family had their château. It was a beautiful seventeenth-century house with lots of rooms, original beams, a large amount of land, and a little stream running at the end of the garden. We had done it up over a few months, and as well as getting a tennis court laid I had also spent time with Dominique furnishing it.

It may seem strange but I've always enjoyed doing that, for all my houses. And with my different wives! Over the years, I would buy furniture, paintings, objects that I liked, and some like a big wardrobe I bought with Tiriac in 1970 go back more than thirty years. In 2003 I bought an apartment in Paris just near the Arc de Triomphe, and Amalia and I are looking forward to doing it up like we want, because that will be the first home that we've arranged together.

I hold on to things, even my cars. I never sell them, I just give them to friends or family. In 1972, I bought myself a 1966 Bentley, which I loved to drive around, and I kept that for years until in the end I gave it to the guy who used to look after my neighbour's house in France. I think he still has it.

When Dominique and I first got married, back in '72, we had rented a nice apartment in Brussels, opposite the Léopold Club, which was the King's club and where the big tournaments were held. That was convenient, because when I was home there was always a Belgian player I could practise with. Brussels was a small place, so I soon made friends with the top Belgian sportsmen of the day, especially Eddy Merckx, the cyclist, and Jacky Ickx, the Formula 1 driver. Eddy gave me one of the bikes on which he'd won one of his five Tours de France, and I gave him one of my rackets – we played tennis sometimes. I still have that bike today. I think I got the better deal. This bike only weighs about 2 kg, which is incredible because they didn't have the lightweight materials they do now to make them. The atmosphere in Brussels was good, we knew lots of people, we went out to dinners, people treated me as if I was one of their own – that was a good period for me. But our apartment only had two bedrooms, and once Nathalie was born, in 1975, it became too small. Dominique's childhood nanny became nanny to our daughter, and she came to live with us, so it seemed like a good idea to buy the French house.

During those last weeks of '76, I spent time at Bazoches resting, getting to know my daughter at last, and playing a bit of tennis with my wife. We did not play that much, because after ten minutes I'd get annoyed with her and would start to hit the ball harder and harder at her until we argued, and one or other of us stormed off court. So more often I'd play with her brother Bernard, who was a good player. Over Christmas, my parents-in-law entertained at the château, and every day a hunting party would be organized – although I always refused to join them – and lunch would then be served for 100 people back at the château. But the rest of the time, we lived a quiet life. Too quiet, in fact. I needed to see people, I needed the noise of the city, and after a few weeks I started to get restless. As Ion once said: 'I give you $100 if you sit still for five minutes.'

CHAPTER NINE

1977

The next time I saw Rosie, two days later, she asked how the party was. All I said was: 'Great!', with a big smile on my face, as if nothing had happened.

On the morning of 5 March, I was in Puerto Rico getting ready to play a $450,000 'winner-take-all' challenge match against Jimmy Connors. These sorts of matches were getting more and more popular, and were a great way for the public to see some top tennis players in places where they did not normally visit. In this match, the loser was still guaranteed $150,000, by the way. Thousands of kilometres away, however, in Bucharest, the earth had been shaken to its core. Not as a reaction to the dollars I was now earning. No. An enormous earthquake, measuring 9.6 on the Richter scale, had shaken the city the night before and had sent buildings crashing to the ground and thousands to their death. By the time Dominique and Mitch were told the news in Puerto Rico, I was on court practising, and so unaware of events in Bucharest. While I was happily going about my business, they were frantically trying to find out what had happened, not only to my house but also, more importantly, to all my family. Luckily, through friends at the Romanian embassy in Washington, Mitch was able to learn that my family was fine, and my house had suffered only structural damage.

Connors's camp, however, had also heard the news. When I came onto court later that day, he made a comment along the lines that I'd better call home because I might not have a house any more. I had no idea what he was talking about and just ignored it, thinking he was just winding me up as usual about the Communists repossessing private property. So we played the match, I lost in four sets (I got my revenge a month later when I beat him in the WCT Challenge Cup final in Las Vegas), and afterwards I found out about the earthquake. Although I was mad about the comment, I just thought it was childish on Jimmy's part and I didn't blame him, because I think his entourage told him to say something to destabilize me. Anyway, I was more worried about all the friends I had in Bucharest than about his remark. I could see from television footage that things were pretty bad.

It wasn't until I returned to the city a couple of months later, to play a Davis Cup tie, that I saw whole blocks where there had once been buildings now reduced to dust. I learned about friends of mine who had been killed running from their apartments as whole buildings collapsed around them. Others had died in their beds when entire floors had given way and they had crashed straight down from four or five storeys up.

It was terrible, and there were about 4,000 deaths in total. Then, people didn't have the mentality to immediately come to me asking for money. Nowadays that's what they'd do. I'm always being asked for money for all sorts of crazy causes and invented problems, and Amalia spends her time trying to work out which ones are genuine and which ones are fake. In those days, people waited for the state to help them. That's why now, the old people – those who have not been able to profit from the new way of life – think it was better under the Communist regime. At least they had a salary, a house, and something to eat. If a tragedy happened, the state would help. Although Bucharest gets regular small earth tremors, this time it had been hit hard, and for a year afterwards there was rubble everywhere.

Ceauşescu, who had already begun his plans for massive reconstruction, speeded them up even more. Over twenty or so years, he built about 20,000 buildings. About one-fifth of central Bucharest, including churches and historic buildings, was demolished. As well as re-housing in new apartments all the people that he had pulled off the land so that they could become factory workers, he had to re-house all the people living in private homes in Bucharest, because they were no longer allowed to live there. Finally, he built huge buildings to accommodate ministries and ministers. The biggest of all, his *Casa Poporului* ('People's House'), which was meant to contain offices for him and his government, was so enormous that it was not even finished by the time he was executed in 1989. It is now the world's second largest building after the Pentagon. For years, roads were blocked off around it, about 24,000 people worked on its construction, and many died in the process.

I went to Rome for the Italian Open in May after a fairly uncontroversial and successful spring: I had won two singles and three doubles titles, and I'd qualified for the WCT finals both in singles (played in Dallas) and in doubles (in Kansas City, though I missed the event due to Davis Cup commitments). By the beginning of May, I had earned $400,000 in prize money alone, aside from my endorsements and sponsorship contracts. This was compared to the $228,000

I had earned in the whole of 1973, my most successful year, when I had been number 1 in the world and the highest-earning player. These figures showed how tennis had exploded as a commercial sport in just a few years.

I made it through to the quarterfinals in Rome and the semis in the doubles. Vitas Gerulaitis had his first really big tournament win that year, when he walked away with the title. Vitas was one of the most colourful personalities and fun guys on the tour. But he was already doing drugs by that stage in his life. He never seemed to sleep, and unlike most players including me, who resisted going out until we got beaten in a tournament, Vitas would happily be out in the discos until the early hours of the morning, knowing he had a big match to play the next day. His final against the Italian Antonio Zugarelli was one of those occasions. Basically he never went to bed. I was told that he'd gone to a nightclub, done drugs until seven in the morning, then come out and beaten Zugarelli in the afternoon. He was probably still high on whatever it was he'd taken. The crazy thing was, he was at the peak of his career – a month later, he had that incredible semifinal against Borg at Wimbledon – and yet he was partying and doing drugs the whole time. It was a mystery, to those of us who were his friends, how he could keep going and play so well.

At Roland Garros, I was seeded 1, with the holder Adriano Panatta at 2, maybe because I'd finished the previous year as number 3 in the world (higher than Panatta at 7). In the 4th round, I found myself against Jan Kodes, the player I played the most in my career, along with Orantes and Connors. In the match, I remember playing the sort of tennis that I sometimes dreamed about. I was fast, I made shots that I only tried in practice, and I even had time to have fun and entertain the crowd. Poor Kodes could only stand and watch, and pray for it to be over – which it was in three straight sets.

The next match, the quarterfinals, I was up against Brian Gottfried. His partnership with Raul Ramirez was the best doubles team at the time. But in singles Gottfried was also a consistently good player and was then leading the Grand Prix rankings. He may not have been very inventive, but he worked so hard on and off court. There's a rumour that he was even practising his tennis the day he got married. Our match started in the late afternoon, the stadium was so full it was unbelievable, and I won the first two sets 6–4, 6–3. Then Gottfried won the 3rd. In those days, players still came off for a fifteen-minute break after the 3rd set in majors and Davis Cup matches, and by the time we came back on I had started to get tight, because I could feel the match turning and it was getting late. I started screaming at Dominique, poor girl, until she had enough and left the courtside. I was calling her terrible names, in Romanian so that only she could understand. She was the closest target, and I needed somebody there for me when I got upset. In the end, she got fed up and left me to it.

By the time we were in the 5th set, I was tired. And it was starting to get dark. I called the tournament referee and asked if we could stop and finish the next day. I knew the winner would play Phil Dent in the semis, and for me that was a good draw. I knew if I had Dent, I could get through to the final. But the referee refused to postpone the end of the match. So I finally lost the 5th set 6–3, Gottfried beat Dent in straight sets (Dent was also carrying an injury), and he then got murdered by Vilas in the final. So I was really disappointed to have lost, because if we'd been able to finish the match the next day I think I would have won, and then anything could have happened. I might well have gone all the way. There is often a bit of luck involved in sport and in winning or losing: sometimes it works for you, sometimes it's against. But when it doesn't work out for you, you get really upset.

Afterwards, I apologized to Dominique for treating her like that, but she was used to it and understood that I wasn't saying it to her in a nasty way. She never complained to me about that, and after this sort of loss she would usually not say anything to me. I had generally cooled down by the time I saw her anyway. On this occasion, we decided to go out to dinner at the Brasserie Lipp, a popular eating place in the Latin Quarter for politicians and other celebrities.

Accompanying us that evening was my brother and the Romanian ambassador to Paris, who was a close friend. They made sure they didn't talk about the match, because they knew I didn't want to. I tried to look OK, as if nothing had happened, but it was impossible. Nobody's fooled. It's the same thing when you're the beaten finalist, and you watch the other player receive the cup. You care very much. Still, going out with Dominique and friends, having a few glasses of wine, starting to joke and pretending you're OK, it's better than what I also had to do more and more, which was going back to my hotel on my own, just sitting on my bed, and doing nothing. Not even watching TV, just doing nothing. That's the worst. And the silence. It starts the minute you get back to the locker room, it follows you to the car, to your room, and when you pack your bag to leave town. But everybody goes through it, even the best. You cannot escape that, it's part of competing.

Our Davis Cup tie against Great Britain in Bucharest was in early June, the week after Roland Garros. It was the third tie I had played in the space of eight weeks. First, in mid April, in order to play against Belgium, I'd had to miss the

WCT doubles finals in Kansas that I had qualified for, along with my partner Adriano Panatta. Then our tie against Czechoslovakia in May meant that I missed another big-money tournament, the Alan King Classic at Caesar's Palace, Las Vegas. Although I was disappointed to be missing these events, not least because I would have made good money if I had done well in them, I knew that playing Davis Cup remained a priority and was the price I paid for my freedom. Also, as all these ties were held in Bucharest, they gave me the only opportunities, other than a couple of weeks at Christmas, to go home and see my family.

By the time the tie against Britain arrived, I was now Major Nastase. I had been promoted to this rank, after a ceremony at the Ministry of Defence, simply because of my age. I was the first to see how funny this must have looked to the outside world, but I'm sure my friend Captain Gibson, at Wimbledon, would have been proud of me.

In the tie itself, I beat John Feaver in four sets, and Dumitru Haradau beat John Lloyd, also in four sets. So we were 2–0 up and needing only one more point out of the three remaining rubbers. Tiriac, who by now was thirty-eight, was still playing doubles, so we paired up against the two Lloyd brothers for the crucial doubles match on the second day. I had always got on well with John, but his older brother David and I were just too different. He took everything really seriously, and during that match I thought he was just looking for an opportunity to complain about me.

Sure enough, half way through the 2nd set, when Britain was one set down, John hit a very angled shot, and I ran and ran and finally got to it and hit it round the side of the net. I couldn't stop my run so ended up in the Lloyds' half of the court. Instead of getting out of the way, David, who was at the net, just stood there, on purpose I thought, so I ended up running into him.

'Are you crazy, fuck you, why didn't you get out the way?' I said to him as I made my way back.

So he marches up to the Spanish referee, Jaime Bartroli, who was a real gentleman, but he was the other side of the court, so he hadn't heard anything.

'Did you hear what he said? Did you hear that?'

'No, I didn't hear a thing,' replies the referee.

'He said to suck his d**k. No, I swear!' Then he screams at me: 'Go on, you tell him, you tell him!'

I didn't say a word. John starts to scream as well, defending his brother, and we're all fighting and arguing. Paul Hutchins, Britain's Davis Cup captain, tries to speak to Bartroli, and my brother, who was our Davis Cup captain, tries to get David to back off. I'm saying to David: 'I didn't tell you to do anything'. David, he's all excited and crazy, he's calling me a liar. The crowd is getting all agitated. The referee doesn't know what to do. It's chaos. Then I see Tiriac, with his long face and his drooping moustache, at the back of the court, sitting on his racket watching us all. Suddenly he gets up, walks over to me and says:

'Nastase, you've had enough?'

'I've had enough but these guys haven't.'

'God, you're starting again,' goes David.

So Tiriac, very deadpan, I can still see him now, he walks up to David calmly and says, very slowly:

'David, my friend, you don't have to suck his d**k if you don't want to. He just said it, you know, but really you don't have to.'

David just stares at him, he can't believe what he's heard, he can't think of anything more to say. John, he starts to laugh so hard, I start to laugh, Jaime Bartroli doesn't understand what's happened, and then we continue the match. And we win in four sets.

We had won the tie, but the British team did not give up. They filed an official complaint to the International Tennis Federation. Although Bartroli did say that David had acted in a provocative manner, a few months later they decided that I should be banned from Davis Cup play for 1978.

As this tie happened just before Wimbledon, I arrived in Britain as number 1 bad boy. When Connors, the other bad boy, missed the champions' parade on Centre Court, which had been organized to celebrate Wimbledon's centenary and the Queen's Silver Jubilee, the press killed him. The fact that he'd been practising on an outside court with me at the time added to the story. Jimmy's mother, Gloria, who was at every major with him and had coached him from childhood, tried to take the blame, saying she'd got the times mixed up, but nobody believed her. A couple of days later, we were travelling back from Wimbledon in the courtesy car, and this big truck stopped at the traffic lights beside us. Inside were these two huge guys with huge muscles, reading the paper. They looked at us, recognized us, wound down the window, and giving us the thumbs up one of them said: 'Well done, Jimmy. Fuck the Duke!' Then they drove off.

Terry O'Neil, the celebrity photographer, had done a photo shoot of me for one of the tabloid newspapers that year and had dressed me up as a Mafioso-lookalike. I was in a white suit, white tie, black shirt, and black fedora hat, and I looked like a guy from Reggio Calabria. It just reinforced the Nasty image, and, by the time I stepped onto court 2 to play my second round match against the Rhodesian Andrew Pattison, my profile was about as high as it had ever been at Wimbledon, particularly among the girls. They'd run after me, screaming my name out, and many of them were still in school uniform, which I found funny. I remember once coming down the steps that led from the players' terrace overlooking court 2 and having to run as fast as I could to the back entrance of the changing room under Centre Court, while I was pursued by hordes of girls. Dominique had been left trailing miles behind me. On another occasion, one girl arrived with a test tube and asked me to spit into it. Dominique thought I was crazy, but of course I duly obliged. I hate to think what the girl did with the contents.

For my match with Pattison, the court was absolutely packed. I didn't want to play him again, because I'd lost to him at Forest Hills in '73 when I was defending my title and I didn't like court 2. Nobody does. It plays softer than the other main courts; because it doesn't get the sun quite as much, the bounce can be a bit more uneven. As a result, I was already tense when I walked on. By the time he'd won the first two sets and was a break up in the third, things were bad. It was then that I was foot-faulted. I was so mad that I asked for the tournament referee, Fred Hoyles (Captain Gibson had now retired). While we waited, I went to the back of the court, where loads of kids were trying to watch the match from under and over the tarpaulin, because there was no room anywhere else. I disappeared behind the tarpaulin as well, poked my head from underneath it, and also went and sat beside the linesman who had called the fault. Some of the crowd were not pleased by the interruption, but I thought I had a right to ask for the referee. To hell with what people thought.

In the end, I won the match in five close sets but was given a police escort off the court, because there were so many people about, so many press and photographers, it was a total scrum out there. I know Pattison wasn't pleased with me, but I take the view that it's too late to regret that sort of incident after a match. I can't go up to somebody and say: 'Sorry, I screwed you.' Firstly he wouldn't believe me, and secondly these interruptions often did more harm to my own concentration than to my opponent's. I didn't plan them, and half the time they didn't help me anyway.

The day after the match, along with all the headlines about my bad behaviour, a story appeared in the papers that my agents, IMG, were no longer representing me. The report made out it was very much their decision and was as a result of my behaviour, whereas in fact we had both come to the decision a few months before. I had always got on really well with my agent there, Eric Drossart, who was a former Belgian Davis Cup player, but to be honest I preferred to be a free agent by then. I just wasn't pleased that the news emerged during Wimbledon, but I guess that as ever the press was responsible, because reporters know a good story when they see one. For this one, they twisted it to suit their needs.

My next match, against the eighteen-year-old American Eliot Teltscher, was scheduled on court 14. To this day, I don't understand what went through the committee's head when they put me out there. Was it to punish me? Had David Lloyd told them that I'd been so nice to him in Bucharest that they just had to put me on that court? Court 14 was about as far away from Centre Court as you could be, and it had hardly any seating. Given how many thousands had scrambled to watch my match on court 2, you'd have thought they would guess that a few people might want to see me play again.

When I arrived, I could not physically get on court because of the crowds. I squeezed on from the back, and waited for my opponent, while girls threw roses at me and others rushed up to try to kiss me. Teltscher eventually made it, after taking twenty minutes to fight his way through the crowds. The match itself went quickly. I won in three easy sets, and I was as good as gold. I never planned how to behave, I could have been worse than against Pattison, but it just happened that in this match I controlled myself. At one stage, though, when one of the flimsy canvas barriers at the side of the court split and panicking girls spilt onto court screaming and crying, I got really scared. I rushed up to the policeman trying to control things and asked the girls to move back and calm down. I really thought somebody was going to get hurt that day, if not killed, because it was such a crush. Apparently, 5,000 people had tried to watch on a court made for 1,500 at most.

Afterwards, I told the press: 'I just don't understand. I'm thirty-one, married, and very ugly.' It's true that this year, 1977, the girls seemed to be even keener on me than before. I have to admit that, like Borg who was getting similar treatment, I enjoyed getting mobbed and I always stopped to sign autographs, even if I'd lost. I went later on to visit a first-aid post where some of the girls were being treated for shock, and when I tried to leave the club that evening, there were so many girls waiting for me at the players' exit (which in those days was the same place as the royal entrance) that their screaming interrupted the doubles match on Centre Court, and police had to hold up barriers to prevent more crazy scenes. In the end, the only way to get Dominique and me out safely was to use three decoy cars.

I kept my concentration really well in my next match against Tom Okker and was lined up to play Borg the Martian – yet again – in the quarterfinals. By then, I think I knew deep down that Bjorn was better than me, after beating me in the Wimbledon final the year before and then in the US Open semifinal. I was probably looking for an excuse and, because I couldn't pick on Bjorn and I couldn't pick on my wife, I had to pick on somebody. And that person turned out to be the umpire, Jeremy Shales. He was a thirty-four-year-old bank official at the time, and, unfortunately for me, I think he had also decided to pick on me, to teach me a lesson. So it was a match that was finished as soon as I got onto court.

I was always on the edge, especially at the start of a match, and sometimes if something happened, a bad call or something, then the tension would not come out the way I would like. It might come out in a funny way, but at other times it would go wrong. I could never predict or premeditate these things. But with this match I was looking for something to happen, if I'm honest.

By the second point, I'd contested a bad line call at the far end of the court. Instead of reducing the tension for me, which can sometimes happen, it just made me lose concentration completely. I lost the 1st set 6–0, with Borg playing brilliantly. I regained some control in the 2nd, moved to a 4–2 lead, but once I eventually lost it 8–6 I just decided to hassle Shales, rather than Borg. I was being a pain in the arse. Not in the neck, in the arse. I flicked a ball gently between Shales's legs at one point, and I complained about points at the slightest opportunity. There were a couple of times when Borg had to retake a serve because of a let cord or something, and on one of those calls I went to the other side of the court, as if the point had been awarded. Shales picked up the telephone on his chair, left his microphone full on so that 15,000 people around the court plus the millions watching on TV could hear, and told the referee Fred Hoyles that I was employing 'delaying tactics'. He then turned to me and said, like a master talks to a naughty schoolboy:

'Nastase, will you please come this side of the court, there's a second serve.'

That was it. 'First of all', I replied, walking angrily up to his chair, 'you don't call me Nastase, you call me Mr Nastase.'

He duly obliged: 'Mr Nastase.'

'That's better, yes.' I jabbed a finger at him, just to make myself even clearer: 'You call me Mr Nastase, you call me Mr Nastase.'

I think he got the message. In fact, the whole world got the message, because after that I started to be called Mr Nastase everywhere. But the damage was done. The match was over as far as I was concerned, and I won only one point in the last two games.

Maybe one of the problems was that, as Dominique said later on, like a lot of people with talent, I was missing something else. Discipline, probably. But discipline was difficult, because that was not compatible, I think, with the way I wanted to play the game. It wouldn't have been me, and people from the outside didn't understand that. To have the talent and the discipline, that would be great. Borg had that. But I could not be something I was not.

The papers the next day were predictably outraged, and my nickname was, yet again, a gift for the headline writers. God, I practically did their job for them that day: 'What a Nasty Way to Go', said one typical headline in the *Daily Mail*. Some did sympathize with the way I had been treated by Shales: 'The Public Spanking', announced another tabloid. But on the whole, it was all the usual stuff: Nasty's got to be taught a lesson, the umpires have to take a firm grip, and he can't be allowed to get away with this.

I did used to read what they said about me, and I don't believe actors, for example, who say they never read what the papers say about them. Sometimes I'd be mad at what was said about me, because it was completely invented or exaggerated, but it was too late. That's the power of the press, it can portray you as it wants. Sometimes, after a match where I made the headlines the next day, I'd go out and buy the papers. At other times Jimmy or somebody would tell me what was in them or tell me to go and buy them. Generally, I'd only be told about the bad articles, not the good ones.

Sometimes I'd give journalists really boring answers just to show them I could be like that too. But the good tennis writers, I knew them all and they were very nice, especially those from Britain: for example, John Barrett, Barry Newcombe, Rex Bellamy from *The Times*, and Laurie Pignon from the *Daily Mail*. They wrote about my game and knew a lot about tennis. Laurie was a friend, I'd call him Laurie Pigeon; he was always dressed in colourful clothes, a pink jacket with a yellow tie, that sort of thing. In France, Jean Couvercelle and Alain Deflassieux from *Tennis de France* were good guys, as was Bud Collins in America. But there were others who were terrible, like Frank Rostron from the *Daily Express*. He always picked on me. He had this big cigar, he smelled of whisky, and he was always giving me shit, provoking me: 'Yeah, Ilie, I've heard this story that you did this and that.' He was awful, he wasn't interested in the tennis, just in the bad stuff.

There was complete hypocrisy in the media about me. They'd write about how bad I was, but really they loved it because it filled their pages. I remember telling one guy: 'If I wasn't here, what the hell would you write about? The linesman, the ball boys? Nice but not as good.'

My sponsors, Adidas, were fantastic. I'm still sponsored by them thirty years later. Horst Dassler, the owner, was a close friend of mine. Sadly he passed away far too young, aged fifty-two, a few years ago. But he never once said: 'If you do that one more time, we're going to end our contract', because he knew I was doing good for him. As did the tournaments and their sponsors, who got people coming to see me who might not have watched tennis otherwise. So really I did a lot of good for the sport, and a lot of people made a lot of money out of me. Yet all along there were people saying that I should be run out of the game. Did that annoy me? Yes.

After Wimbledon, I moved the whole family, including our nanny and Dominique's brother Bernard and sister Nathalie, to Los Angeles, because I was spending the summer playing Team Tennis for the Los Angeles Strings. This time the contract, worth $250,000 a year, was a whole lot better than returning to Hawaii. I was renting, at $5,000 a month, a huge five-bedroom house in Beverley Hills, which had previously been lived in by Richard Burton. It came complete with cook/housekeeper, swimming pool, and a big garden, so at least Dominique and my daughter were happy with the luxurious life, even if they hardly saw me all summer, thanks to the crazy Team Tennis schedule.

Team Tennis had teams all over the country, and top players had signed up, such as Borg and Gerulaitis, Chris Evert, Rosie Casals (who was with me in LA), and Billie-Jean King, who was the one really behind the whole thing. The problem was the travel. A couple of weeks after starting with them, by which time I'd already flown all over the country, I had to return to Paris for a Davis Cup tie – the final of the European zone A – against France.

I arrived jet-lagged, went straight to honour a lunch at the Romanian embassy in Paris, then had barely two days' practice before playing François Jauffret, a guy who for some reason I never managed to beat in the competition, though I beat him on all other occasions we met. Something used to happen to him in Davis Cup, and this time was no exception. I was comfortably two sets to love up, and was 4–2 up with a break in the 3rd, when, I remember very clearly, I had an easy overhead to put away but I tried to play a drop shot instead. I missed. Then the match turned. On that one point. I didn't plan to fool around, it's just the way I used to play, whatever the score, whatever the match. But that was enough. He climbed back to two sets all, and won the match. Tiriac and I won the doubles, and I won my second singles, but it was not enough and we lost the tie. So I felt really guilty and upset. In fact, I remember breaking my racket I was so mad.

Afterwards, I went out to drown my sorrows with my friend Mitch. We ended up in Castel, the nightclub, where I met Claudia Cardinale, who I knew through Nicola Pietrangeli. Jean Castel, the owner, was a friend of mine and he loved tennis, so I was always welcomed there. The nightclub itself is in the Latin Quarter, and it's like a private house. It was very exclusive, and we loved going there during Roland Garros when Jean used to throw lots of parties for the players. In those days, if you were a member and you had a child, they gave you a bottle of whisky with your child's name on it, and they kept it there until they turned eighteen. So I had two bottles there at one stage, one for Nathalie and one for my son Nicky. Then Jean sold the club, and things changed. Inside the club, it's all velvet everywhere, there's a salon and bar to the right of the entrance. Then, below, there's the discotheque and another big seating area with lots of couches. Above the salon there's a restaurant, and on the top floor a kind of cinema for movies. The whole thing is on about four floors, so it feels very intimate.

As Claudia and I were still deep in conversation, we decided we'd carry on the evening and move on to another club, Le Privé, owned by former tennis player Jean-Noel Grinda. After his tennis career, Jean-Noel had become a professional backgammon player, married a beautiful Scandinavian model, and in the end started up this nightclub that was just off the Champs Elysées. So off I went, with Mitch and a couple of actor friends of Claudia keeping us company. By then, I'd had a few glasses of wine and thought, to hell with it, let's have a dance (a slow one, mind you), so we ended up on the dance floor, in the early hours of the morning, and the thought obviously crossed my mind that we might take things one step further. But no, I didn't ask. She was a friend of mine, and to be honest it was easier just to pick a woman up at a disco or a tournament. Also, I was still being pretty good then, and I was exhausted after the previous few days. So we went our separate ways in the end, and I flew back the following morning to the next part of the crazy Team Tennis schedule that included, in the week to come, one-night matches in Salt Lake City (Utah), Boston (Mass.), St Louis (Missouri), and New York. There wasn't even a word to describe how I felt by the time I finally arrived back in Los Angeles a week later. Jet-lagged certainly didn't cover it.

One of the best things about playing Team Tennis, though, was having a sense of belonging to a team, and I got on well with all my fellow LA Stringers, especially Rosie Casals, who I had played mixed doubles with so much in the past. Everybody knew Rosie was gay, it was an open secret, just like we knew about Billie-Jean King, even though she was married. What we didn't realize, until Martina Navratilova bravely came out a bit later, was that half the tour was lesbian. Personally, I find it very sad that people don't feel they can say if they're gay, because honestly who cares? But for men, it's still so unacceptable, because winning is part of proving your virility. I have to say nobody ever accused me of being gay, except in Romania, and then I just said: 'Send me your sister, you'll see if I'm gay.'

Rosie used to have all these parties that summer in her home town, Sausalito. It's about 30 km from San Francisco, it's very nice, very European. But if you think San Francisco is gay, you haven't been to Sausalito. I remember she invited me and Mitch once, in '77, to one of her parties after we'd played a match against the San Francisco Gaters. We were the only two guys there. The rest were women. To be honest, I think it would have been more promising for me to check out Mitch than the women. I remember Rosie had a swimming pool, and they were all jumping around naked in the pool. I didn't dare go naked, so my excuse was that I couldn't swim, although I would probably have been ignored even if I'd jumped in. It would have been like: 'Huh, what the hell are you doing in here! Goddam you bastard, get outta here! We're going to have to disinfect the swimming pool!'

There was Chinese food at the party and some cookies, and, because I'd come straight from our tennis match, I was starving. This girl was handing round the cookies, so I put a whole one straight into my mouth, then went to take another.

'Hey, you're strong. You know what you're eating?'

'No.'

'They're called funny cookies.'

I shrugged my shoulders and wandered off, not knowing what funny cookies were. Then I realized. I started to feel funny. I wasn't sure if it was the Chinese food or the cookies, but not long after my head started to hurt like hell. Mitch and I eventually left, and by then I was feeling completely sick and dizzy as well. Mitch too felt so terrible that we went to the hospital, and when we left there, on the way home, he nearly crashed the car into a lamppost. Jesus, I thought, this could all end badly. That gave me a real fright. Back at the hotel, I couldn't stop throwing up, I felt dizzy, and I didn't sleep all night. My head felt as if it had a band all around it, and it was throbbing so much I thought it was going to explode.

I never told anybody, certainly not Dominique, but those cookies had obviously been laced with marijuana. Somebody told me that, once you cook it, it becomes three or four times stronger. I had no idea because I'd never done drugs before – and never since. I'm not sure Rosie knew what was going on at her party, although maybe she thought if I ate some I might change my mind and go for a lesbian. I wasn't going to jump on her, that's for sure, much as I really liked her. We used to call her Rose Butt, because of her big butt. Anyway, the next time I saw Rosie, two days later, she asked how the party had been. All I said was: 'Great!' with a big smile on my face, as if nothing had happened. What I really felt like saying was: 'Great. I had a fantastic time, met all sorts of naked women, and ended up throwing up afterwards. Always the sign of a good party!'

I always enjoyed watching the women's matches, particularly those of Rosie, Billie-Jean King, Margaret Court, and later on Martina Navratilova and Chrissie Evert. I played with Rosie, so I liked to watch her matches out of interest and friendship. I was also good friends with Billie-Jean. She was very nice and very American, but she was also a bit like me: she was very emotional, she put a lot of passion into her game, and she had a beautiful style. The way she or Margaret Court played, their performance level and skill, it was great. Some men players are stupid, because they say women's tennis is terrible, but it's just different from men's. And I'm sure that if they'd had the same rackets as they have nowadays, their game would have been different too. These women had the talent, the skill, to play the Williams sisters today. No problem. They'd maybe need to train and prepare differently, get stronger. But the ability was there, no question.

As for the issue of equal prize money that Billie-Jean spent her life fighting for, this never bothered me. In fact, I used to say to her: 'You're stupid, why don't you ask for more? That would really get you noticed. You just need to give the reasons why you think you should be paid more. You're more feminine, you have better legs, anything!' Billie-Jean would laugh: 'It's too late, I settled already.' Personally, I didn't care. It wasn't coming off the men's purse, so if they could have more money than us that would be great.

We were two different circuits by the mid-Seventies anyway: they had their Women's Tennis Association (WTA) and their Virginia Slims circuit, we had our ATP with our WCT and Grand Prix circuits. Although Wimbledon still does not give equal prize money to the girls, the US Open did so by 1974, and that was good. Still, Billie-Jean said to me recently: 'Ilie, sometimes I think I was an idiot to do all that, because the players of today they don't give anything back to me. It's not that I want anything, I just want to be thanked.' She gets no appreciation for all she fought for, to allow the girls of today to have the money they do and the tour they have. Do you think any of the women today, like the Williams sisters, ever say in their victory speech: 'I have to thank Billie-Jean King, because she was the one who made sure we have equal prize money'? No, they don't care. There's no respect from anyone for those who came before them.

Team Tennis continued through July and August '77, and when we were playing in Los Angeles we'd regularly get the local film stars coming to watch us at the Inglewood Forum, where the famous basketball team, the LA Lakers, was also based. We would meet these guys before and after the match, because the Forum had a restaurant and bar next to our dressing room, and under instructions from the owner of the team, Jerry Buss, we'd have to mingle. So I met Jack Nicholson, who was a big fan of mine. He asked me if I wanted to play golf with him, because he's a golf fanatic, but I told him I didn't play. Ryan O'Neal would often come over with his daughter, Tatum, who was eleven or twelve at the time. She was a spoilt brat, and when she got together with McEnroe some years later, I'm not sure who was worse out of the two. Ryan was crazy about rollerblading, and he was always trying to show me what he could do, like he was showing off. Also, he was always trying to be a boxer, shadow-boxing the whole time. He was very cocky, I thought. Richard Harris also came over a lot with his young girlfriend, because he liked my game, and although he was wild he was a really nice guy as well.

Through Billie-Jean, who was playing Team Tennis in Philadelphia, I also met Elton John, because he was a huge fan of hers. He wrote his song 'Philadelphia Freedom' for her. After that, I met him many times, in LA, Paris, and New York. Elton's obsessed with tennis, and I've played a couple of times with him in charity events. One year, he invited me to a concert he was giving in New York with Billy Joel, and I went along to the pre-concert party, where he told me his mum really loved me. That made me feel old. Elton's a great guy, though, he's done work for Agassi's charity for kids in Las Vegas, and in June 2003 he came to do a concert for me in Romania. It had been my dream for years to bring him to

Romania, and finally the radio station I now run there arranged for him to come over. Unfortunately, it was during the French Open, so after all that I couldn't make it to the actual concert, because I was playing the seniors' tournament every day. Even if Elton had laid on his private jet, it just wouldn't have been possible, so I was really disappointed.

All these people, they became friends, not close friends, sure, but guys that we would hang out with, and they accepted me straight away, although I was a sportsman and they were actors. In the end, they're just people, like everybody else. If you treat them normally, they're fine. The problem comes with their minders and hangers-on. They think they should make it impossible to talk to the guy they're 'protecting', that they should be treated differently. But I've never done that.

It's like with Muhammad Ali, who happens to be one of my all-time sporting heroes. But he's such a nice, funny guy. One year, I was playing a tournament at Caesar's Palace and he was filming something in the casino there, so in the end I met him when he was surrounded by cameramen, photographers, and TV.

'You're the big boy of tennis, I know that,' he said. 'But I've also heard you've got a big mouth. You see this mouth? It's bigger than yours.'

Then he turned to the photographers: 'Take a picture of the bad boy of tennis.'

So they started snapping away with their cameras, and he pointed to my head and said: 'You're pretty but I'm prettier than you.'

He then put my fist in his face: 'You see, Bad Boy', which is what he always calls me, that or Big Mouth, 'you have your knuckles in my face, because I want it, but I could easily have it the other way round.'

I liked that, he was joking away very naturally with me from the start, and we've always carried on in that way whenever we meet.

The US Open at the end of August was the last to be held at Forest Hills, and it was over for me in the 2nd round, when I was beaten by the Italian Corrado Barazzutti. I was really disappointed, even though I had not played much in tournaments. I didn't see at the time that this was the beginning of the end of my serious involvement in majors. Although I was already thirty-one, I couldn't accept defeats like this. That took a few more years.

That was the year when I first started to go to Studio 54 in New York, which was the new discotheque to be seen in. Dominique was not with me then, and it was there that I met Bianca Jagger, who had already split up with Mick and was very good friends with Andy Warhol and the dress designer Halston. They all used to hang out there as well. Bianca looked a lot like Dominique, and she was fun and cool but nothing ever happened between us. In later years, when I would go to Studio 54, Bianca was often there, along with Margaret Trudeau, the ex-wife of the then Canadian prime minister. As well as going out with Mick Jagger, Margaret also spent a couple of nights with me. She was in the middle of rebelling against her marriage, and I guess I was too, so it suited us both. Most of the evenings I was there, Vitas was also there. Sometimes, he and the others would go up to the top of the gallery to do I don't know what, but I always stayed downstairs. I'd watch the show, with all the dancers and sometimes these white horses would also come on. The music was great, and Steve Rubell, one of the owners, who loved tennis and would come to the US Open every day, would also do the rounds and talk to everybody. It was fun, and for me it was a way of forgetting that I'd been beaten in the tournament and admitting to myself that my best days were probably behind me.

The autumn of '77 saw me win a tournament in Aix en Provence, in southern France, which made headlines in the tennis world. A new racket had been tried out the week before at a tournament at the Racing Club in Paris by a couple of Frenchmen, Georges Goven and Christophe Roger-Vasselin. Nicknamed the 'spaghetti' racket, it had double stringing and it made the ball go completely crazy. In fact, I had lost in Paris to Goven, and I'd never lost to him before. Then Tiriac and I lost to Roger-Vasselin and some other guy in the doubles final. So I thought I'd test this racket, and in Aix somebody lent me one. It was horrible to play with, it put twice the amount of spin on the ball, because it kept the ball inside the strings for longer. You just had to put your serve in play, you couldn't go for an ace or anything because it was so soft. You couldn't hit topspin either, you could only slice, otherwise the ball was uncontrollable. So it was not easy to play with, but I won the tournament with it against Vilas, who was driven crazy by the racket.

By the end of the week, Philippe Chatrier, who was now President of the ITF, decided that the spaghetti racket was bad for tennis, and he banned it. He saw I was doing OK with it, and he thought it would be dangerous for the sport. If I hadn't won, who knows what would have happened, because I would have kept it and then it would have crept in more slowly to the sport. So he was right to ban it quickly, because if he'd allowed it everybody would have switched in the end. The irony is they should have done the same with the larger rackets, but, because they were never banned at the beginning, it was all too late after that, and tennis is now like ping pong on a large court. The game has changed, and now there's no going back.

CHAPTER TEN

1978–1980

For John, it was life or death out there. For me, too. But afterwards I became a completely normal person straightaway. He couldn't understand that.

Having finished ninth in the world rankings the previous year, WCT signed me up again at the start of 1978 to play their circuit from January until May, this time for a guaranteed $250,000 a year for the following three years. I may not have been winning big titles any more, but I was pulling in the crowds wherever I went and therefore making money for the organizers. I was the only player to sign such a contract, and, just after, WCT became part of the Grand Prix circuit, so there was no longer any need to sign players up to ensure they played that circuit rather than the Grand Prix.

I was pleased that, despite the guarantee, I also played well enough to qualify for the eight-man play-off finals in Dallas in mid May, even though I lost there to the tough Miami-born Eddie Dibbs in the 1st round. I had also partnered during the season the best-behaved guy on the tour, the tall, graceful Chilean Jaime Fillol, and we had qualified for the doubles finals in Kansas at the beginning of May.

The River Oaks Country Club, in Houston, Texas, was

not one of my favourite stops on the tour, however. This was the sort of club that did not allow Arthur Ashe to play, because he was black, nor Harold Solomon, because he was Jewish. I only played there once, but that was enough. They were such snobs that I wore jeans and old shoes all week just to provoke them. I got to the final that week in April, even though I was playing Team Tennis simultaneously. I was flying between Los Angeles and Houston every day, playing indoors in the evening in an air-conditioned arena in LA, then dashing to Houston and playing outdoors in the sun. In the final, I was playing against Brian Gottfried. It was very hot, and I had been going backwards and forwards all week. I won the 1st set, but then lost the 2nd and started to get annoyed, because there was this lady sitting behind my chair in the first row, wearing a beautiful white hat, and she was clapping all my mistakes. Every one of them. So I let her do it at first, but then I started to get really mad, and I went up to her and asked:

'Lady, what do you do when I do a good shot, because you're clapping my mistakes? Who do you clap for?'

And she went: 'I'm a spectator, and it's my right to clap your mistakes.' You know, rights in America and all that.

So I said, very slowly: 'If you don't shut up, I'm going to have rights too. You know what I'm going to do? I'm going to shit in your hat. Your big white hat. Because that's my right too.'

So she became all red, she stood up, stormed off, and reported me to the president of the club. She even reported me to the police, I think. Anyway, I lost the match, there was a party, nobody mentioned anything. Then the next day, the headline was: 'Nastase, banned from ever coming back to River Oaks.' What a relief.

By the time Wimbledon came round (I had missed Roland Garros because of Team Tennis) I had had no grass court practice and had gone over the $3,000 fines permitted in one season, largely because of the River Oaks incident and various other situations where I got into trouble for bad language and protests against bad calls. So I knew that the Pro Council was planning a tough punishment. The Pro Council was made up of nine members taken from various bodies of the game including the ITF and the ATP, but I had no idea, when Wimbledon started, what they would do or when. Helpfully, the day before the tournament started, one newspaper carried the front-page headline that I might receive a $10,000 fine and – what was worse – a one-year ban, and this might in effect end my career. That was not a good way to start the tournament.

Dominique, by now, was travelling a lot less with me. She would be there for the majors, for example, plus any tournament that led up to them, but at other times she would stay home for several weeks at a time before rejoining me again for a few weeks. We'd decided, from the beginning, that Nathalie would not travel around with us, because we didn't think it was good for a kid to live like that. That meant, though, that Dominique was either at home in Bazoches with Nathalie while I was travelling around on my own, or she was with me, in which case Nathalie was at home with her nanny. Either way, it was never an ideal situation.

During the Wimbledon of '78, Dominique was with me, and that allowed me to stay reasonably calm despite what was going on with the Pro Council. They had asked me to attend a hearing on the middle Sunday of the tournament, so that I could defend my case, after which they would decide on my punishment. I refused, because I was still in the tournament and there was no way I was going to get all uptight about the meeting before playing the next day. So I wrote a letter to them instead and tried to concentrate my mind on the tennis.

On the second Monday of the tournament, I met Roscoe Tanner in the 4th round. With Centre Court full to bursting point for this eagerly awaited last encounter of the day, I played a fantastic match. The crowd was really behind me, and I was reading his serves so well that I was sending returns back to his ankles, which he did not know what to do with. Meanwhile, I was serving like a demon and mixing up the pace and pattern of my rallying. Tennis seemed easy once again and my worries forgotten as I beat him in four sets 2–6, 6–4, 6–2, 6–3. With the tournament behind schedule because of rain, I had no day off and had to play Tom Okker the next day in the quarterfinals. I played well, and the crowd saw a great match – it was voted by many journalists as the match of the tournament – but Okker played unbelievably well and it was his turn to beat me in four sets. As I came off court, I went straight to be interviewed by the BBC's Gerald Williams. It was then that somebody from the Pro Council handed me a letter. This was obviously a pretty bad moment to be informing me that I was to be fined $5,000 and suspended immediately for three months from all Grand Prix tournaments. Well, they're not very diplomatic these guys.

So I put out a press release accepting the decision but adding that 'given that I am imperfect, then it should also be recognized that those who sit in judgement over the players both on and off the court are also sometimes imperfect. Yet it seems I am the only one who is forced to pay for their mistakes. If all umpires were professional like Frank Hammond in America and Bertie Bowron in Europe, I would not get so upset.'

The fact was, I would have preferred to have had good umpires and no Code of Conduct, because a lot of my anger was directed at the really bad level of umpiring that existed while I was playing. That didn't improve until after I'd retired, when proper, professional umpires started travelling to all the tournaments. That was a huge step. If you know the guy is going to do his best because it's his job, he's paid good money, and he's not just there to watch the match, then you respect him and he respects you. He's not just some local part-timer who starts to laugh when he makes a mistake – that reaction used to send me berserk in one second flat. And I felt sure that some umpires or linesmen were out to screw me. OK, I had fights with them anyway, so it's difficult to say whether they did it on purpose. But Fred McNair, the American doubles specialist, once told me, after one of my matches against him, that one of his friends had been on the middle line, the service line, and sure enough this guy had given me such bad calls that I'd got mad at him. So things like that got me upset. Anyway, by the end, every time I walked out on court I thought everybody was against me. Put it this way: if a point had to be replayed or was not clear, they would give it to the other guy, maybe because of my reputation, maybe because I screamed at them. But they never gave it to me, that's for sure.

I accept that sometimes there was no excuse for what I did on court. Whether it was because of pressure, fear of losing, crowd problems, bad umpiring, whatever, I have to confess I behaved like an arsehole at times. It's a strong word but there's no other word for it. Sometimes, I know I asked for it, I went too far and deserved to be fined or disqualified. As I have already said, tournament directors in the early days had no Code of Conduct to go by, so they would let me get away with things because I was one of their biggest attractions – if not the biggest. Then, when the Code of Conduct came in, at the end of 1975, things changed but I guess I didn't.

So after my '78 Wimbledon was over, I went to dinner at San Lorenzo in Knightsbridge with Dominique and a few friends. We met up with other players like Vitas Gerulaitis and Chris Evert, who were also having dinner there, and I tried to forget about the suspension. I then stayed on in London for a few days to shoot some scenes for the film *Players* with Ali McGraw and Dino Martin, Dean Martin's son, who was a good player. In the film, I had to lose to him in the semifinal of Wimbledon, and for this match I was as good as gold and did exactly as I was told. Although I had fun shooting the scenes, the experience was a one-off as far as I was concerned. Films were not for me – I preferred my own real life drama every time.

The next day, with Dominique returning to France, I jetted off with Vitas to the States to continue the Team Tennis season, which we were both signed up for. First, though, to add to the crazy travel schedule, we stopped off in New York to play a $300,000 invitational tournament at Forest Hills. Half way through the week, we then flew to Las Vegas for a Team Tennis evening match, then back to New York in the early hours of the next day in time for the semifinals, which we had both qualified for. I think Vitas got a couple of hours' sleep, but, despite trying to sleep in the aisle of the plane and on the floor of the airport terminal, I swear I hardly slept all night. Then I walked straight onto court to face the nineteen-year-old John McEnroe, who was by now an established name since reaching the Wimbledon semis the year before as a qualifier. Despite my exhaustion, I somehow managed to beat him in straight sets. 'If you can do it, so can I,' Vitas told me after watching me play, so he too got rid of his semifinal opponent, the Pole Wojtek Fibak. Unfortunately, in the final, Vitas seemed more awake than me, and he beat me easily for the title.

Then it was straight over to Los Angeles for the rest of the LA Strings Team Tennis season. This year, the owner Jerry Buss had made me coach as well as player. I know a lot of people thought that was the funniest thing they'd ever heard, but I really enjoyed the extra responsibility. I had great players in my team: Chris Evert, first of all, then Stephanie Tolleson, who went on to work in the tennis division of IMG in London, the Japanese–American Ann Kiyomura, and the two Amritraj brothers, Vijay and his younger brother Ashok.

I had a very relaxed team atmosphere. I was a friend not a coach, and, although Vijay and Ashok weren't big on practice, Chris certainly was and that was fine with me, it kept me in shape. I'd practise with her for hours: lobs, smashes, anything she wanted. At first, she took it all pretty seriously and would get upset if she lost one of her one-set matches, but soon, as she's got a good sense of humour, she relaxed and the whole team had a lot of laughs together. I remember one match, in New York, I had to come in as a substitute half way through – you could do that in Team Tennis – and I had my tracksuit on but had forgotten to put my shorts on. Vijay knew that, so he started pulling my tracksuit down but I only had my jockstrap on underneath. Once Chris realized that, she leapt in, trying hard to pull my tracksuit down as well. Sometimes, I'd shout at her: 'Come on Chris, hurry up, get out of the dressing room!' but other times I'd just go in, they'd all be naked in there. But they took it the right way; it was a joke.

Of course, I knew her very well because she'd been engaged to Jimmy Connors, so we'd been out a lot in the past anyway. But to give an idea of how crazy the people were who came to the Team Tennis matches, one evening when Jimmy came to watch – he was living in LA at the time and had stayed friends with Chris – one guy started shouting out: 'Hey, Jimmy, how's Christ Evert in bed?' Jimmy was so mad he was chasing the guy all over the place. I too went berserk at some matches, screaming back at some of the unrepeatable insults that people shouted at me. I would chase after guys in the stadium, I'd complain to the linesmen, the umpire, they'd throw me out. In a way, I quite liked all that craziness because I was allowed to do things on court that I could not do in tournaments. Then I'd go to Wimbledon or the US Open and it was all so perfect, so quiet.

There was pressure on me to win, though, not just as a player but as a coach. My team had to win. Because of my reputation and the atmosphere in our team, the other nine teams in the league didn't take us too seriously. But we played well and were attracting the crowds wherever we went. Some of the other teams had good players, like Vitas, who played for the New York Apples, and Martina Navratilova, who played for the Boston Lobsters and who had just won the first of her nine Wimbledons that year. Even so, we found ourselves in the play-offs, the finals in other words, against the other most successful team, the Boston Lobsters. Played over a best-of-five series, we won 3–1, to the surprise of a lot of people, and became Team Tennis champions. But that was as good as it ever got, because that was the last year I played Team Tennis and the last year they operated under that format at the time. By the end of the season, most of the teams went under.

Martina is a player and a person that I've always respected. Like me, she had to adjust to life in the West, but whereas I had Tiriac, she had nobody. So she found things a lot harder at first. She would eat badly, spend madly, and get really unhappy. It wasn't until she got to be friends with Chris Evert and Billie-Jean that she sorted herself out. When she first appeared on the tour as a teenager, she was skinny. Then she got fat and then she got muscly, but throughout she had great touch and she was a great sportswoman. And she came to the net – it was unusual to see that in a woman – so she brought the real serve-volley tactic into the women's game. I loved watching her matches, especially those against Chris, because the two were such a contrast of styles, and those against Evonne Goolagong-Cawley, because, like Martina, she went to the net. Martina played in such an unusual way, the way she moved around the court, the way she put passion into her game like Billie-Jean. She would scream on court, she'd fall down, she'd express her feelings. She was a bit like me – though with more control – because she'd complain to the umpire and to the crowd. That was new for the women. I also thought it was really brave of her to come out about being gay, because she was the first to say it. All the others who were gay had never said anything, and many today still deny it, even though I don't think it matters at all who people are attracted to. But I think it was natural for her to say it, because by then everybody knew and also that's how Martina is: she's a very honest person.

During the summer of '78, I continued to be based in LA, and Dominique stayed most of the time in France. I had an apartment this time and was going out more. I had met, over the years, actors such as Clint Eastwood and Kirk Douglas, and whenever I was in LA I'd call one or other of them up and we'd go out for dinner. I'd been to Michael Douglas's birthday party when he was thirty, and, because Kirk's wife Anne was Belgian and spoke French, we all got on very well. I'd go to his house in Palm Springs to play tennis or we'd go out for dinner. I had met Clint a few years before in Las

Vegas. He always kept a low profile wherever he went: he'd walk slowly, he'd talk quietly. I remember once we met at the Hyatt Hotel in LA for breakfast – I was staying there during a tournament – and he pulled up in a beaten-up old Ford, like the New York taxis, wearing an old T-shirt and jeans. He was trying very hard not to attract attention, but because he's so tall everybody noticed him when he slowly made his entrance.

In New York, in the late Seventies and early Eighties, Vitas and I would go to Studio 54, where we became good friends with Andy Warhol, who was always there. Andy, maybe surprisingly, also used to go to watch the tennis during the US Open almost every day. He told me he liked me, the way I played, the way I made him laugh. Usually, if you sat next to him he wouldn't say anything unless you started to talk to him. But with me he talked quite a lot, although he had a very soft voice so it was not always easy to hear what he said when we were at the night-club. Maybe because he's also from Eastern Europe, from Slovakia originally – his real name is Andrej Warhola – he felt we had something in common. He also had this little camera, and every time he was interested in something he'd take a photo. He did one of his series of multicoloured screen prints of Chris Evert, and he asked me if I wanted to come over to do a shoot for him as well, but stupidly I never found the time. He did give me, though, as a birthday present one year, a signed lithograph of one of his Campbell Soup images. He was very pleasant, very nice to everybody. He never screamed or swore at the people who used to grab at him, even though he was very small and used to get jostled around quite a lot. He never tried to be the centre of attention, unlike Halston, who was Jackie Kennedy's favourite designer when she was First Lady. He was always talking, gesticulating, with a cocktail in one hand and a cigarette in the other.

I never got really into the whole scene like Vitas did, going there every night, doing drugs, going to each others' apartments afterwards to do more drugs. Sometimes we'd go to Halston's house on Park Avenue. It was an incredible place, made of steel and glass, with a huge staircase and a ceiling-to-floor living area, which at the time was really unusual. We talked, we had fun, some people drank, smoked. I don't know what, and I didn't care. But nobody bothered me, trying to make me take drugs. It was cool. The fun for me was to be there early, like 11 p.m. or midnight. I'd stay a couple of hours, but then I would think I'd have to practise the next day or play a match, so I'd leave. I knew my limits very clearly. Vitas's limits, though, were completely different. On one occasion in New York, I left him at a party in the hotel we were staying in, and I went to bed. It must have been around midnight. The next day, when I got up, he was still partying. He'd never been to bed. But he played his match that day just the same, perfectly normal.

By the late Seventies, I also started getting invited onto chat shows more regularly. I'd done *The Johnny Carson Show* in the early Seventies, soon after my Forest Hills win in '72. I then did his show again in '77, when Adidas started to market my Nastase tennis shoes, which are still in production in the States and are being brought out again in France. Johnny was a fan of tennis and would come to watch Connors and me play a lot at Wimbledon and at the US Open. I have to say that I didn't get nervous, because I knew that the questions would be about tennis rather than about the politics of my country, for example. Johnny might ask me what it was like to bow in front of the Queen at Wimbledon or why I did certain things like pulling my shorts down or arguing: 'You're a nice guy, I know you off court, you're not like that' Carson would go, but I'd be ready with the answer: 'When you're at work, you're different. When you're here, are you the same as when you're home with your wife?' 'No', he'd reply, pretending to get angry like me.

Over the years, I did all the big American talk shows, as well as shows in France and Britain. In Britain, I still enjoy doing *A Question of Sport* every year – the current captains Frankie Dettori and Ally McCoist are crazy and fun to be with, although I can hardly understand Ally with his Scottish accent. It's hosted by Sue Barker, who's fantastic, so I always have a great time. I also did *They Think It's All Over* a couple of years ago with the craziest guy of all, Jonathan Ross, who happens to be a big tennis fan. At one stage, he dressed up as Serena Williams with high heels, boots, and he was almost naked on top, with big boobs. Half the stuff he said had to be cut when the programme went out, it was too dirty. He's really nuts that kid, but I love him.

At first, it was special for me to do these shows, but now I'm used to it and I'm more comfortable, although I have to admit that I'm never as comfortable as on a tennis court. Put me in front of 15,000 people on a tennis court, with a television audience of millions, and if I'm playing tennis I thrive. I feel like I'm on my stage, and I love being the centre of attention. But if I have to give a speech in front of people, I hate it.

My three-month suspension in 1978 from Grand Prix tournaments ran from July until September, but it did not affect me very much because I was contracted to play Team Tennis for most of that time anyway. The only big event I did miss was the first US Open to be played in its new venue, Flushing Meadow. Financially, though, I made more money from various exhibition matches that I played during that period. That's how stupid the system was. So instead of playing Grand Prix tournaments in September, I played a series of exhibition matches, mainly in Holland and Belgium, with players like Borg and McEnroe.

I remember, I was always the driver. When I played against Borg, I would drive and he would be asleep all the time. Once we were supposed to go to a place called Mons in Belgium, which is about 50 km from Brussels. Sure enough, after about ten minutes Bjorn is fast asleep. So I go on the motorway and follow the signs to Mons. Then, about 2 km from Mons, I suddenly see signs for Bergen. Mons? Where's Mons? No Mons any more. What the fuck is this, I think to myself. So I turn around, go round and approach it one more time. I see Mons, then the exit says to Bergen. Again. So I turn around again and think, hell, I'm not going there, I'm going back to Brussels. This is in the days before mobile phones, of course. So I drive all the way back to Brussels. At that stage, Bjorn wakes up: 'What's happened? We've played already? Did I sleep through the whole thing?' 'No, we went, but I can't find fucking Mons. Call the guy and ask him if this Mons exists.' So we call the guy and he explains that Mons and Bergen are the same place: Mons is just the French version, and the motorway exit was just inside the Flemish part of Belgium. That's why the name had suddenly switched.

The year after, I had a similar episode when I was playing a tournament in Tel Aviv. The guy who organized it was a Canadian friend of mine, Gerry Goldberg, and he said:

'No problem, I pick you up at the airport, I'll fix the hotel, the visa, the guarantee, everything. Just take the plane.'

So I arrive, we set off in his car and I ask: 'Where are we staying?'

'The Hilton, you'll see, it's beautiful, by the sea.'

So we get talking and by now it's dark. Then suddenly we arrive in front of a high gate. A guy comes out in uniform, with a machine gun.

'Where are you going?' he asks looking at us suspiciously.

'We're trying to get to the Hilton.'

He looks at us as if we are nuts. Then he just starts to laugh: 'This is Jordan, not the Hilton.'

In the end, we make it to Tel Aviv, but instead of going straight to the Hilton, Gerry insists on taking me to the Sheraton. That's where the action is, he says. So he's drinking beers, and, as he's a nervous, manic guy, moving all the time, he's fetching more beers the whole time. In the end, by about one or two in the morning, he's left and I'm talking to various girls, but I'm completely smashed because I'm not used to drinking like that. Then I realize I can't remember where the hell I'm staying. Plus, Gerry still has all my gear in the back of his car. So I check into a nearby hotel – not a very good hotel it turned out – and crash out. The next morning, the phone wakes me up at about eleven o'clock. 'You son-of-a-bitch', I can hear Gerry screaming, 'I was calling every single hotel in Tel Aviv trying to track you down. Your stuff's at the Hilton, and you're playing Colin Dibley at twelve.'

I just made it in time, and after that he invited me many times. In fact, I visited Israel with him – the Dead Sea, Jerusalem, the Wailing Wall – and I loved all of it. It was just the first trip that was the craziest.

The travel, by that stage in my career, was really constant. Team Tennis didn't help, but I think all players were travelling and playing too much in those days. Tennis had not really got itself organized, and there were too many competing circuits, too many points to chase, too many dollars to be won. The game was in full explosion. In 1978, even with my suspension and Team Tennis (plus I was banned from Davis Cup that year), I still played twenty-one tournaments. But a big part of me had a need to play tennis, and that's what people couldn't understand a few years later when they said I should retire. I didn't want to leave the sport, and still don't. That's why I still play now and always will, as long as I can and as long as people want me to.

I was never motivated by money. If I had been, I would have shut my mouth and saved myself a lot in fines, disqualifications, and suspensions. In fact, I was not ambitious with my money. I kept most of it in a bank in Luxembourg, because my in-laws had contacts there. It would earn some interest, but at least it was safe. I'd pay my taxes in whichever country I'd play, then put the money in the bank. That's one of the things Tiriac taught me. Once or twice I invested in business ventures that didn't pay off, and once I'd done that and lost money I decided it wasn't worth doing any more. Luckily, I never lost big amounts like Borg, although his former business partner and the press exaggerated the amount he lost. He told me it was about $1 million, whereas they said he'd lost everything. In those last couple of years in the Seventies, Dominique's brother Daniel was looking after some of my financial interests, and I had the banker in Luxembourg who would also advise me. He'd give me a summary once a month, and I'd call him and ask him how I was doing. I didn't have hundreds of millions anyway, but I was happy with what I had made, considering I had started with absolutely nothing. Money gave me the power to know that I could buy anything I wanted, but although I liked to live well I never went crazy. I have never gambled; even all those times I'd been in Las Vegas, I'd resist. Connors, Dibbs, they'd all have a go, but I never went near the gambling. I was afraid that, once I started, I wouldn't be able to stop. If I wanted to buy a watch, I'd buy one, not twelve, like some of today's top sportsmen. But I was pretty relaxed about money. I didn't feel the need to keep spending it or to count how much I had. One year, my American Express gold card that was in Dominique's name went missing, and for some reason I never bothered reporting it. Then one morning I was woken up in my New York hotel suite by two cops, who told me they'd arrested a pickpocket and he happened to have Dominique's card on him. How long had it been missing? 'About six months', I replied, unsure. 'Why didn't you report the loss?' they asked. 'Because whoever stole it was spending less than my wife.'

It's true, I had high living expenses. I was supporting my family in Romania, not because they expected it but because for me it was natural to do that. It's not like they weren't working and were just waiting for me to pay for them. But I wanted to help and share what I had, so sometimes it meant paying for them to come to France, other times buying things for them in Romania to make sure they had a nice life. I also had my wife and daughter to support and homes in France and New York, where I had bought an apartment on 72nd and 3rd, which was a convenient base for all the times I was there. By 1980, for tax reasons, I bought an apartment in Monte Carlo as well. When I travelled, I was staying in nice hotels and flying first class, because I wanted to enjoy being able to do that, to live well, not like I used to live when I had nothing. When I flew to and from the States, which at one stage I was doing almost every two weeks, I would fly Concorde, which was expensive. But the plane was so fast, it was essential for me. Nobody gave me money, I didn't inherit any. That's why I don't feel guilty about the money I have or the way I spend it. I think I worked hard for it, and I deserve what I earned.

Although I flew the whole time everywhere, I could never

sleep on planes. Not properly so that I was unaware of what was going on around me. So I was suffering, that's all, and I'd arrive exhausted without having recuperated, especially if there had been turbulence, because that made me really nervous. Sometimes, because of my schedule, I'd get straight off the plane and play the same day. Nobody knew, but I really didn't feel like playing, I felt sick. Also, in those days I didn't drink. Nowadays I have a little drink sometimes to help me relax on flights, but then all I could do was watch the in-flight movie and read the paper, because I've never had the patience to read a whole book. I'd start but never finish. Ion was always trying to get me to read. He'd read in English to improve his fluency, and I know that I would speak the language better now if I'd followed his example. Dominique loved to read, and Amalia does too. She taught herself English by watching English movies on TV and reading books, and now she speaks better than me. But my temperament was not suited to books. I'd always be getting up after ten minutes and doing something else. It's something I do regret.

All the travel meant that, when I did go home to Bazoches to see Dominique and Nathalie, I'd often be there for a few days only. I'd arrive, go straight to see my daughter who I often had not seen for weeks, see my wife, then crash out and spend the rest of the time trying to rest and recover before setting off again. Sometimes I was not in a very good mood, because I'd lost in a tournament somewhere – that's why I'd been able to go home in the first place – so I was not always very good company for my wife and daughter. When I went home, the nanny was always there, Dominique's family was also there a lot, and probably it was difficult to have time just to ourselves. My daughter now says that she has no recollection of her parents being together, although she adds that this is why our separation and divorce did not affect her at the time as she did not notice any difference.

By the end of the Seventies, Dominique knew that I was no saint when I was away. She didn't need to ask me questions when I got back, go through my pockets, or peel off the long blonde hair from my jacket (more likely the white hair from the Studio 54 horses). I think she just wanted me to be discreet when I was away, for her sake and for the sake of Nathalie. So I suppose I took advantage of that, although I'm not proud to say it. She knew my reputation before we were married, and we had both agreed that she wouldn't travel with me the whole time. Dominique now says that she was maybe too influenced by the nanny, who told her it was bad for her to be away from Nathalie for very long. But that's life, you make those decisions and there's no point in regretting them. Anyway, even if she had travelled more, I still think our marriage would have ended. Life just started pulling us apart. She had her calm life in Bazoches with Nathalie, the nanny, her family. I had my restless, crazy life jetting around hitting tennis balls in all four corners of the world, and that life appealed to her less and less. I still enjoyed it, and after a few days of quiet at home, I would be ready to go off again. I'd have my bags packed in the hall a few days before I was actually leaving, and she'd think I was nuts, but I was happy to keep travelling. It's the only life I knew, and despite the bad sides I still loved it.

The last two years of the Seventies went by in this way. I'd be away, Dominique would sometimes join me, I'd play tournaments, exhibitions, I'd win some and lose some, I'd get into trouble in some matches, and make people laugh in others (sometimes in the same match). Slowly but surely, though, I began to slide down the rankings. I finished sixteenth at the end of 1978 and won two singles titles and was runner-up in four. By the end of 1979, I was fiftieth and had won five doubles titles but no singles. At first, I didn't want to admit to myself that this was happening, because a lot of the problem was in my head. I'd lost confidence. Instead of hitting a shot instinctively, I would think about it beforehand, and that's never good. Sometimes, though, I played so well in a match that my confidence would return, and I'd still feel able to beat anybody. Physically, at that stage, I was still as fast and as strong as before. By then, also, I'd be getting provoked by spectators because they knew I had a big mouth on court. It got to the stage where if I didn't respond to their insults – 'Commie bum' was a favourite one in the States – they'd think: 'Hey, what's going on?' And I'd find it very difficult to say nothing. Then, as soon as I raised an eyebrow or said anything to an official, the public would immediately take great pleasure in whistling, heckling, and slow-clapping me. That would be OK if I was winning, but if I was losing, things would quickly turn sour, I'd get into trouble, and it would all go wrong from there.

For the other players, I was now beatable, and if you don't beat them they don't respect you. When you're number 1, they're hoping they can beat you maybe once. When they know they can beat you regularly, it's like wild animals that smell blood: they come more and more. So when, through lack of confidence, I started to lose more often to players who I didn't think were very good, that was tough. It takes years to admit to yourself that you're no longer the same player, and even once you admit it to yourself, you don't want to admit it publicly when the press asks you questions, although there comes a stage when you cannot argue with the facts.

None of this did much good for my relationship with Dominique. When a sportsman starts to go towards the end of his career, his relationship with his wife or girlfriend also has to change, and usually it doesn't improve. You're seeing each other more, you're having to think of doing other things with your life, and for me I found it difficult to accept spending a long time at home. That, plus the worry about the lack of results. I think that's one of the reasons that so many marriages go wrong, not only in tennis but also in other sports, when the sportsman comes to the end of his career. The only thing I regret maybe was that Nathalie was not born later on, so that I could have seen her more. Because for the first five years of her life, when I was still with Dominique, I hardly saw her, and when I did, it was hard for her to become close to me, because she didn't know me. Luckily, we had a nanny who brought her up right and who explained to her the situation, before and after we got divorced, so Nathalie has always understood the reasons for my absences. That's one of the reasons I have a good relationship with her now.

In 1979, I missed Wimbledon through injury, then went to Flushing Meadow for the US Open. Now being played on hard courts, the tournament had a totally different atmosphere from Forest Hills. It was much bigger, much noisier. The planes taking off and landing every few seconds from nearby La Guardia airport meant that often you couldn't hear yourself hit your own shot, never mind hear your opponent's, which is not good, because it's important to hear as well as see a ball being hit, so that you can anticipate what sort of spin is being put on it.

The crowds there are really noisy. They shout at you when they want, they don't wait for the change of ends to wander around, eating their hot dogs and drinking their Coke. It was in that atmosphere, in my opening round against a Finn, Leo Palin, that I scored a fashion first by changing my shorts beside the court during a changeover. I was on the Grandstand Court, and the day was incredibly hot and humid, like they can be in New York. I was leading 7–5, 6–5, but I was sweating all over, and the sweat kept pouring down my back and into my shorts. I'd got really uncomfortable and couldn't play, so I asked one of the ball boys to go fetch me another pair, which he did, obediently. Out he came with a nice dry powder-blue pair of shorts. And at the change of ends, what else could I do but strip off? I have to explain that I was wearing a skin-coloured jockstrap, so I was not completely naked, but still I did say 'excuse me' politely as I stepped out of the sweaty old pair, kicked them aside, and put on the new pair. I did a little bow to the crowd, and on I went with the match. I won the game and the 2nd set, then Palin retired with an injured leg. Well, I'd enjoyed myself. Nobody had done that before, not even me. As I walked off court, in a final flourish I pointed triumphantly to my backside, accompanied by the whistling and clapping of the crowd.

My next match was less funny. It was against John McEnroe, the number 3 seed, who would go on to win his first US Open title. We were scheduled on the main Louis Armstrong Stadium as the second match of the evening session. It was a hot and humid night, and by the time the previous match, a women's singles, had finished, a lot of people had drunk a lot of beer. When we came on, it was already nine o'clock, and the 10,000 capacity crowd was already in an excitable mood. They were ready for a show. The press had built the game up as if it was a boxing match. Well, that's almost what they got. Strangely, because McEnroe was a local boy, the crowd were behind me rather than him. Maybe they sensed that I was the underdog. In any case, the local bad kid versus the original bad boy of tennis made for a great event as far as they were concerned.

I had hired my favourite player, Roy Emerson, to practise with me the week before the Open – I'd gone to California especially – because I was not in good shape. I was not too ashamed to ask him for help, because I knew I needed to improve – not to win the tournament, because I knew I couldn't, but to do as well as I could.

I knew the match itself was not going to be easy or quiet, and that either me or McEnroe – or both – would get into trouble. That's why they gave us Frank Hammond as umpire, because he was the best. He was the only one who could control us. He'd talk to us as people, not as naughty schoolboys, as most of them did. He'd say: 'Come on, Ilie, let's play, the ball was out, trust me.' And we always had a chance to tell him calmly if we thought there had been a bad line call.

The tennis was actually good for the first two sets. We were both playing well, angling shots away, making each other run for impossible balls, entertaining the crowd. Then, with the score level at one set all, some loud hecklers in the crowd started to get to me. They wouldn't stop, and I started to yell back and get annoyed. I also got a few bad line calls. I started to complain to Frank, who seemed to be losing control of the match and not knowing what to do. He got all serious and changed his tone. It's true it was not an easy situation. When I was a break up in the 3rd, I stalled at one moment, saying I wasn't ready to receive serve. He docked me a penalty point. The crowd got mad, and it took a while for play to start again. But, when it did, my rhythm had gone, and I lost the set 6–3.

In the 4th set, McEnroe went 3–1 ahead, with my serve to follow. I stalled again. I admit, it wasn't good, but I was losing control myself and I started to shout at Roy and

Dominique, who were at the courtside. OK, the next step after a penalty point is a penalty game, but I didn't think Frank was ever going to do that. But suddenly, Frank awarded the game to McEnroe. Then the crowd went completely nuts. They didn't think it was fair. John also got involved, and we both went crazy. It was total chaos. For seventeen minutes, while cans, cups, garbage, and even bottles were being thrown onto court, and the police arrived in case there was a riot, I argued, John argued, the crowd screamed at Frank, and Frank lost control completely. He kept ordering me to play, and I kept yelling that it was too noisy. How could I have played? I couldn't even hear my own voice. Then Frank defaulted me. Just like that. That should have been the end, but it wasn't. Things just got worse. The crowd wanted his blood. They wanted a match, after all. They'd waited for this one, and they wanted to see the end of it. So two minutes later, I got reinstated, and crazily it was Frank who got taken off by Bill Talbert, the tournament director, and replaced by Mike Blanchard, the tournament referee. That was the end of my match, though. After everything that had gone on, there was no way I could play properly again, and McEnroe closed the set out 6–2.

By the time the match was finished, it was about 1 o'clock in the morning, almost four hours after we'd first gone on court. Afterwards, in the locker room, I had my shower and, as usual, I calmed down straight away. As it was late and neither John nor I had eaten, I just went up to him, totally naturally, and asked him if he wanted to join me and my party for dinner. I know he was completely shocked that I'd asked, but that's how I am and I can't explain it. For John, it was life or death out there. For me, too. But afterwards I became a completely normal person straightaway. He couldn't understand that. Anyway, I'd never had a problem with John during the whole match. He too had gone crazy at one stage, because they'd called a foot fault off him, so he too was waiting for a situation to happen to fire himself up. But, unlike me, he was able to stay aware of the situation on court, whereas I could not think: 'Hey, I've really got to stop and calm down.' Once I started, I had no choice but to keep going. So he joined me and Dominique and Roy for dinner in Manhattan, and we all had a very nice time. Dominique and Roy didn't say much to me after the match. What was the point? She was used to it by then – although it turned out it was the last major she ever went to – and Roy was my coach for my tennis, not my behaviour.

The other reason I made the headlines during that 1979 US Open was that I played mixed doubles with Dr Renée Richards. I'd known her in the Sixties when, as an amateur, she was Dr Richard Raskind, but after years of painful treatment she'd re-emerged on the women's tour as tennis' first transsexual player. Mitch, my friend, had suggested I play with her, because all the women had refused do so, either in the singles or doubles, and the men wouldn't play with her in the mixed. So I felt sorry for her and thought it wasn't fair, after all she'd been through. Not just the operations but all the problems before and after, not feeling either a man or a proper woman but wanting to be a woman. So I was thinking why doesn't somebody give her a chance and play with her? I asked her if she wanted to team up: 'but let's make it fun', I added. So that's how we played. And she was a good player, strong as well and very tall, and sometimes she carried me or played like me. I remember her feet were bigger than mine, she had big hands, but she tried to be feminine and was trying to change her voice at the time, to talk more like a woman.

Not surprisingly, I got teased the whole time by all the

players. 'Only you can play with that person, not man not woman,' they said. But for me it was important to help a person who nobody else was helping. The girls were saying they would boycott, they wouldn't play against her, which was stupid and biased because she was already forty-two when she returned to the circuit, so they had no need to be afraid of her. Also, half of them were lesbians, so they should have been more aware of fighting prejudice. Anyway, we had good fun. I remember, the first point of the match we played, I put away an easy overhead, and she came and hit me over the shoulder: 'What a boy, Nasty!' So I fell down on the ground, as if she'd hit me really hard, and everybody laughed. And the whole match was like that. In fact, we got to the semifinals of the mixed doubles and were only beaten by the number 1 seeds and eventual winners, Bob Hewitt and Greer Stevens, his fellow South African. We did so well and had such a good time that we played together again at the US Open the following year.

In the spring of 1980, Dominique finally told me that she had had enough and that she was filing for divorce. There wasn't any one particular incident that had made up her mind. It wasn't because we hated each other. We never got to that stage, and in many ways we still had feelings for each other. It was more that she realized that what she and I wanted out of life was always going to be different, and that there was no chance of things changing. She wanted a quiet life and I didn't, basically. I know it was more my fault than hers, because I know I was very difficult to live with in those years – even now, I'm not easy, as Amalia knows. Still, it was difficult for me to accept the reality at first, because, particularly with my first marriage, I thought it would last forever, like my parents' had. But nobody can guarantee that, and we were both sorry our marriage had broken down. It didn't matter what the reasons were. Of course there was some screaming and fighting, but in the end I saw that there was no going back, and we began divorce proceedings.

It was bad because it was just before Roland Garros and not long before Wimbledon, and we had to put out a press release as the papers kept asking me where Dominique was. In fact, I didn't play the French Open that year; there was too much going on in my private life, and it would have been too difficult to concentrate on a match.

In all divorces, the beginning is the toughest, and we tried very hard to keep it '*à l'amiable*', as the French say. But it's harder when you are well known, because the media inflame things very easily. And the British press are among the best in the world when they smell a good story that will sell papers. With me, during Wimbledon, they were like animals after their prey: they followed me absolutely everywhere. They kept showing photos of me with different women, even though none of them meant anything to me, and I lost count of how many times I made the front page of the newspapers. I had always been very patient with the press and happy to talk to reporters. But the build-up of tension in my private life over the previous few weeks, as well as this relentless and unwanted media attention, meant that I felt very fragile and upset. And that's when I lost control and did what I had never done to anybody before or since: I publicly lost my temper off court and hit somebody.

CHAPTER ELEVEN

1980–1984

At one stage, I got fed up. I put my arm around the grey-haired old lady sitting next to me and told the photographers: 'Hey, guys, meet my new girlfriend.'

The hitting incident happened when I was really at the end of my patience, after two weeks of hounding by the media. One reporter, who was staying at the same hotel as me in Kensington, just wouldn't give up. He came knocking at my door two, three times, and when he finally turned up at 8.30 one morning and asked: 'How about the divorce?' I got really mad. I smacked him and stupidly broke his glasses. It had never happened to me before to lose control like that, and I was really upset. I was shocked at what I'd done and couldn't believe what was suddenly happening to me. But, of course, that incident alone made yet more headlines the next day.

The pressure on me had really started the week before Wimbledon, when Romania played the semifinals of the European Zone B Davis Cup tie. This was on grass at Bristol. Having been 2–0 up after the first two singles, my friends the Lloyd brothers had taken the doubles, and Buster Mottram had equalized by beating our player Andrei Dirzu, whose grass-court experience was almost nil. So at 2–2, it was once more all down to me against John Feaver in the final rubber. The match lasted two days, because rain interrupted play, and I squeezed through in five sets on the Monday to win the tie for Romania. But on the way, because of the tension I was feeling for personal and professional reasons, I was a very bad boy and was given various official warnings for abuse and bad language. I don't know what it is about the Davis Cup and Britain, but again, after the tie, I was suspended from the competition, this time for eighteen months. So that was not a good start to my stay in England.

I had an Italian friend with me, who everyone called Bambino. I'd first met him through Panatta, who he was good friends with, but as he was a big 140 kg guy he became my unofficial travelling companion and bodyguard during what was a tough time for me. After the match against Feaver, Bambino pretended to shoot me with a fake gun when we were in the changing room. It was just a joke, and I fell to the ground, saying: 'I don't want to play Wimbledon, they're going to throw me out, it's better to kill me now.' But of course, for the press, this just added to the story of the day – my bad behaviour. So Feaver, who had not yet recovered from his match against me, was driving from Bristol to London when he heard on the car radio that the Wimbledon draw had been made. 'And who do you suppose I was meeting in the first round?' he told me afterwards in his terribly British accent, 'You! I couldn't believe it! I had to hold on hard to the wheel, because I swerved at that moment and almost hit a lamppost.'

So, on the first Monday of Wimbledon, after Bjorn had won his opening match, I walked onto Centre Court to face Feaver, for the second time in a week. Davis Cup on a bad provincial court was one thing. Wimbledon was quite another, and I was on my best behaviour, beating him easily 6–2, 6–3, 7–6. I did allow myself a little bit of joking, though, with the 'magic eye' black box that was being tried out for the first time on the service line. It was positioned to the side of the court, so at first I just circled warily around it. Next, I started gently bouncing balls on it to test it out. Then, in the 3rd set, after a doubtful service-line call, I walked over to it, got on my hands and knees, peered into it like a cat looking into a mouse hole, and told the machine: 'You must have been made in Russia.'

After the match, I was in a hurry to get back to my hotel in London, where I was meeting somebody. The car company Austin Rover had given me a Mini to use during the tournament. Painted on the doors in bright yellow letters was the slogan: 'FAST AS NASTASE WITHOUT THE RACKET: The New Quiet Minis.' It was fantastic, because I could park it in the Wimbledon car park rather than wait for a courtesy car, and I could park it anywhere in town, even sideways. Driving on the left was also great fun. I was in the car with Bambino, and I was sweating like mad and my hair was all dishevelled, because I'd just taken a quick shower. I was going fast, and we'd come from the club and were just coming up the hill towards Southfields tube station, when I saw these two huge police cars stopping everybody. This policeman jumps out in front of the car and stops me. He was really upset, because I guess I was going fast. In fact, I didn't see him, and I almost hit him. So he says, in his very British accent – I love the British accent, it's so unique:

'Goodness me, why are you dr . . . Oooh, Mr Nastase. How are you? Oh dear, what happened to you? Is this how you drive in your own country?'

So I look at him and say politely: 'No, sir, I'm sorry. But I'm rushing.'

'But why are you going so fast? What seems to be the problem?'

'Sir, I'm rushing because I have to go to Wimbledon to play a match, and I'm nervous because I'm late.'

'But Mr Nastase, Wimbledon is that way', he says, pointing behind me, 'you've just come from Wimbledon, haven't you?'

So I stare at him for a few seconds, and then we both start to laugh and he lets me off. But I was more careful after that on British roads.

What really got me the headlines during the tournament was my private life. Reporters had decided that I belonged to them and that they could ask me anything they wanted to, usually along the lines of: 'Can you comment on your divorce?' or 'How many girls have you slept with this week?' Half way through the week, the then Miss UK, a very beautiful girl called Carolyn Seaward, turned up at the players' hotel – I'm not sure why she was staying there – and I met her and ended up having a drink and dinner with her. The next day, of course, I invited her to the tournament, and she turned up because for her it was just fun. I'm sure she had no intention of going any further with me, unfortunately. But immediately the press went crazy, taking photos of us as we sat watching Virginia Wade's match on Centre Court, and saying I was now going out with her. At one stage, I got fed up. I put my arm around the grey-haired old lady sitting next to me and told the photographers: 'Hey, guys, meet my new girlfriend.'

But they just wouldn't let me go. There was another young woman who I was seeing, not seriously, and again they just kept provoking me by asking me questions the whole time. I was getting really angry about having my private life invaded like that and started to shout back at reporters who were following me. Part of me accepts that if you've been number 1, they're going to write about you and want to know everything about you. You can't escape it. But I still don't think the media should be able to ask and do anything it wants. I know journalists have to sell papers, but when they started to make things up about me, and I wasn't even divorced yet, I really was not comfortable with that.

Soon after Wimbledon, I went to Romania for Bjorn Borg's wedding to my compatriot Mariana Simionescu. Like me, Mariana had had to get special dispensation to be allowed to marry a Westerner. Bjorn was riding high, after winning his fifth Wimbledon title in a row, and everything was looking up for him. So it was a slightly difficult and strange time for me to be going home, because the same could not be said about my own life. Vitas had organized a stag party in Miami not long before – to which I did not go, though I can't think why – where he apparently invited all the girls that Bjorn had ever known. I don't know if that was true, but I heard it was a pretty wild party. So now, for Bjorn's wedding, and with my marriage ending, I was thinking in my head 'Don't do it', but of course people have to find out for themselves.

The wedding was a huge affair. Régine, the French night-club owner and society hostess who was a friend of mine, hired a plane to take everybody over. Vitas was there, and IMG organized it all because Bjorn was one of their biggest clients. The wedding itself was at a monastery, by a lake, about twenty minutes north of Bucharest. It was very traditional. Mariana wore a dress by the tennis designer Teddy Tinling, and all the guests made a procession behind the bride and groom, who were sitting on a cart pulled by oxen, like they do in traditional Romanian weddings. Except that I remember it was not easy to walk behind the cart because the oxen had shit all over the road, so we got it all over our shoes. But apart from that, it was lovely: lovely weather, lovely wedding – and lovely shit. In the evening, there was a huge party with lots of food and wine, and an orchestra playing Romanian folk dances. Vitas and I danced together, and I remember he was so full of energy he ended up leaping into my arms.

In the meantime, my divorce was getting difficult with Dominique. Not because of her but because our lawyers were getting nasty with each other. She never said bad things about me, she was reasonable, she was a lady, and I couldn't have complained about her in any case. But the lawyers were arguing about everything. Suddenly, though, mine, who was an experienced old lawyer, said: 'Come on, guys, let's finish now because it's getting stupid. Let's cool it.' So we worked out an agreement and after that it was OK, and we started to talk almost normally. Still, I think it took Dominique a few years to get over her time with me, because one day, many years after, somebody asked her why she had never remarried (she only remarried in 2001), and she replied: 'Not after him. I can't.' It was such an interesting experience, once was obviously enough. That was a good line, I thought!

Her family were really fantastic all the way through. They were sad, but, however difficult things were, they always understood the reasons for our separation. I kept the house in Bazoches, although Dominique lived there for a few years after the divorce and I only sold it at the end of 2003. I still stayed in touch with the Grazia family, especially my brother-in-law-Bernard, who I got on best with. And sometimes I'd go up to the château and have lunch with my daughter Nathalie and my mother-in-law, who I stayed on very good terms with until her death in 1989. In fact, when I heard she was dying of throat cancer, I made a special trip to visit her, and I then went to her funeral. I felt very much that I owed it to her, out of respect for her and also for my daughter.

From 1980 onwards, I was no longer winning tournaments, so I decided to enjoy myself. I had finally accepted that I was no longer a top player, and, because I knew I'd been number 1, I was satisfied with how things now were. There was no point in chasing after something that was never going to happen again, but, just because I was now losing much more, it was not a reason for me to go away.

Throughout my career, when friends of mine did well, it didn't bother me, because it didn't matter what they were doing, what mattered was what I was doing. I might be frustrated by my results, particularly in the later years, but I didn't have a problem when, for example, Connors did better than me in the singles. When we played each other, he took a loss to me much harder than I did one to him, especially as overall I beat him more than he beat me. He found it very frustrating that somebody who never practised and who didn't take the game as seriously as he did could beat him. And when I was playing doubles with him later that day after playing him in the singles, it was tough, so I had to try to block that out. But I never tried anything on him, because we were friends and it wasn't worth screwing the friendship. Sometimes I shouted at his mum Gloria, and once I shouted to Jimmy: 'Gloria should come and play for you', because I was upset, but we never stayed upset with each other for long.

Considering how competitive he was, it was strange that Jimmy liked to have such fun when we played doubles. We won two grand slam titles, Wimbledon and the US Open, we were finalists in the French Open, and we won a lot of tournaments together. All the time we enjoyed ourselves. Sometimes, things would turn sour and we'd get into trouble, but we never took the matches too seriously. Jimmy had a good game for doubles: he had the best return of serve in the game at the time and a great volley. I could never understand why he didn't volley more in singles, because he played so much from the baseline. If he'd been able to serve bigger as well as go to the net, he would have been an unbelievable player. We complemented each other well as a team. He played in the ad-court – the left one – and, because of his fantastic service return, he would set up the point. I would be covering the net, jumping around, poaching, putting away volleys and smashes, creating angles. I played the same way when I was with Tiriac, because it's important to have the best returner of the pair playing in the ad-court. Jimmy and I never got upset with each other when we played, even if one of us wasn't playing well. We just kept talking and kept relaxed, although some of our joking got on our opponents' nerves and got us into trouble. Compared to doubles teams like Gottfried and Ramirez, or Smith and Lutz, who used to practise all day, we did well as we never practised and we still became one of the top doubles teams. In the end, Jimmy decided to stop playing doubles with me, because he gave so much of himself in the singles that it was too much for him to play the doubles as well.

Jimmy had an attitude to tennis that was hard for me to understand. He'd practise the same way as he'd play a match, 110 per cent, as if he was playing a Wimbledon final. He told me one day something I'll never forget and that sums him up. He was playing the young American Aaron Krickstein at the US Open in 1991 on a typical New York hot and humid day. Jimmy had turned thirty-nine that day, and he was down and out in the match. Somehow, he got himself out of an impossible position and won the match, in five sets. It made the headlines all over the world: this thirty-nine-year-old who never gave up. After the match, he was dead. He went on a drip on the massage table with doctors swarming around him. So I said to him, while he was lying there: 'Are you fucking crazy? What's wrong with you, you've already won this tournament five times. Now you're old, you want to die on the court?' He looked at me and said: 'Nastase, you don't fucking understand anything. You're European, you're a bullshitter like all Europeans. For me, the five wins don't count. It's the last one that counts. This one. And I'm still here.' And that was amazing. Here was a guy who was at the end of his career, trying as if it was his very first tournament.

Some people, like Steffi Graf, quit at the top, but I could never have done that, partly because tennis was still what I loved doing the most and partly because I didn't have anything else lined up. I didn't want to start doing something that didn't particularly interest me, just for the sake of it. I have to be committed to do something. So by 1980, I had started to play doubles more again and had some good results, winning tournaments with partners as different as Buster Mottram, Yannick Noah, Adriano Panatta, and the Argentinian José-Luis Clerc.

Adriano had always been a good friend of mine, and particularly in Europe we'd hang out together off court as well. He was a typical Italian: he liked to enjoy himself, he liked football, good food, beautiful women. Once, we were playing a tournament in Florence, and there was a whole group of us and we'd decided to go to watch a soccer game. So we had dinner, and this being Italy and Italians of course we were late. So we rushed off. We were in three cars, six in each car, I'm in front, he's in the car behind. From nowhere, he stops the car in the middle of the road. Everybody jumps out and runs into this bar. And I'm left stranded on my own. What the hell are they doing? '*Abbiamo dimenticato il caffè!*' they shout back to me. They'd forgotten to have their essential coffee after dinner! So they dashed in, *caffè stretto*, nice and strong, dashed back out one minute later. Then back into the cars and off, as if nothing had happened.

Being Italian, Adriano was also unbelievably superstitious. In the early Eighties, Tiriac and I were playing the Monte Carlo tournament one April, and again we decide to go out to dinner with Adriano and a big group of guys. Once again, we're in several cars, going up a windy mountain road to La Chaumière, a well-known restaurant. Adriano was in the first car, and I'm following behind. Suddenly, he stops the car and leaps out. So we all stop too. 'What's happened, what's wrong?' I shout over. '*Il gatto nero, il gatto nero*', he screams, gesticulating madly, '*è andato davanti alla macchina. Non si può andare più. Finito.*' Apparently, a black cat had crossed the road in front of the car. So that was it. We had to turn back. Some of the guys were English and American, and they couldn't understand what was going on. But I knew we had no choice. Back we went, all the way down to the bottom and back up some other route, a very long way round.

Another time, at Roland Garros during the French Open, Tiriac and I were playing Adriano and his chubby compatriot Paolo Bertolucci. I said to Ion: 'I think we can make it easier'. 'What do you mean? What the hell are you planning?' he growled back suspiciously. So I went to the dressing room to find this guy Mabrouk, who'd worked there for years, and I said: 'Mabrouk, I give you 500 francs if you find me a black cat.' So he goes roaming around the area, which is a very leafy, bourgeois neighbourhood with beautiful houses and apartment blocks, and he finally kidnaps a skinny little grey cat. So I feel I have to give him 500 francs. 'Well, Mabrouk, not great, we'll have to spray him.' 'You can't spray him! You're crazy!' 'OK, then find me a black cat!' So out he goes again to search for a black cat and finally he finds one. And 500 francs more go to him. Except now I have to hide the bloody cat in the changing room. So I put him in my tennis bag, which starts to move around strangely. Luckily, we're playing on Centre Court, which is a huge court, so it's harder for the spectators to see the bag moving around.

Ion was going crazy: 'You can't do this, you're crazy', because we'd had a lot of discussions with Philippe Chatrier, the tournament referee and President of the French Tennis Federation, and he'd warned us that if we did anything more that was bad he'd never put us on the Centre Court again. Anyway, I go on court with the cat, wriggling away in the bag. We toss the coin, and Adriano decides to serve first. We warm up, and when the umpire says '*Messieurs, vous êtes prêts?*' ('Gentlemen, are you ready?'), I pretend my racket is broken, I run over to my chair and, literally, let the cat out of the bag. Of course, it dashes straight across the court to the other side, while Adriano rushes around, shouting: '*Stronzo, stronzo, sei una merda*' ('You idiot, you idiot, you're such a shit'). And we beat him and Bertolucci quite easily.

In 1981 and 1982, I played doubles at Roland Garros with José-Luis Clerc. In the first of those years we reached the semifinals. José-Luis was like me, always joking during our doubles matches, but we tried hard as well. He hit hard and I was at the net jumping around, so we complemented each other well and everybody used to come and watch us. He was a good singles player as well, and in both those years he was a semifinalist at Roland Garros. In '81, though, we played Alex Cano from Argentina and Pablo Gimenez from Spain, on Centre Court. Both are quite short, so we were teasing them by lobbing them the whole time. We kept lobbing, we didn't stop. Finally, Gimenez went to get a chair beside the umpire and stood on it on court. All four of us were laughing, the whole crowd was laughing. It was as if it was rehearsed, but it wasn't.

By 1982, I'd bought a Parisian apartment almost opposite the stadium, in Avenue Robert Schuman. This was lucky, because for one match I was still asleep just before we were due to play, at 11 a.m. We'd been out to Castel the night before. Usually you phoned through at nine o'clock in the evening to find out when you were playing the next day, but I hadn't because I'd just been beaten by Guy Forget at the end of the day, 9–7 in the 5th. It had been a really long match, so I never expected to play first match the next day. I remember José-Luis turning up at my apartment at 10.30 to tell me we were on in half an hour. I couldn't get out of bed, I was exhausted, so he dragged me out, put me in the shower. 'Come on, let's go, let's go,' he kept saying. We rushed off to Roland Garros, luckily just one minute away. There was no time to practise, we went straight on court. I was sitting on a chair and Jose-Luis said to me: 'You OK?' and I was mumbling: 'Where am I? I have to have a coffee. I can't start the bloody match without a coffee.' We start to warm up. Just as we were about to start playing, Bambino waddles onto court like a typical Italian waiter, with something in his hand covered with a beautiful white napkin. He takes the napkin off in a flourish to reveal an espresso. Fantastic. But the umpire goes berserk: 'What are you doing?' 'Mr Nastase told me to go and get him a coffee, so I brought him a nice strong *caffè*.' All that was missing was the croissant. After that, I woke up, and we won our match.

Another evening, we went out to dinner in St Germain, in Paris, with Connors and Vitas. It's the Latin Quarter and the streets there are very narrow, plus they have cars parked on both sides, so the wing mirrors on my Mercedes were constantly getting clipped. At one stage, it was so narrow I couldn't get through because there's this Fiat blocking my way. So Bambino said: 'No problem, no problem.' He got out, put his back against the Fiat, and just lifted it up against the wall. That's very Italian. As for Connors and Vitas, in the back, they were speechless.

By the time Borg had lost his Wimbledon final to McEnroe, in 1981, aged twenty-five, I think he was beginning to tire of the sort of serious life he had led since he had first played on the tour at fifteen. He started to come out with me, Vitas, José-Luis, and others, and would be out late, dancing, drinking, and having fun. At first, we were surprised to see him, because he'd never done that earlier. But once he stopped winning absolutely everything, he started to go nuts, catching up on his lost teenage years. In Monte Carlo, where the parties went on all week, we'd go out, then go off to Régine's nightclub, now called Jimmy'z, and have a good time. The Italians too knew how to organize good parties, but the best ones were in Monte Carlo, as it was the most relaxed, glamorous place on the tour.

One night, though, in 1981, my evening almost ended behind bars. I'd gone out with Bambino, and we were just coming back to the hotel. I was driving my brand-new black Mercedes, when on a bend in the road I came up to a Mercedes convertible. I tried to pass it, but the minute I did that the guy driving it carved me up, scratched my car as he went past, then stopped, blocking my route. I leapt out and shouted:

'You son-of-a-bitch, what's wrong with you, what the fuck are you doing?'

At this point a huge guy, maybe 2 m tall, got out of the car: 'What did you say?'

Slightly stupidly, I repeated what I'd just said, but just to be safe I woke Bambino up who was sleeping in the car.

'Get out of here', said Bambino, 'just go.'

But the guy was charging towards me, because he was mad. He looked as if he was going to hit me. Just before he did so, Bambino, who was not tall but was quick, jumps out of the car and takes a punch at him and knocks him out cold, onto the pavement. So the woman in his car gets out and starts to scream:

'They've killed my husband, Nastase is a mafioso!' – I had an Italian numberplate on my car – 'Look, his bodyguard is a mafioso!'

This all took place outside the police station. So the police come out, take one look at the guy who's lying there looking dead, while the wife is telling them that her husband is very important. I'm now getting worried. I explain to the police what happened. It's chaos in the street, cars are stopped, it's almost midnight, and I'm playing Vilas the next morning at eleven. The guy wakes up while we're talking and lunges at Bambino, but the police decide that Bambino and I are the ones who have to go back to the police station to continue the report, while the guy has to go to hospital, to get a certificate that he was beaten up. So we go to the station and make statements. One of the policemen recognises me and says 'Ilie, this is bad luck, because that guy, we have trouble with him almost every day in Monte Carlo. But he's very powerful.' He explains to me that he and his brother are two of the biggest builders in Monte Carlo, they own banks there as well, they sponsor everything. They're huge. In the end, it's well past midnight, they let me go home but they keep Bambino overnight in jail. They take all his belongings and in he goes. Then they go back to the hotel with me, gain entry into Bambino's room, check every inch of it, including under the bed in case he has a gun. I explain that he only has one in Italy where he has a licence. 'Can I go to bed now, I have a match to play tomorrow morning?' 'No, first we have to check your room too for guns.' So they go through that too. Eventually I get to bed at 1.30 a.m. But then, every half an hour, somebody calls me, then hangs up. I don't know who it is but it's really scary and I could not sleep all night.

By 8.30 the next morning, I'm back at the police station with an Italian paper and a croissant for Bambino. I try to make it a bit nicer for him. Then I call Prince Albert, because by then I knew him very well. I also knew Prince Rainier, Caroline, the whole family. I explain what happened and say it wasn't normal what they were doing to Bambino. So Albert arranges for Bambino to be released that afternoon. By the time I get on court for my match against Vilas, I'm so exhausted and stressed that I can hardly hold a racket. And that's when I get the worst score of my career: 6–0, 6–0. Naked in front of the world, that's how I felt. Except that nobody knew the story behind my performance.

My last Wimbledon, in fact, turned out to be in 1982, when I lost in the 2nd round to an American called Lloyd Bourne. As José-Luis did not play on grass, I did not enter the doubles. That was it for me at the All England Club, though I did not know it at the time, which was probably just as well. I had played there since 1966 and had only missed two years, through illness or injury. Despite never winning the singles title, I loved the tournament and still do. That's why I play the seniors' event there every year, and hope to do so until they stop inviting me.

One thing, though, that makes me sad is that I am still not a member of the All England Club. About twenty-five years ago, once I realized that I was never going to win the men's singles title, which qualifies a player for automatic membership of the All England Club, I applied to become a member. So I got my three sponsors who were already members, and I went onto the waiting list. And I've been waiting ever since. But now I don't think they'll ever make me a member. Players like Ken Rosewall, Tony Roche, and Fred Stolle have all become members in the meantime, even though they never won the men's singles. I have nothing against them becoming members but maybe I should become Australian, like them. That might help. I have, though, won the other titles there: the doubles and mixed doubles, and I was a popular player whenever I played, I brought in the crowds. I still do, when I play my seniors' matches. I even saved their 1973 tournament and got fined $5,000 by the ATP for the pleasure of playing that year. So I don't understand what more I could have done to help the tournament and the game, both of which I love so much.

I did ask them once when they thought I might become a member, and they replied: 'Well, rules are rules, and there's a waiting list', but it's clear they bend those rules to let some people in. It doesn't upset me as much as my kids. When my son Nicky came a few years ago, he asked me why I couldn't go and watch a match on court 1: 'Because I don't have a ticket'. 'But you were number 1 in the world.' He couldn't understand. If Bobby Charlton wanted to go watch a football match at the Stade de France, somebody would always find him a seat.

But now it's too embarrassing to ask again, even though I get on very well with the people who run Wimbledon now: Tim Phillips, the chairman, Chris Gorringe, the chief executive. They are all very nice to me and have invited me, as president of my tennis federation, to have lunch at the club and to sit in the Royal Box. I had lunch there in their members' restaurant on the first floor, just behind the terrace that overlooks the main entrance. I sat with Bobby Robson, the football manager, and had a lovely time. Unfortunately, I had to dash off after lunch, because I had a match to play, so I didn't get to sit in the Royal Box.

But all I want is the opportunity to come back and watch the tennis when I'm no longer playing. To come back with my kids and show them the place I loved coming to for all those years. And to mingle with the public and share my enthusiasm for the sport. I just hope one day I'll be granted my wish.

If not, I'll just have to carry out the threat I made to a journalist who came to interview me back in 1973. He asked me how I wanted to end my career: 'By smashing my racket over an umpire's head at Wimbledon and taking the net from Centre Court with me.' The trouble is there would be too many umpires for me to choose from.

After losing at Wimbledon in 1982, I went off to Tramp's, where I liked to go whenever I was in London. Johnny Gold ran it for years and he made me a member, so that whenever I turned up, bringing other players with me, it was always: 'OK, no problem, Mr Nastase, you just need to sign.' I liked that. Also it was a nice club, private, not many people could get in. The club is laid out so that everything is downstairs. On the right is a big restaurant, and on the left a big dance floor, with a bar and a DJ. And I would meet lots of people there I knew already, like Michael Caine or Sean Connery.

If you're well known, even if you've never met the other person, you just go up to each other and say: 'Hi'. The contact is always easy, there's no need for introductions. Sometimes you feel like saying to them: 'I'm a huge fan of yours', but usually I would wait a bit and say it later. And they'd usually do the same thing. You don't want to appear too uncool. I've met Michael Caine several times, and I went to a party of his in his London house a couple of years ago with Amalia. He's very nice, very straightforward and informal. As for Sean, I've known him for years. He's a big tennis fan, and he came to the Royal Albert Hall seniors' event, which I always play, and to the Laureus Sports Awards at Monte Carlo that I'm associated with. Mishter Nasty, he calls me, with his Scottish accent.

At the 1983 Monte Carlo tournament, Borg announced that he was playing his last professional tournament. We were all shocked and couldn't believe he was retiring when he wasn't even twenty-eight. He said he was getting threats on his life, but I've always thought if that was true he'd get killed whether he was on court or off. But something unbelievable must have been bothering him to make him retire. Maybe it was pressure, maybe he was just fed up with the game, with having to sacrifice so much to stay at the top. People don't realize what winning all the time did to Bjorn. He was playing every single week and usually winning. He was using more energy than anybody else, because as well as the matches, he'd practise five hours a day. He'd been playing since he was fifteen and that's a lot of tennis, a lot of matches, and a lot of pressure. He was more professional than anybody, he'd be in bed sometimes by 7.30 p.m., watching TV or reading comics, which is what he liked to do to clear his mind. And he was always in complete control of himself.

Happily surrounded by a sea of women and girls at Wimbledon, 1973.

RIGHT: I am the Master. Joy at winning my third Masters title in a row, Boston, December 1973.

BELOW: Bjorn Borg took over from me as the fans' favourite at Wimbledon.

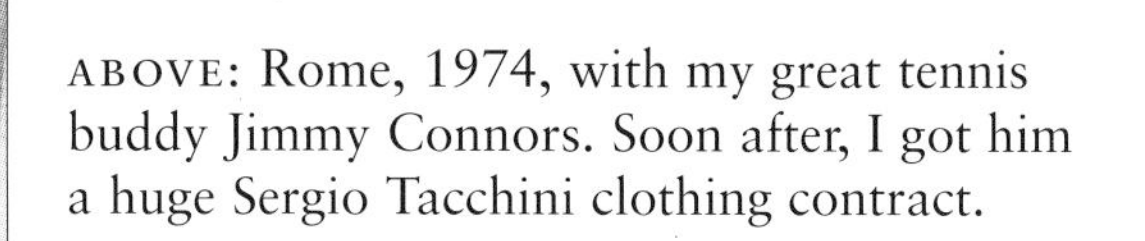

ABOVE: Rome, 1974, with my great tennis buddy Jimmy Connors. Soon after, I got him a huge Sergio Tacchini clothing contract.

LEFT: My parents Elena and Gheorghe, outside my house in Bucharest in the late seventies.

RIGHT: Creatures of the night: Vitas Gerulaitis and I admire model Cheryl Tiegs' dress at New York's Studio 54 in 1978.

LEFT: A white-suited Bianca Jagger pays me a surprise visit at Queen's Club in 1978.

ABOVE: Having a laugh with President Clinton at Roland Garros, watched by French Tennis Federation President Christian Bimes.

LEFT: Eyeballing Robert Mitchum, watched by Barbara Sinatra, during a party she threw for her husband Frank in Los Angeles.

The sort of headlines that accompanied me throughout my career. My Nasty nickname was a headline-writers' dream.

NASTASE AND WOMEN -BY HIS WIFE

'He is rivetingly handsome—olive green eyes, a jaw like a Greek god and the most fantastic legs'

Nasty mobbed on outer court

Nasty's nastiest moment

ILIE WALKS OUT ON TITLE

THE LOVE NASTASE LEFT BEHIND

...g on Dominique's finger

ABOVE: Masters Tournament, Stockholm, December 1975. Arguing with the umpire, moments before Arthur Ashe quits in disgust at my behaviour.

BELOW: 'Between you and me, sir, I'm sure the ball was out.' I wasn't always so polite during my 1977 Wimbledon match against Andrew Pattison.

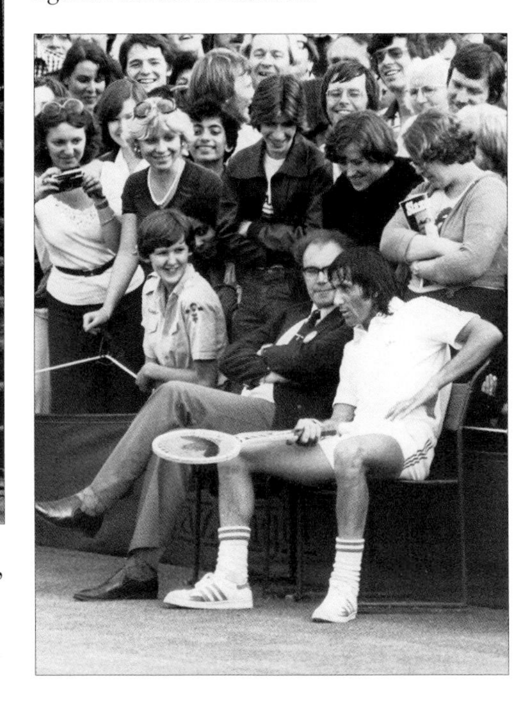

Wimbledon, 1974. It was drizzling, so I thought, 'Why not borrow a spectator's umbrella to keep myself dry?'

'You can't see the line? I'll move your chair to where the sun doesn't shine'. Laughing at the lineswoman's errors.

Wimbledon, 1977, quarterfinal against Borg. Questioning calls from the first point. 'You call me Mr Nastase,' I asked umpire Jeremy Shales.

US Open, 1979. Grand Prix supervisor Frank Smith tries to regain control during my match against John McEnroe. Jimmy Connors' bodyguard and a cop listen intently.

LEFT: Marriage number two, to Alexandra, New York, September 1984.

BELOW: New York, 1988. Cooking a traditional Romanian dish of cabbage and sausages at Le Relais, one of my favourite restaurants.

LEFT: Joking with Mansour Bahrami, one of the stars of the seniors' circuit, during the Honda Challenge at the Royal Albert Hall.

RIGHT: I met these steel workers during my campaign to be elected Mayor of Bucharest in 1996.

My three elder children, Nathalie (right), Nicky (left) and Charlotte (centre).

ABOVE: Nicky, aged two, on the balcony of my house in Bucharest. The bread is almost as big as him.

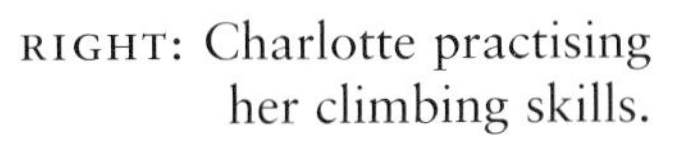

RIGHT: Charlotte practising her climbing skills.

LEFT: The Brazilian Bethy Lagardère, widow of my great friend Jean-Luc Lagardère, held a party at her Paris house on the day of the Brazil v Germany World Cup final in 2002.

ABOVE: Marrying Amalia, July 2003, days before our daughter Alessia was born. With us, my daughter Nathalie, Ion Tiriac and his son, Ion-Ion.

LEFT: My wife Amalia holding our newborn daughter Alessia, August 2003.

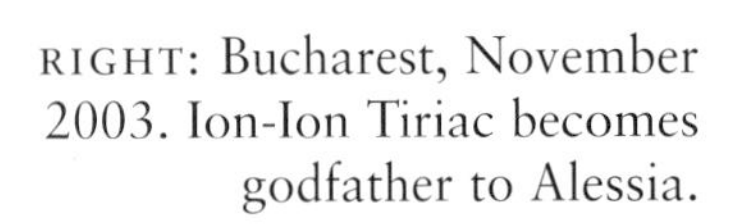

RIGHT: Bucharest, November 2003. Ion-Ion Tiriac becomes godfather to Alessia.

So I think that in the end Bjorn had just had enough, he wanted to live a more normal life. But he's never told anybody, not even me, although I would consider myself a close friend of his. He doesn't talk about that sort of thing and never has. He said he felt he was like a book, with everybody always trying to read him, and he hated that. Even his wife Mariana found it difficult to talk to him about his problems, as he retreated from her when he had worries. Anyway Bjorn retired, and Mariana told some people that, if he had not quit, he could have ended up in a mental hospital. He was looking so tired and drained by the end. For some years, he never came near tennis. Nobody saw him at tournaments, and he didn't touch a racket. He was like Greta Garbo: he wanted to be alone.

Bjorn must have regretted his decision, because in 1991 he tried to come back. He was still playing with his small wooden Donnay rackets at a time when everybody else had switched to larger graphite ones. He even asked Wimbledon for a wild card, and they said, no, he had to qualify. In fact, I think tennis treated him unfairly, because I was getting wild cards – not to Wimbledon, of course – but to Roland Garros in '84, for example. And I hadn't won as much as Bjorn.

By this stage, he was no longer with Mariana. They had split up in 1984, and, although I too was divorced by then, I felt uncomfortable trying to talk to Bjorn about his problems at the time. For a start, I hardly ever saw him in those years, and when I did I never felt Bjorn wanted to discuss his private life. Also, it was hard because I knew Mariana very well, and whenever I saw her she would ask me a lot of questions about Bjorn. She always wanted to know how he was, what he was up to. It was clear to me that she still had feelings for him. So I felt caught between the two of them, and I thought it was better not to discuss anything with him.

In the early Eighties, after I separated and divorced, I enjoyed myself a lot with women. And at least now I didn't feel guilty. There were always a lot of tennis groupies around at every tournament, and they didn't care whether you were happily married, happily separated, or happily divorced. They just wanted to have fun with a tennis player, so now that I was unattached I made the most of it and slept with as many women as I could. Like a sailor, I had women in every town. For a while, that was great and just what I needed: lots of no-strings-attached sex. But deep down, I didn't enjoy that I was not married, and after a time I realized that I was not necessarily happier. Then, towards the end of 1981, some friends invited me out to dinner when I was in New York, and it was there that I met Alexandra, who was to become my second wife.

She was different from Dominique – well, she had to be. Somebody once asked me what I looked for in my wives, and I replied: 'Something the previous one didn't have.' After all, what's the point in marrying the same one as before? Alexandra was six years younger than me and was an American model and actress. She'd once shot a film with Marcello Mastroianni, who coincidentally I knew quite well through Nicola Pietrangeli. She was born in France and grew up in Lyon, where her father, who was a diplomat, was posted, so she spoke perfect French, and some Italian too because she'd modelled in Milan. It was important to me that she understood the European way and spoke French, so that she could enjoy spending time there and could communicate with Nathalie. Right away, we got on well, she was fun, so we kept in touch over the next few months.

By the spring of '82, she started to travel with me when she wasn't modelling. I first took her to a tournament in

Milan, then to Monte Carlo. What was good was that she knew nothing about tennis, and unlike Dominique she would never ask me why I was losing. She also never asked me when I was going to retire, she let me do what I wanted, even though I was not doing well. So although she came at a difficult time in my career, she never put any pressure on me. She was also very understanding about my past and the fact that I had a daughter who I wanted to see. Nathalie used to come over to the States for a month in the summer, during her school holidays, and at Christmas. By then, I had my apartment in Monaco, and for seven years, until the mid Eighties, was resident there for tax purposes. An added advantage was that, as a Monaco resident, I didn't need a visa for France and that made it much easier to go and visit Nathalie.

Although I was not spending much time in Romania, I knew that things had got worse since the Seventies and were now very difficult for the vast majority of my countrymen. I was in a difficult situation. The Chief of the Secret Police, General Stan, was president of the Romanian Tennis Federation. I have to say that, other than sometimes having to play tennis with him early in the morning before he started work, I was always left alone by him. In fact, he was good for tennis in Romania. Because of his influence, he'd get visas for kids so that they could play abroad, and they had more favours done for them than other kids in other sports in Romania. So apart from being permanently bugged, I had never had a problem with the regime and was always treated more than fairly. My parents didn't have any problems either. They could have what they wanted and could travel to see me when they wished, though they took care never to abuse the system. If I'd complained about the situation for the rest of my fellow Romanians, that would definitely have been the end of my freedom. And it would have had no effect anyway.

I could see that there was less and less food to buy in the shops, that people were queuing more and more, that there were shortages of everything that people take for granted in the West. But my current wife Amalia, who grew up in Bucharest and was a young girl in the early Eighties, tells me that there really was nothing to eat. Her parents had good jobs – her mother was a nurse and her father was an electrician – so they had money, but they couldn't spend it because there was nothing to buy. They would queue for bread, eggs, everything. Meat? That was a rare luxury for everyone.

They lived in a small two-bedroom apartment, in a typically grey Communist-built block of flats. They would have hot water once or twice a week. Even cold water was not always available. Electricity would get cut off at ten o'clock at night, so after that hour there was no light, no heating, and in winter it was freezing cold. Although she did not know anything better and she had a happy childhood, like my parents when Romania first became a Communist country, Amalia too knew there was another world out there. She says it felt like a distant planet, and she never thought she would go there. She remembers going on holiday with her parents to the Black Sea when she was young. There were lots of foreigners, East Germans, who were the ones from the Eastern bloc who had a bit of money, plus Westerners, and shops that only foreigners were allowed into. Her parents used to take her in but they would tell her to shut up, not to speak a word of Romanian, otherwise they would get arrested. Although her parents had the money to buy what was in the shops, it was against the law, they'd get put in jail. So they'd go into these shops and it felt to her as if she was going to a museum: she'd look at the sneakers and the clothes, but couldn't touch. She says she found it thrilling.

I knew this was the situation for most Romanians, so I was still shy when I was home, I didn't want to show people that I had money, and I made sure I never threw my weight around and treated people badly. I'm proud of the fact that I stayed the same. For me, that's as good a reward as anything.

One of the other reasons that I was aware of what was going on was that I have always liked to read the papers, to keep in touch with what was going on in the world. Maybe it was because I was European and was more open to the world in general; maybe it was because I was Romanian and I couldn't get newspapers there, at least not ones with the truth in. Either way, wherever I was in the world, I'd always buy the *Herald Tribune*, or the *International Herald Tribune* as it was called outside America. Even in America, rather than buy the *New York Times* or *Washington Post*, it was always the *Herald Tribune*, because it gave the best coverage of events around the world. In France, I'd also buy *l'Equipe* for sport as that too gave the best worldwide coverage. It would give little summaries of everything that was going on. There were some players like me – Ashe, Smith, Richey, Orantes– who were interested in other things, not just tennis.

Also, even though we were upset if we lost a match, it was not like today's players, who don't want to see the guy who's beaten them for weeks. We were OK about it, I don't know why. We didn't hate each other. On court, it was different, we all wanted to win. But off court, we'd still be friends, we'd go out together, talk to each other.

I spoke lots of languages and I now had a high profile, for good or bad reasons, so I also crossed over into other worlds. I got to meet people outside sport, so possibly that too made me more open to things beyond tennis. Nicola Pietrangeli was the first to introduce me to all his well-known friends. As well as Claudia Cardinale, he brought Gianni Agnelli to tennis and Marcello Mastroianni as well. Marcello adored Nicola, so at Wimbledon or in Paris we'd meet up with him if he was there. I remember going to dinners at his mews house in London, there would always be loads of Italian friends, food, and wine, because Marcello drank quite heavily, I have to say. It would be like a party atmosphere, and he was phenomenal, always full of energy.

One of the dangers when you are successful and famous is that people take advantage of you. It was always better when I was married, because all my wives have been good at spotting people like that, but I have to say that, during my career, I was usually too wrapped up in my tennis to notice what people's motives were. And part of me didn't really care. I like having people around me, I'm very sociable, and as long as I was having a good time I didn't notice so much what else was going on around me. Of course, there were always people who were ready to tell me how wonderful I was. They're starfuckers, and if you're not careful you end up believing them. Then when you retire you get a shock, because nobody says that any more. I did notice that people I hardly knew would be quick to tell me I was great, I was the best, but even I could see that they didn't mean it. So I was lucky, as I didn't associate for long with people like that, and I don't think I ever got big-headed in the sense that I believed I was fantastic and everybody else wasn't. I liked being well known, I liked to be liked – I still do – because it made me happy, in a very basic way. Maybe that was down to having started with nothing. Somewhere, I suppose I was just happy to have got to where I had in life.

By the end of 1982, I had slipped to 118 in the ATP rankings, and by the end of the following year I was down to number 169. I was thirty-seven years old, so that wasn't bad but I was now at the stage where I was no longer gaining automatic entry into the majors. I knew I was not the player I used to be, unlike guys such as Connors or McEnroe, who went on believing, for years after they were past their best, that they were still the same player. They just couldn't admit that things had changed. I like their attitude, but then they have to put their money where their mouth is and compete against guys who are twenty years younger, then see what happens. So sometimes, sure, I'd get upset with the way I was performing. The worst was when I lost confidence and heard the crowd go: 'Ah', every time I missed a shot. That's the worst feeling, and it comes to all players. But, in the end, I accepted the fact that I was declining.

I got frustrated and worried, though, when in 1983 I thought I had to retire. I no longer had the pressure of winning, but I got a buzz from going out in front of people, playing a match, getting applause, entertaining, then moving onto the next place. The idea of not travelling was as tough to accept as the idea of no longer playing tennis. I wasn't clinging onto my past glories, I was comfortable with what I now was, it was just that I wanted to carry on living the life on the circuit. The idea of stopping terrified me.

In the spring of 1984, as a bit of fun I made a pop single in France. The guy who produced it had insisted for so long that, in the end, I just thought why not? I had no intention of doing like Yannick Noah, who has become one of France's most successful singers. I just did it for the hell of it, because I can't really sing at all. The result just proves what can be achieved with technology. I was given a voice coach, who did everything he could to get me to sing better. Then we recorded the song, called 'Globetrotter Lover' (what else?), which was really a happy summer pop song, with a slow, talking B-side. I had some girls as backing singers, and, when the record came out, my first thought was this can't be me, it's incredible. Even more incredible was that it got to number 2 or 3 in the French charts. I know there's not too much competition in France, but still that was enough to attract the media. I was invited to sing on the biggest prime-time show at the time, called *Champs Elysées*, hosted by Michel Drucker, one of France's star TV presenters. I almost died of nerves. It wasn't live, so I sang in playback, but that's a technique in itself so it didn't make things any easier. It just meant that, if I forgot the words, the music would still continue until I remembered them again. Princess Stephanie of Monaco, who I'd known since she was about six, was on the same show and was really encouraging: 'Come on, Ilie, you can do it!' she kept repeating before we went on air. I was sweating away, I almost forgot the words, and I swore I would never do this ever again. A bit like women say after a difficult birth: no more kids. Definitely more nerve-racking than playing a big final.

I did sing it once more, though, and this time live, at the players' party at the Monte Carlo tournament that year. Back in the Sixties, they used to get the players to put on a show, but during the Seventies and early Eighties they no longer did this. In 1984 they revived the idea, so I was persuaded to black up, to look like Yannick Noah, who'd won the French Open the year before, while Tiriac and Pietrangeli dressed up as women in blonde wigs to look like Marilyn Monroe. Then on I went, with those two as my backing singers, to sing live in front of everybody at the party. Luckily, I think most people were too drunk to notice that I gave the performance of a lifetime.

The last time I heard the song was a couple of years ago. I'm now chairman and chief executive of Romania's biggest radio station, and as a birthday surprise the director decided to play it on the radio. She and some of the staff had organized a meeting in my office, they made sure I was listening to the radio, then, when the music started, they all chorused: 'Guess who's singing?' 'The boss!' I replied, laughing.

Later in the summer '84, I had some more serious business to attend to. I decided to get remarried. It had taken me more than three years to have the courage to take the plunge again, and it was almost as daunting as retiring. Strangely, I did both at the same time.

CHAPTER TWELVE

1984–1991

Suddenly, in the distance, I saw a tank and heard people screaming. Then I saw them running. So I started to panic.

After Alexandra and I had been together for three years, she started to wonder what my plans were for the two of us, as she was thirty-two and had never been married. She was a very open person, very approachable, and I felt we had a future together. So we made the decision to get married, and planned the ceremony to take place during the 1984 US Open, even though I would not be playing, because there would be a few tennis players who I wanted to invite that were in town that week.

The wedding itself took place during the second week of the tournament. Jimmy was supposed to be the best man, but, aged thirty-two, he'd still got to the semifinals against McEnroe. As they started the match at 1 p.m. and the ceremony was scheduled for 4 p.m., it was all too tight, even for somebody as determined as Jimmy. So another friend of mine, Gerry Goldberg, the guy who'd taken me to the Hilton in Tel Aviv via Jordan, stepped in at the last minute. It didn't seem to matter to the priest that he was Jewish. We'd got permission to marry in an Episcopalian church on Madison Avenue, although I myself am Greek Orthodox (the Romanian Orthodox church follows the Greek Orthodox rite), so the whole thing was a mixture of religions anyway.

Alexandra looked very beautiful in a traditional white dress, and I was in morning suit, along with Bambino. Before the ceremony, I'd joked to him that I was putting my head in the noose again. That was pre-wedding nerves, because really I was happy. I felt I'd found somebody who understood me and who put up with me in what was not always an easy time. Jimmy made it to the reception, despite losing his semi, as did Stan Smith and a few other players. My three sisters came over, but my mother was not able to. She was getting too old to travel, and my father had died a few years before. Nathalie was not there either, as she was back at school in France by then. Altogether we had about seventy-five people at the reception. We danced, we had a good time, and it was all over too quickly, which is always a sign that you have enjoyed yourself. We didn't go on honeymoon, though, as we were still travelling a lot anyway.

Although I was not playing official tournaments, I had played Davis Cup that year as well as a lot of exhibition matches, tennis clinics, and special events. In fact, I was in such demand that I was still travelling as much as I had been when I was on the circuit. That was good, because it made the transition to retirement easier. It didn't mean I was sitting at home wondering what to do. That would come a little later. For now, I had a new wife, people were still paying to see me play, and I was keeping busy.

I was also spending more time in New York. The incredible thing was that wherever I went in the city, people would come up to me and say: 'We loved your matches at Forest Hills. That's great you live in New York, you belong here.'

They're right, and probably if I'd lived there when I was at my peak I would have been like McEnroe. I would have been the local guy, and everybody would have gone crazy for me. After you start to live there for some time, you feel you belong there. I love New York, because everybody is screaming and gesticulating the whole time. It's always noisy. In some ways it's not that different from how people are in Romania. Also, there are people from all over the world in New York, and I like that. I just used to come in with a visa. In the early days, before I knew Alexandra, I had to renew it every month. Then it was every three months, six months, then a year. By the end, I had a visa for five years, so that was fine. I never got a Green Card, though, as I never saw myself as American, much as I liked New York. I was never like Martina Navratilova or Ivan Lendl, who both became American citizens. I'll always stay Romanian, no matter what.

We'd bought a big apartment in Manhattan, up near Central Park, between Park and Madison Avenues, and we spent time doing it up. Then, in 1986, we also bought a beautiful country house in Bedford, in upstate New York, about an hour's drive from Manhattan. We'd go there at weekends and meet up with other players like Arthur Ashe, Mats Wilander, and Wojtek Fibak, who all had houses there or in Greenwich, Connecticut, which was only a few miles away. Ours had a big garden with a swimming pool and tennis court, and I liked it very much.

During 1985 and 1986, I had a lot of time to think about the fact that I was, in effect, retired from tennis. I was still playing exhibitions, mainly in the States because I didn't want to fly over to Europe for a day or two. I was Director of Tennis at an exclusive tennis club in Miami Beach. I also had my contract with Adidas, so I had appearances to make for them. Gradually, I found myself with periods of two or three weeks when I was at home. Then it was terrible. I'd sit around, watch TV, have a few beers, and get very depressed. I no longer had a clear purpose. My level of desperation was such that I even started to like American football, which normally I hate. I knew I had to get used to this new life, that I had no choice, and that the good life I'd had before was not going to come back. But it was still really tough.

I knew that I did not want to throw myself into the first thing that came along. I didn't need the money, so for me it was important that, whatever I did in the future, I had to put passion into it, just as I had done with my tennis. I was waiting for something to come along that would give me that desire. I did not want to commit myself to something that I could not give the time to or take seriously.

I was lucky, though. At least I was still able to play tennis. Some sportsmen, when they retire, that's it. There are no possibilities for them to keep going in their sport. I was still fit and could play. It was less but at least it was something. I was also lucky because the very first seniors' tournaments began around then.

Some people thought I should coach, but I had no interest in that because it would have meant becoming like a player again, without the competing but with all the pressure. You have to travel, wake up with the guy, go to practise with him, eat at the same time as him, then you get fired if he doesn't win. I'd like to coach because I have ideas on how to do it and on how to play the game, but I'd hate all the other stuff, especially the pressure. I knew I had to disconnect myself from that.

I was never clinically depressed. I never let myself go completely. I kept busy. But deep down I knew something was missing. I had to become a normal person, and that was tough. That's the hardest thing for sportsmen to come to terms with, and one of the reasons so many of them have problems when they retire. I have to say that I missed the tension of getting up and thinking about my match, the tension of preparing before the actual match, the ritual of putting on the socks and shoes, then the shorts and shirt. I missed the tension of being in front of a big crowd, the applause, the entertainment, the thrill of competing, and, of course, the best feeling in the world: winning.

The other thing that happened was that, although my name remained very well known, I got recognized less. At the peak of my career, I would get noticed not only at tournaments but also when I was walking down the street and in everyday situations. It can be quite addictive to have people coming up to you the whole time off court or staring at you. In the same way, it was a good feeling to be applauded and cheered on court. It showed people were reacting to me. That was the upside of being well known, and I have to admit that I liked that. Luckily, though, I didn't miss it too much, because it was at that moment that I began to get more compliments, more people talking about my game, and appreciating what I had done. So I never got to the stage where I had to applaud myself in the bathroom mirror while I was shaving or suddenly leap up and cheer when I was watching TV: 'Ilie, you're great, nice shot.'

When I first went into tennis, it was never because I wanted to be famous. Firstly, the best names in tennis in the Sixties were not household names, and their fame did not go much beyond the sport itself. Secondly, I loved the sport and never thought about what it might bring me, either financially or in terms of fame. So when I started to get followed by girls, recognized in the street, and asked for autographs wherever I went, I enjoyed it. If people were nice to me, there was no problem. I didn't think about the downsides of fame, which came more when I began to have problems on and off court.

That was in the late Seventies and early Eighties, and that's when the non-tennis press started to show more interest in me. They'd ask me things, and I'd have to give an answer. Then, when I didn't give the answer they were looking for, they'd provoke me to say things I didn't mean, or they'd just misquote what I'd said. But I didn't worry about that since there wasn't much I could do about it.

The paparazzi also followed me more. They'd always be photographing me in nightclubs, dancing with women, even though none of the women was ever a girlfriend. Cheryl Tiegs, the highest-paid model of her time, was photographed several times dancing with me at Studio 54, the implication being that we were more than just friends. Those situations just became normal for me, and most of the time I just ignored them.

Once, though, I was in Stockholm in the Eighties to watch Connors and McEnroe play Davis Cup against Sweden. We all went out for dinner, and there were a few beautiful girls around the table. The paparazzi were swarming around, and I told them not to take pictures of Jimmy with the women, because his wife was back in Los Angeles and they were going through a difficult time in their marriage. One guy didn't stop, and even though I asked him again and again he still carried on snapping away. So I really got mad. I grabbed his camera, broke it open, ripped out the film, and gave it to Jimmy. The guy didn't even do anything. He knew he'd gone too far. When I handed his camera back to him, he just snatched it and left, without saying a word. But I did it to protect Jimmy. We were just talking to the girls, but that's how rumours get started in papers. When I was divorcing, in particular, I'd had a lot of that, so I knew the dangers. The worst had been during that Wimbledon in 1980, though I suppose I asked for it sometimes by sitting next to a beautiful girl or going out to dinner with her. Those were the downsides to fame and success.

Mostly, I was comfortable with being well known. When I stopped playing, I didn't go overnight from being on TV every day to never being shown and being anonymous. That would have been very hard. But I'd get noticed in some places and not in others. I was no longer getting mobbed every time I went back to Bucharest, for example. I remember once, in the early Seventies, I had my Lancia parked somewhere in town. I had only just bought it, and there were like 1,000 people all around it. They just looked at the car, looked and looked, because there weren't many cars like it in Romania at the time. I turned up and tried to get into my car, but it was completely impossible. So I tried to push this guy out of the way and said: 'Excuse me, I would like to get into my car.' 'Yeah, sure', he went, barely glancing at me and moving to block my way. 'No, really, it's my car.' I had to struggle to get into my own car, because once the people recognized me it was even worse. It was crazy. I had realized by the early Eighties that it was not normal to live like I had been living in the ten years before. It was impossible, and I would not have wanted it to carry on for ever.

In 1990, I was given a prize during Roland Garros that summed up my love–hate relationship with the media. Every year, the 1,250 accredited journalists and photographers at the tournament vote for the player who is the most '*sympathique*', or nice and fun. He or she gets the Prix Orange. I won the first-ever prize back in 1981, and other past winners have been Henri Leconte and Lindsay Davenport. The same 1,250 then vote for the player who is the most unpleasant or sour. He or she gets the Prix Citron. Past winners of that include Marcelo Rios and Yevgeni Kafelnikov. In 1990, I did the double: I got the Prix Orange and the Prix Citron for the entire decade before, for being '*roi des courts et du fair-play*'. I assume they could not be serious about the latter. The whole thing is a proper publicized ceremony, with sponsors, a website, everything. I saw the funny side of scooping both titles, especially as my prize was to receive my weight in Château Giscours, one of the best Bordeaux wines. In fact, I made sure I added on a couple of kilos. Then I went in a chauffeur-driven car to order the wine at the château itself, stopping at Château Margaux to order some from there as well. I still have a magnum of the Château Giscours, which I will open at a suitable time.

Before we had got married, Alexandra had been very honest with me and had told me that she could almost certainly not have children. She knew she had a major problem. For her it was not a good feeling, because when a woman cannot have children I think it is the hardest thing to accept. In addition, some men would find that an obstacle to marrying, but if you love somebody and you want to go far with them, to marry them, then you accept their problems. It was not a major worry that stopped me sleeping, and we weren't the first couple who could not have children. It was bad luck, and it didn't matter whose fault it was. Anyway, I had a child already, so I felt I could help somebody by adopting. Alexandra, though, found childlessness much harder to live with.

We first looked at adopting in Romania, and we took a paediatrician with us from France to advise us. But he was not very reassuring about the children in the orphanages. Many were already infected with HIV and had AIDS, even though this was in the early days of the epidemic that affected so many Romanian orphans. Even the others were in a very bad state of health. We didn't feel we could undertake such an enormous task, given my lifestyle. So we decided to try and adopt in America. Even in rich countries, there are people with problems who cannot keep their children, for whatever reason. A kid is a kid, and it doesn't matter where they come from, you can still give them a home, love, and education.

We made enquiries to find a good lawyer who specialized in adoption, because it's not so much the agencies as the lawyers who are important in America. They're the ones who do all the paperwork, who make enquiries, who check everything out. The lawyer we found was based in New York. A few years later, when Arthur Ashe told me he had adopted his little girl, Camera, I discovered that he too had used the same lawyer. That was something else that brought us closer.

Alexandra was the one who was driving the whole thing, although I supported her throughout. She was the one who really badly wanted a baby. All our friends had kids, and she was desperate to have one as well. So I'd go to all the meetings, I'd go to the social workers' enquiries when they ask you in detail about the sort of life you lead. They would then come round to the apartment and look around, then ask you more questions about how you live. I think they were trying to make sure you were not an alcoholic, not doing drugs. They wanted to check you out socially and financially. But it felt incredibly intrusive all the same. And of course it's no guarantee that you won't start to do all these things once the kid is adopted.

The most difficult thing Alexandra had to do was to go and talk to women who are pregnant and who are thinking of giving up their baby at birth. That involved so much pain on both sides. She'd go and see them, then talk to them on the phone. In the end, she found one woman, she talked to her a lot, who told her that she would give up the baby, and everything looked settled. Then, as soon as the baby was born, the woman changed her mind. That was terrible. Alexandra was devastated. But she was determined, and with time, patience, and more strain for the two of us, we finally found another person. This time, she was a young kid, thirteen years old, who had accidentally got pregnant with a friend from school. She lived in San Antonio, Texas. Her mother was taking care of her while she was pregnant, but she had decided to give up the baby for adoption because she wanted to return to school and carry on her education.

On 1 July 1987, she gave birth to my son, who we named Nicholas. Because I was away, Alexandra went with her cousin to pick up the baby at the hospital, when he was a day old. It was really tough for her to face the mother who was giving up her baby. In fact, it was not easy for anyone who was there. But later that day, Alexandra called me to tell me the good news, and I was really happy. It didn't matter that he was not genetically mine. It never has, not with him nor my daughter Charlotte who was adopted in 1990. The closeness between parent and child quickly develops. Adopted children take on your personality, and sometimes they can even start to look like you. Nicky, because he is blonde with blue eyes, looks like Alexandra. Charlotte, who is darker, with brown eyes, is more like me.

Soon after Nicky was born, I had to do all the paperwork, apply to the courts to put him in my name, and swear certain things, including, again, that I wasn't an alcoholic or a drug addict, that I was a normal person, whatever that means. Some adoption contracts require you to stay in touch with the birth mother, but ours did not. So finally, after a long wait, we were a real family.

I loved having a baby at home. Because I was less busy, I spent much more time with Nicky in his first two years than I had with Nathalie. I suppose I'd waited so long to have another child – something I would have wanted to do with Dominique but life decided otherwise – that I made the most of it. I would change him, play with him, take him for walks, go to the market. I'd carry him on my back and go to this restaurant, Le Relais, on Madison Avenue, run by a friend of mine. I'd walk in with Nicky on my back, everybody was looking at me. I'd stand at the bar because I couldn't sit down, and I'd have a beer. Jimmy Connors was his godfather – I'm also godfather to his son Brett – and he'd see the two of us joking around, doing what we'd call French kissing: we'd kiss on the cheek but with the tongue. So Nicky started to do that, and every time Jimmy saw him he'd say: 'Nicky, how's the French kiss?' Whenever a beautiful girl would walk past, I'd go: 'Nicky, French kiss', and he'd wag his tongue around, and the woman would turn round and look very surprised because he was only a couple of years old. Once, though, when he was about four, I said: 'Nicky, French kiss, come on', and he just looked at me and said: 'Dad', in a sort of exasperated and bored way. He'd already developed a mind of his own. But he's like that. He's cute and bright. He likes to have a joke but not too much.

After a little while, we decided we did not want him to be an only child, because he had started to become a bit spoilt, so we started the process to adopt another baby. It didn't matter that we'd already passed the tests once. We had to start all over again. At one stage, I got really fed up, and I said to Alexandra: 'No, I'm not going through that again', because they make you feel like you're doing something wrong, that you're a bad person, that you're trying to take advantage of a child. But if you want another child, you've got to put up with that, and you go back for more. Again, we had a very unpleasant time while our life was examined in detail. The crazy thing was that the social worker who handled our case was blind. So she'd come round and ask: 'How many rooms? Where's your bedroom?' It's true, I'm not kidding. She came accompanied by somebody, but still it was strange.

In the end, we found a woman in Miami. She already had six or seven children, she was in her late thirties and could not keep this one. So that's how we got Charlotte, who was born on 14 March 1990. She was really good for us too. It felt as if she was completing our family, and for a while we were all very happy together. My life felt fuller and more joyful than it had done for some years. I continued to play tennis where I could, but I also had more time to enjoy my two wonderful kids. We'd move between our house in upstate New York, our apartment in Manhattan, an apartment I had in Miami, our house south of Paris, the apartment in Paris, and our house in Bucharest – so I didn't have much time to get bored!

In the meantime, things in Romania had changed dramatically. The situation had evolved from when Ceauşescu had first come to power in 1965. This had been after the death of his predecessor, the leader of the Romanian Communist party, Gheorghiu-Dej, who had been the puppet of the Russians and had let them do whatever they wanted. Ceauşescu though was very stubborn and resisted. As well as publicly condemning the Russians when they crushed the uprising in Czechoslovakia in 1968, he was like a mediator between Russia and China. As a result, he was isolated among the other Communist countries. But, importantly for him, he became the darling of the Western world. President Carter said he was his best friend. The Queen received him on a state visit to Britain, and he had been paraded around London in her open-top carriage. He could do no wrong in the eyes of the West. Although the situations are not identical, there are similarities between how he was treated by the West and how Saddam Hussein was, in the days when Iran was the enemy of the West. The latter now awaits justice at the hands of his people, just as Ceauşescu received it from his. In any case, by the time he was appointed president in 1974, Ceauşescu was a very acceptable leader, both inside and outside Romania.

Then, he started to make more and more visits to China and North Korea, where he saw the cult of the leaders. By the end of the Seventies, he had flipped completely and turned into a megalomaniac. His personality cult meant that his wife, Elena, and various members of his family rose to high positions in the government or administration. He tried to control things too much, unlike President Tito, who had managed to hold Yugoslavia together without turning into a dictator and without plunging his country into ruin. In the late Seventies and early Eighties, Ceauşescu had this crazy idea that no other Communist country had: he wanted to repay Romania's debt to the West, which had been accumulated from the accelerated industrialization of the previous decade. He thought this would gain him favour with the West and would help to maintain his independence from Russia. He set himself a target of repaying something like $15 billion in three years. Nobody had ever done that before. So although the country was producing a lot, he ordered that most of Romania's agricultural and industrial production should be exported, and all the money made was to go towards repaying the debt. As a result, Ceauşescu squeezed the nation completely, and that was its ruin. There was absolutely nothing to buy, nothing to eat, no energy, no medicines, for the vast majority of the people.

By the late Eighties, the situation had got very bad. So bad in fact that when Ceauşescu paid a visit to, say, a market, they would rush round in advance and spray the fruit to make them appear all ripe and beautiful. Or they would just put in huge arrangements of fake fruit and vegetables. He knew the situation was not good, because he could see the people in the streets had nothing. But it's also possible that those around him did not dare tell him how bad it was. Maybe they deliberately misinformed him about the scale of the disaster. We'll never know. Either way, the worst thing he did, of course, was not to take care of his people, and that is unforgivable.

In 1989, one by one, the other Communist regimes began to fall. The Berlin Wall came down on 9 November, and Russia began its change towards a more open, capitalist society. That December, I was due to come over to Bucharest to spend Christmas with my mother. Normally, I would come over for a couple of weeks, but that year, because Nathalie and Nicky were in Paris, I was planning to go back to Paris to spend New Year's Eve with them there. As I boarded an Air France plane at Charles de Gaulle airport, about a week before Christmas, a stewardess told me that there had been a big anti-Communist revolt in Timisoara, a town north-west of Bucharest. I didn't pay much attention, I have to say. I arrived back in Romania, and life seemed to carry on very much as normal. Whenever I was home, I spent all my time catching up with friends and family, so I had no time to find out what was going on.

A few days before I was due to leave, I went to reconfirm my Air France booking. The airline offices are just next to the Intercontinental Hotel, right in the centre of town. Suddenly, in the distance, I saw a tank and I heard people screaming. 'What the hell is this?' I asked myself. I was a bit worried. Then I heard this noise, like a big bang. I saw the smoke. The guy had obviously fired from the tank. Then I saw them running. So I started to panic.

I came straight home. My mother was already watching events on TV. Romanian TV was saying everything was OK – of course. But a few years before, I had been allowed to have satellite TV – I'd said it was because of sport – so we were glued to CNN, listening to what they were saying. Across town, in their little flat, Amalia tells me that she and her family were listening to the BBC World Service under the bedclothes. They knew they'd be arrested if they were found out, but that was the only way, through the BBC's Romanian service, to find out what was really happening.

I remember seeing Ceauşescu make a speech from the balcony of what is now the parliament. He began to speak, and the people started to boo him. He continued, and they booed and jeered him more and more. Eventually it was so loud that he had to stop. I couldn't believe it. In fact, the atmosphere turned so much against him that in the end he escaped by a helicopter that came to get him and his wife from the roof of the building. He wasn't fleeing Romania, he was fleeing the crowd.

As soon as I saw all that, I decided I should leave as soon as possible. We could hear helicopters circling above the house, because it's almost in the same street as the state TV station. The army was trying to defend it from the rebels, because the television station is always one of the most important places to capture. My mother was insisting that I leave. She was worried and didn't want me to take chances. We didn't know how people would react to me, given that

I knew Ceauşescu, his son, and his senior ministers. You never know what can happen during times like this. People can go crazy, they can lose all sense of reason and justice. The Securitate, the secret police, also wanted me to leave right away. They thought I might be threatened. I remember a guy who I'd never seen before came to my house and said: 'When are you leaving? Let's go. Come on, go, go.' I was 100 per cent sure he was from the secret police. My mother, though, was over eighty then, and she didn't want to leave. Nor did my two sisters who were living there.

So I called the French embassy immediately. There was no reply. I then went straight round to see what was happening, because they knew about Air France flights. They said they had a plane coming in – flights were still coming in and out of the country – and, even if it didn't make it in, they had a special plane for French nationals. I was lucky: the next day, 23 December, when they drew up the passenger list, I was on that flight. On the way to the airport, the army was everywhere. They were also checking us thoroughly at the airport itself, because they had quickly taken control of the whole place. Helicopters were circling above noisily. Meanwhile, Ceauşescu and his wife were being captured. And I was just happy that I was going to be able to see my kids again.

As we sat in the plane on the tarmac, some shooting broke out between soldiers and guys that were probably rebels. This was a very tricky situation. The Securitate wanted to put people against each other, to kill each other, like in a civil war. They thought this would weaken the revolution. Stupid, really. But I remember the pilot saying to us that, in the plane, we were on French soil and not to worry. That there was nothing that could happen to us. In the end, we were cleared for take-off. Our flight was the last Air France one out, and when we landed at Charles de Gaulle airport many people started to clap out of relief and happiness to be back in France. For me, it was a really stressful experience. I had been part of events, I had seen what had happened, and I was just glad to be out of there, safe.

That evening, in Paris, I had dinner with Ion, who asked me what things were like. I said it was very bad. But Ion is his own man, and he insisted on going back. He had his own reasons that I have never discussed with him. So he flew in the next day to Bucharest, along with many of the world's press, who were covering events. There were lots of flights going in, and not many coming out.

On Christmas day, Ceauşescu and his wife were condemned to death by a military kangaroo court and executed immediately by firing squad. They were given absolutely no trial, no possibility of defending themselves. I didn't agree with shooting them like that. It was barbaric and inhuman. It went against all human rights. Also, conveniently, by shooting them, the truth could never come out about what had really happened to the country. Because those who took over misinformed the people. I'm not trying to defend Ceauşescu. What he did was terrible. But I think the Securitate had a big part to play in events around that time. It was as much a *coup d'état* as a revolution. Because they didn't want the truth to come out that not only Ceauşescu but also many others who were high up in the government arranged for the country to be bled dry. Money went abroad to Switzerland, and it was not just Ceauşescu who knew about it and who arranged it. By killing him, and without a fair trial, none of that came out. Those who took over in the chaos and confusion immediately afterwards were involved in running the country beforehand anyway. So that's why the truth will never come out: they didn't want to be judged over their involvement. They had participated in the corruption, that's for sure, because it needs more than just one person to bring the country to its knees.

In a way, we're all guilty. I'm guilty, now that it's all finished, because I didn't say anything at the time. But I had family there, and I could not afford to complain for their sake, even though I could always have left the country, even defected, if things had got really bad for me. Of course, now, all these people are coming out with books in Romania saying they were dissidents. Thousands of them. All supposedly dissidents inside Romania. A bit like the French: anybody over seventy years old now says they were in the Resistance. But that's all bullshit as far as the Romanians are concerned, because nobody could say a word against Ceauşescu. The only dissidents we had were either in jail or abroad. Period.

After Ceauşescu's overthrow, it was chaos. I deliberately stayed away until things settled down. Some people took advantage of the times, they came back and now they have hundreds of millions of dollars. Tiriac was like that. He saw the opportunity. Now he's got a bank, an airline, insurance companies. I'm not like that. I'm not saying I wished I did it, because I don't think like that. But I didn't want to take the risk at the beginning. I was afraid that people would either think that I was a friend of the old regime, or that I was now coming back to profit from the new, so I stayed away for a couple of years. I kept in close touch with what was going on, and I started to talk to the Prime Minister, Petre Roman. It was he who kept insisting that I had to come back. When I returned, in 1991, I noticed that the situation was much better, the country had settled down and was starting to work normally, even if it was not good. There was some sort of democracy, and there were more rules.

Straight after the revolution, the military had been in

charge. An interim president was appointed, Ion Iliescu, and an interim government. In fact, with the exception of 1996–2000, Iliescu has been the president ever since, even though now it's the prime minister who's got the power. In the first couple of years, the police, who are called the Militia, had no control over the population. They were terrible. They used to beat all these people up in jail during the Communist years, so the population hated them and they were right.

After the revolution, people had no money, so they were reduced to stealing, in particular, food to eat, and crime was high. The Militia, because they were hated, could do nothing. The government kept trying to find a tough guy to be Minister of the Interior, to handle the situation, but it was chaotic. Those who had been in the Securitate were swearing they'd never been in it. I think the biggest mistake our president made was to allow these people to hide or deny their past. He should have done like in East Germany, where they opened up all the files of the Stasi. Instead, all the files were burned, and the records destroyed. After that, nobody knew who had been in the Securitate any more. That's still the case today, and it has not helped to rebuild trust in our country.

Before the revolution, people had nothing to buy even though they had money, and I used to help my family out financially, not on a regular basis but to make their life easier. After the revolution, there were things to buy but they had no money, so I have had to help them on a regular basis. Otherwise, it would be impossible for them.

In the late Eighties, I started to get to know one of France's biggest industrialists, Jean-Luc Lagardère, and his Brazilian wife, Bethy. He owned a whole range of businesses, from military aircraft to publishing. Jean-Luc became a friend through his passion for tennis. He was always at Roland Garros, and he loved to play tennis with me when our schedules allowed. Bethy is a very energetic and warm person, and we also got on very well.

In 1991, during the Monte Carlo tournament when Borg made his attempted comeback with his wooden racket, Bethy called me from Paris. She wanted to see the match, was there any chance I could get her a ticket? She'd called Tiriac, she'd called everybody. But everybody wanted to see this match.

'No problem, come down.'

'How are we going to go to the club?' she asked.

'Bethy, don't worry, we have cars, I even have my own driver.'

'You're sure?'

'Listen, you know me, I arrange, I deliver. I'll pick you up at your hotel tomorrow morning.'

So the next day, I get to her hotel, the luxurious Hotel de Paris, next to the Casino, at about ten o'clock. We have breakfast together. 'My driver's coming at eleven,' I explain. The hour comes and goes. Still no driver. Bethy's getting nervous. The match is starting at twelve. Ten minutes later, she says: 'Who is this stupid driver? He's an idiot, you told him eleven, why isn't he here?' As soon as she's said this, two big black Mercedes cars sweep up at top speed. They stop dead in front of the steps. Police jump out of one, Prince Albert of Monaco leaps out of the other, shouting: 'Ilie, I'm here, I'm so sorry I'm late.' 'This is your driver?' goes Bethy, alarmed. 'Yes, this is my fucking driver.' She goes all red, and we get in. She's in front, with Albert, and I'm in the back. The policemen are in the car behind. We're heading towards the tennis club, which is at the top of a winding road lined with pine trees and which overlooks the bay of

Monte Carlo. It's the most fantastic setting in the world for a tennis club. But as we approach, we come to a halt. We can't get close. There are cars and policemen everywhere. Albert, rather than saying who he is and insisting on being let through, doubles back and goes down, up, and round, and we finally reach the club through a back route. All along, Bethy is behaving very nervously and looking at me, worried that I might tell Albert what she'd been saying to me about him. Because she knows I'd be crazy enough to say: 'Hey, Albert, guess what Bethy was saying about you just before? Ha, ha, ha.' We finally arrive at the club, Albert asks Bethy if she wants to join us for lunch upstairs. 'No, thank you, I'm not hungry,' she lies and she scurries off. 'Don't you dare tell him what I told you', she whispers to me as she leaves. 'Come on, Bethy, I wouldn't do that!' I did tell Albert some time later, and he fell about laughing.

Albert is like that. He's not at all into status and playing on his name. I call him Albert or sometimes Colonel Bebert, because he has a slight stammer. We speak in French or English, because like his sisters he's fluent in both languages. He always has crazy answerphone messages, with him either singing, or speaking in a funny voice. In the early Eighties, when I was resident in Monte Carlo, he'd regularly ask me to go bowling with him late at night in Nice, down the coast.

When my sister Gigi had a small apartment in the same building as Albert, she could tell me exactly what his movements were. She called me once:

'I've just seen Albert in his Jeep, entering the building with a beautiful blonde.'

So I called him: 'Albert, how are things?'

'Fine', he'd reply, 'I'm watching TV.'

'No, you're not, because I've just seen you entering your building with a blonde.'

'You saw me? Where are you?'

'In New York.'

'Are you are a Romanian spy? What's going on?'

That freaked him out completely. I had to explain, otherwise he would have gone crazy.

In 1991, I was inducted into the Tennis Hall of Fame. As a European it didn't mean much, but for the Americans it's the ultimate achievement in your sport. It's like being knighted in Britain. Sir Ilie of Tennis. I didn't realize how seriously they took it until I went to America. All the country's media are there, every TV channel. It means you've done something for your sport. There are Halls of Fame for all the big sports, and for tennis the Hall of Fame museum is at Newport, Rhode Island. There's a tournament there each July, and that's where and when you're inducted, during a big ceremony. The place itself is very New England, colonial, with grass courts and an old wooden clubhouse. And the museum is inside that.

The presentation of the plaque that you're given takes place in front of guests and other Hall of Famers. I made a speech, along the lines of: 'You're not going to hear my best speech today, because my best speeches are X-rated and done on court. Today I'm going to behave.' Though actually I nearly gave an unplanned performance anyway. The wife of Jimmy Van Alen, who invented the tie-break, was there. She was about eighty years old. At the party later, after the dinner, I was there with Alexandra, friends, and committee people, when Jimmy Van Alen's wife came up to me and said:

'Mr Nastase, I have to say I don't like the way you behaved on court.'

'Why, what's your problem?'

'Well, I was in Romania in 1972, during the Davis Cup final, and you called me a bitch.'

'I did?! I swear to God, I never said that! Especially in Romania because they would put me in jail. It's just not possible.'

Everybody started to laugh uncomfortably, but she insisted: 'No, no you really did call me that.'

'Well, you must have done something for me to say that. What did you do?'

'Well, every time you missed a shot, I clapped.'

'There you go, like I said, you see, you deserved it!'

Everybody was looking at me, shocked. I mean, I'd just been inducted. But why couldn't she tell me this later on? Anyway, it's a big deal in the US. I don't say it, but others now say: 'Ilie Nastase, Hall of Famer'. It's like my title in America.

CHAPTER THIRTEEN

1992–1998

I asked for her phone number. She said she didn't have one. She did, but I discovered that later. She just didn't want to give it to me. This one was smart as well as beautiful.

On 8 April 1992, something happened that shocked everybody in tennis. Arthur Ashe announced that he had AIDS. He had felt obliged to reveal the information because a newspaper was about to go public with the news. Rather than give them that satisfaction, he felt he had no choice but to speak to the world himself. As with everything in his life, Arthur showed a lot of courage. This was not the first time he had had to face serious illness. His father had died of a stroke, and in the early Eighties Arthur himself had developed a serious heart problem. In the end, in 1983, he had undergone a major heart operation, during which he had received a contaminated blood transfusion. Five years later, in 1988, when his little adopted daughter Camera was only two years old, he learned that he was HIV positive. He and his wife Jeannie decided to tell no one.

When Arthur eventually went public, he showed incredible dignity. He never said: 'Why me?' Instead, he said: 'Why not me?' I thought that was the best line. It's one I now tell myself often whenever anything happens to me that isn't good. Not 'Why me?' but 'Why not me?' As Arthur said to me when we talked about his illness: 'What if I was sick with another illness, like cancer? It's bad too. This is no different, it's just another disease. Why should we be afraid to say we have AIDS?' In those days, though, it had such a terrible stigma. Everybody thought you were gay if you had it, even though it doesn't matter how you caught it. It's the same disease, whether it was got through gay sex, straight sex, drugs, or infected blood. If it had been me, though, I don't think I would have admitted it. But Arthur was really courageous. Probably many people who didn't know the truth thought he was gay.

When I heard the news, I was unbelievably shocked. It took me a long time to accept what he had said. I kept telling myself that maybe he could get better, or that he could still live a long time. I then realized why, in the previous few years, he had been so busy. He already knew he was HIV positive, so he had tried to do as much as possible in the time he had left. He was anti-apartheid, he'd been arrested for protesting in Washington, he'd promoted tennis projects for poor, black kids, and he'd done things with the United States Tennis Association to help kids get started in tennis.

Once Arthur had full-blown AIDS, he knew that his death would follow quickly. We didn't. We thought maybe he could last longer. I saw him at the US Open in September 1992, and although his face looked a bit thinner he didn't look ill. He was always skinny anyway. I remember I saw him in the car park at Flushing Meadow, where he was promoting one of his tennis projects. I had a beautiful red convertible Ferrari then, and he was joking with me: 'Jesus, not bad for a Commie, having a car like that. Did you buy it? Mortgage your house?' 'No, Negroni, I bought it with the money from beating you at the US Open!' and we both had a good laugh. I always used to tease him. He and his wife liked me a lot, and they lived a couple of blocks away from us in New York. Their house in Connecticut was about 5 km from mine, so we'd run into each other quite a lot. Arthur was always in a world of his own, though. I remember he had a bike in New York, and he'd sometimes cycle right past me, without noticing. One day, I ran after him, and said: 'Arthur, you stupid, you don't remember me?' He looked at me, surprised: 'Oh, Nasty, how are you?' He obviously hadn't seen me.

Then, one day, on 7 February 1993 to be precise – I remember it very well – I was in Paris, and the phone rang. It was a journalist I knew. He told me that Arthur had passed away the day before. I was really upset. I never thought he could go that quickly. Not after I'd seen him looking fine a few months before that. I sent a telegram at once to Jeannie, I talked to her on the phone, and she said I didn't have to come to the funeral because there would be lots of people there. Donald Dell, the agent, was organizing everything. I couldn't go because I had tennis commitments in France, but I really wish now that I had been able to make it.

Arthur's death made me think about all the matches we'd had together – about the good times and the not-so-good times. All these things came to mind. What I'd done to him in Stockholm in '75, how I beat him at the US Open in '72. I remembered some of the great laughs we'd had. The time in Myrtle Beach, South Carolina, when Jimmy and I had presented him with a cream cake for his birthday, and had ended up covered in it ourselves. There were also a couple of occasions in Japan when we'd played doubles together. Once, in a tournament sponsored by Canon, we'd each been given nice small cameras. Finally, someone showed me how to use mine, so I put it in my racket cover and took it on court. At one point, I got the camera out and said: 'Arthur, I want to do something to you. Please, can I?' 'What do you want to do?' So I ran to get my little camera, and I asked him to pose for me, like Fred Perry: 'Put your racket higher, like that. Good.' And I snapped away. All the time he was saying: 'No, no, you can't do anything, because I'm going to have to fine you $200 for this', because he was President of the ATP. Like, he was going to have to fine his own partner.

Another time, the Japanese guy calling one of the lines was giving us a load of bad calls. I'm swearing at him in English and the linesman didn't understand, so he started to laugh. Being Japanese, even if you're telling them 'Fuck you', if they don't understand they'll still smile back and say: 'Thank you, thank you, *Nastase San*, Mr Nastase'. Arthur was going: 'No, please be careful, stop swearing, I'm going to have to fine you, default you.' So I replied: 'Arthur, if you fine me, or default me, you have to do the same to yourself, because we get fined as a pair.' So that shut him up.

This guy was still giving us bad calls, so I asked the umpire if I could have some matches. 'Matches?' 'Yes, matches.' When I got the matches, I broke them in small pieces, and I went to prop up this guy's eyelids. Arthur did his nut: 'Nasty, I'm not ever going to play with you again!' I made him nervous, because he never knew what I was going to do next. And he was very serious. Normally, he didn't even talk to you when you were playing doubles with him. But he had a great sense of humour as well. Whenever anything happened in the dressing room, not just to him but to anybody, he would shout: 'Nasty. Go get Nasty, because I'm sure he did it.'

So all this came back to me when he died. This guy was here, now he's not. Next time it's you maybe. That's what he said. It could happen to anybody. The reason doesn't matter. Could be cancer, could be AIDS. We know we are mortal, but we never really think it. It's stupid, though. When you're a kid, you just want to be older. Then when you're older, you see time going by very quickly. You see people dying, like Arthur, who are young and just a couple of years older than me, and you think: 'Jesus Christ'. When you have kids, you think of death even more. To tell the truth, for me it's better not to think about these things too much, because I get too depressed and I can't do anything.

I stayed in touch with Jeannie, and have tried my best to support the AIDS charity she set up in Arthur's name. She received enormous support from all of his many friends around the world. But Arthur's death remains one of those that affected me very deeply.

The other one that also upset me a lot – for very different reasons – was the death of Vitas Gerulaitis, nineteen months later, in September 1994. What was so shocking was that Vitas did not die of a drugs overdose, something that many people feared he would. He died because he inhaled, in his sleep, massive doses of carbon monoxide from a faulty heating system in a friend's guesthouse, where he was staying. It was such a stupid death. He was young, barely forty, and he seemed to be getting his life back on track after having been so dependent on drugs for so long.

For years, I'd been telling his mother and his sister Ruta: 'Look, Vitas has to stop.' I'd tell him as well. So would Jimmy Connors, Bjorn even, and Fred Stolle, who was close to him. We'd all try. I used to tell him, particularly in the early days, when he was doing a lot of drugs: 'Vitas, don't do it, because you're going to die young. You're not going to make it past forty.' And he'd go: 'Ah, come on, Nasty, I'm not doing much now like I used to do. It's OK.' So I'd try to scare him, not to be nasty, but to shock him. It never made any difference. Once he was addicted, it was too late to stop him.

Apart from the fact that he would sweat a lot and not eat much, he seemed normal. He had tremendous energy, but that's what coke does to you. You don't eat, you don't sleep. That's why generally people who take it are all so skinny. They never close their eyes. He was very lucky, as well, because he only drank ginger ale. Probably if he'd been drinking alcohol, he would have died much earlier. For what he was doing, he was in good shape, he was fit, running around. So when I heard he'd died, my first reaction was: 'Vitas did something last night at one of his wild parties.'

What was strange was that, like Arthur's death, it was announced to me on the phone by a journalist, and I was once again in Paris when I heard the news. This time, though, it wasn't a few months since I'd last seen Vitas. It was a few days. But again, strangely, it was at the US Open. I was playing the seniors' event, and when I was in New York I always practised with Vitas, on an indoor court in a club. That was not easy in New York, but he knew the owner. A couple of days before the end of the tournament, I noticed he had this little phone with an earpiece, and I asked him where he got the phone because I wanted to buy one as well. I asked him how much it was. 'I don't know – $300 or something. Come on, let's go, I'll take you there.' So we went to this store, and in typical Vitas fashion he paid for the phone – I didn't have any credit cards or money on me at the time. Then we went back to Flushing Meadow, and I promised him I'd repay him the next time I saw him. A few days passed and I didn't see him again, and I then went back to Paris.

The very first time this new phone rings, the very one that Vitas had bought me, it's a journalist on the line to tell me that Vitas had died. I couldn't believe it. He had to repeat it several times. I called his mum and his sister at once. 'Ilie, it's over. We're devastated.' Again, though, I had an exhibition match the day of the funeral so I couldn't go, and I really regret that too. But they had a lot of support. Bjorn went and many other players as well.

I called them again a week later to see how things were, because Vitas's mum had been very nice to us when we went to his house. He had a tennis court, and she was always fixing us sandwiches, taking care of us. We'd practise there, for hours, because Vitas, despite his lifestyle and reputation, practised a lot. He had a huge problem with his serve. He didn't know how to serve. The ball toss was wrong, and he would try to practise it every day. In fact, he never had a powerful serve, or one he could rely on. By the end, it did get better but it was never much of a shot. But he was very quick, all over the court, so he compensated for it.

Like with Arthur, all the times we'd had together came to mind. Dancing together at Bjorn's wedding, evenings at Studio 54 in New York, dinners in Paris at Castel's. He had this white Rolls Royce convertible, with all these girls always in it. He was generous, he loved having fun, enjoying life. So after the sadness and shock, I started to remember the good times, because that's the only thing you can do.

By the previous year, 1993, I had agreed to become Romanian Davis Cup coach, so I started to have links again with my Federation and with the country. I was still spending only about one month a year there, but for me it felt good to be involved with the competition that I had played for eighteen years, and in more than 146 rubbers. I am very proud of that. Only Nicola Pietrangeli has played more Davis Cup rubbers than me.

About a year later, I met the future Prime Minister, Adrian Nastase (no relation to me) at a reception in Washington. He was already a senior official in the governing party, the PDSR, which is our social democratic party. Towards the end of the long dinner that followed the reception, he asked me what I was doing and would I be interested in working with them? I thought that was a good idea. It might mean I could be a bit more involved with helping to rebuild my country, though I did not plan that my involvement would be very much. I also thought I would understand a bit more about how things were being run, and that would be good too. So I joined the PDSR.

One day, Adrian Nastase called me to say they didn't have a candidate for the mayor of Bucharest elections that were coming up in April 1996. Would I stand for them? With my fiftieth birthday coming up that year, this would be a challenge and something completely new for me. I talked it over with Alexandra and some of my friends, who encouraged me, so I decided to say: 'Yes'. Bucharest was my home town. However much I loved all the cities I had lived in – Brussels, Paris, New York, Monte Carlo – deep down, 'home' meant Bucharest. That's where I felt the greatest attachment. So the whole family moved to my house in Bucharest, and the kids went to the American school, which was close by. Nicky in particular started to learn Romanian very quickly because he made friends with other kids in the street, and they'd cycle around and play together outside. Charlotte, who was younger, learnt less because she stayed indoors a bit more, but she too settled in well to her new life.

Then the campaign started. We had to raise money. I put

in some money from my own pocket – something not many politicians would do, I think – and I started to work hard. I was told I just needed to start one or two months before, but I insisted on starting four months before. I would get up at 6 a.m. and go to the markets and the factories. I would talk to people in the underground on their way to work, and accompany the police at night when they visited drug centres. I really wanted to understand people's lives, what their problems were. And I wanted to do things properly, because that's how I am.

At the beginning it was good. I was doing something I had never done before, and everybody was very nice because it was not yet close to the elections. I also had a good team, with some enthusiastic young people to help me. One of them had an ad agency, so we made a lot of noise. Too much maybe. That's when the other parties started to wake up, because I was way ahead in the polls. So the other parties decided to form a coalition against me as that was the only way they could stop me.

Then the campaign got really nasty. The closer to the election it got, the worse it was. The opposition started to attack me with lots of personal things. They weren't saying what policies they had, what they were going to do. They'd just attack me. I found that hard to understand. They also started to promise crazy things, and people will believe anything, especially during an election. My main opponent, a guy called Ciorbea – which means 'soup' in Romanian – had been a high-ranking judge under Ceauşescu, part of the Communist elite. He didn't have any policies, other than empty ones.

Just before polling day, we had a huge TV debate, just the two of us. I was nervous, but also I knew I had experience of the media. He sat on a squeaking chair, and started by complaining to the moderator: 'You gave that chair to me, not Mr Nastase, because he's famous, he's a star.' That set the tone. And the moderator kept asking really stupid questions, always gossipy or minor things. Then Ciorbea started to talk about my private life, that I was a womanizer. So the debate degenerated, and we never talked about politics. Finally, at the end, he got a cheque out: 'I have here this cheque', he announced, waving this piece of paper around, 'from a company that wants to give me $10 million to rebuild this city in 200 days. I just need to sign it as the mayor, and we'll get to work.' So I just said: 'I can't make that promise, and I'm not willing to. But if Mr Ciorbea thinks he can, then good for him.'

You can't be normal to be a politician. It's bad, but that's how it is. When the opposition were making their promises, my camp wanted me to make some as well, like mending all the holes in the road in three months. I didn't think the roads problem was important anyway, and I was not prepared to lie. I did have policies, though, and I worked hard to show the people I wanted to do something. One of my ideas was to have a law passed that would promote the individuals' right to own their own shop. There are about 50,000 shops in Bucharest. Up until then, all the shops belonged to the City Hall. I had a lot of support for this. In fact, five days before the election, the Prime Minister signed a law giving people the opportunity to buy their shop. Fine. Whoever was the mayor had to sign the paper allowing the sale of a shop. The guy who got elected, Ciorbea, was mad at the law, and for four months he never signed a single sale. Nobody could buy a shop. Then, after four months, he became the Prime Minister himself.

The people of Bucharest, though, didn't seem to understand what was going on. Democracy and elections were totally new ideas for them. They kept saying to me, when I visited the markets: 'You have to give us more money for pensions.' I'd try to explain that this was the business of the government, not the mayor, but they still got mad at me. They didn't understand the difference.

I was determined to be honest and true to myself from the start and that became a problem, not so much for my team as for the PDSR. They would argue with me, saying I had to promise certain things. I refused and insisted on saying what I wanted. I'd say: 'I can't promise you this, but I can help on that.' Here, as in many countries, the more a politician lies and the more promises he or she makes, the better they are considered. Then the senior people in the PDSR realized they could not control me, and they neglected me towards the end of the campaign. They switched their attention to Ion Iliescu, who had presidential elections coming up at the end of the year. So I had abuse from the press, abuse from my opponent, and in the end I was left alone to take it. I was different, not like a politician should be, and they couldn't handle that.

I don't actually think the mayor should be a politician. He should be independent. That's why I thought I would have made a good mayor. I had money, good contacts, a name; I would have attracted investors and helped to renew the city. I didn't think my lack of political experience was a problem. I'm used to thinking quickly, I'm happy to work hard, to learn. But in Romania all that was not enough. If you're not backed by a party, you're not going to make it.

In the end, I was beaten by two per cent of the vote, so it was close. I was disappointed because I had put passion into it, and I was honest. I saw others win who were not honest. If it had been a fair election and you lose, OK. Fair game. Like in sport. You win or you lose. But in politics you have to make all sorts of concessions to win. And I wasn't used to doing that, and wasn't prepared to either. So it was the opposite of sport. Also, people in politics are usually there for personal ambition. I had none. I had wanted to do something for the city I was born in, but they didn't want my services, and for that I was disappointed. Afterwards, I announced that I was not going to be involved in politics any more. Adrian Nastase probably didn't appreciate that, because those around him then said: 'You see, we should never have used him.' They thought I was not committed, whereas in fact the opposite was true. It's just I wasn't a career politician.

Romania is still a young democracy. Before 1990, the idea had never existed, because before Communism we were a kingdom. For Romania now, it's a bit like leaving prison at six in the morning, blinking in the sunlight. You don't know what to do, because the guard hasn't put your breakfast in front of you. You can see it's there, but you don't know how to go and get it. Politicians cannot be born in twenty-four hours, and Romania as a democracy is still only fifteen years old. It was normal that ex-Communist career politicians filled the important posts in government in the years following the revolution, because nobody else had any experience. It will take time for others to learn what to do. But I hope that the young people of today, those of my baby daughter Alessia's age, will live in a country that has a fresh new generation of people running the country, and that we will all have learned more about how democracy works. In the meantime, I don't look back at my time in politics with regret. It's done now, and I learned a lot in the process.

As for General Stan – what happened to the ex-head of the Securitate, who was the president of the Romanian Tennis Federation? He got out of politics, and bought a pharmacy in Bucharest. He now spends his days doing good where he can.

A few days after the mayoral election results, I was asked if I wanted to be President of our Tennis Federation. 'Sure,' I replied. A quick election was organized, with about 400 people voting – all the coaches, presidents of private clubs, plus some others. And I was elected unanimously. All was done in the open, no long campaign, no personal attacks – nothing like the mayoral elections. So I flew off in May 1996 to Roland Garros as the new President of my Federation. I was pleased about that, because again it strengthened my links with tennis. Every four years we have elections, and three times a year there are ITF meetings in various places around the world. If I can, I go.

The other thing that happened at that time was that my marriage to Alexandra was in serious difficulties. Once we had Nicky and Charlotte, Alexandra stopped travelling. She stayed at home to look after them. I didn't have a problem with that. And Nicky and Charlotte remain two of the best things that have ever happened to me. The greatest thing Alexandra did for me was to bring those two kids into my life. I adore them, and they're fantastic. If it was left up to me, I'd be spoiling them the whole time. But as with Nathalie, I didn't think it was a great idea to take kids travelling around with me, especially when there were two of them and they got a bit older and started going to school. I also think that once women start to have children, particularly after the first baby, their priority becomes the child. They become like a cocoon around that child, they want to give him or her everything. That's natural, it's not a criticism. It's just that for me, in those days, I don't think I had really understood that. Now I do, because I'm older and I've finally matured a bit, so I don't worry if Amalia is like that with our daughter.

With Alexandra, I was still away quite a lot and her attention was mainly on the children. Plus, I have to say, I still needed to have sex. There's no denying. And if I was away for long periods of time, then I'd try to get it. Some women would tell me they didn't approve of what I was doing. And that was fine. But mostly I didn't get that sort of reaction from the women I approached. They were quite happy to sleep with a married man.

Like Dominique before her, Alexandra knew very well what was going on, and she accepted it as inevitable. Of course, it wasn't great for her, but she felt for the kids that it was better to stay married. So while she stayed based in Bucharest for the couple of years around the mayoral election and the start of my time as president of my Federation, we began to lead more and more separate lives. Eventually, in early 1998, she moved back to New York, partly because Nicky was ten years old by then and it was time that he moved back to school in the States. I went to see them as often as I could, but I also understood that we had arrived at a sort of arrangement with our marriage, which allowed me to do more or less what I wanted. As long as I was reasonably discreet.

About eighteen months before, in 1996, I had gone to a concert in Bucharest given by Sting. It was in aid of Romanian orphans with AIDS. I remember going to fetch him at the airport, and he was a very nice, straightforward guy. I've met him several times since, in Tramp's in London, in the States, and, although he's not a close friend, we get on very well whenever we meet. He's very easy to talk to.

At the concert itself, I was approached by a very striking young woman. Very tall and slim, with long dark hair and huge eyes and a lovely smile, she offered me a cigarette. She was working for British American Tobacco as a cigarette sampling girl. Ironically, one of the brands she was pushing was called 'Lucky Strike'. She had been told that, if she saw anybody famous, she should go up and offer them a cigarette. Then, if that person was photographed smoking that particular brand, it would be good publicity for the company. So I told her I didn't smoke, and then asked if she had a ticket for the concert. 'Of course not, I don't have the money', she replied. So I gave her a ticket. Then we got chatting. Her name was Amalia, she was twenty years old, and she was studying economics and insurance at Bucharest University. This was one of four part-time jobs she did during the week to try to make ends meet. I was impressed. And I liked her. I immediately felt she was different. Before long, I asked for her phone number. She said she didn't have one. She did, but I discovered that later. She just didn't want to give it to me. This one was smart as well as beautiful.

A few days later, I asked a friend of mine to track down Amalia through the cigarette company. Sure enough, I got her phone number. A few weeks went by. One evening, I decided to call her:

'Do you know who I am?'

'No', she said.

'I'm the guy who gave you the ticket to the Sting concert.'

'How did you get my number?' she answered, suspiciously.

'I can't tell you that.'

And what did she reply? 'If I didn't give you my phone number it was for a reason. It's because I don't want to talk to you.'

How cool is that! She told me, years later, that she thought she had nothing to gain from giving me the number. She knew I had five girls a week – her words, not mine – and she didn't feel like being number six. I was forced to admit that five girls a week was, even for me and my reputation, a bit of an exaggeration. I think I've slept with about 2,500 women, but, if I was doing what she thought I had been, even that number would be way too low.

Anyway, the phone conversation ended soon after, and that was that. Over the next couple of years, I'd occasionally phone to see how she was, but she always told me that she was fine, she had a boyfriend she liked, and that she was enjoying her studies. That was all. Actually, I was getting a bit fed up with hearing about the boyfriend.

Then, in spring 1998 I called again: 'Can't you dump your boyfriend for me?' I asked. 'I'll see,' came the non-committal reply. A few weeks later, my phone rang. It was Amalia: 'I did what you asked me to do,' she said. She had calmly waited for things to take their course. She also had not wanted to get involved with me until it was clear that I was separated from Alexandra. There was no official separation, because I did not want to upset the children. But we were clearly no longer together.

So it was not until almost the middle of 1998 that Amalia and I really began our relationship. Very quickly, I knew she was totally different from all the other girls I had been seeing before. She obviously wasn't impressed by my name, and she was fun to be with. I felt very at ease with her. She was also very straight talking and incredibly mature for her age. Now, although she's thirty years younger than me, she'll say to people 'Meet my child', and they look down, expecting to see a little child. Then they realize she's talking about me. It makes me laugh.

In fact, she was the one who had to meet my two younger children the year we first got together. And like everything she does, she was very open with them from the start. I'd tried to say to them that Amalia was my secretary, but later that day Charlotte made it clear what she thought of my ruse: 'That's your girlfriend, daddy, not your secretary.' My son, who was eleven by then, had started to believe me because he's like that. He has an innocence about him that many boys have. But my daughter, who was eight, was like so many girls of that age – eight going on eighteen. She immediately said: 'Yeah, yeah, that's your secretary. Yeah, yeah.' She wasn't taken in. She then went straight back to her mum and said: 'Daddy has a new girlfriend.' Well, at least Alexandra knew.

The kids have always been great about Amalia, and they have a very good relationship with her. She has always made sure I stay in touch with them. For that, I'm lucky. She's very flexible, very understanding of the situation. It's not always easy with my life, and it was made harder at one stage, when I was going through the divorce with Alexandra.

Later that year, she also met my elder daughter, Nathalie, who is one year older than her. But they got on really well from the start. Nathalie is a very warm, friendly person, but she could have had a big problem about Amalia being younger than her. Instead, she considers her like a really close friend. They email each other every day, they talk on the phone. In fact, she confides in her more than she does to me, because Nathalie and I are both quite similar. We're quite private, so Nathalie has never really talked to me very much about anything that is worrying her. She'll tell Amalia, rather than me. That way, she knows it will get back to me.

Amalia's first trip abroad with me was to the soccer World Cup in France in 1998. We were invited to watch a match in my friend Jean-Luc Lagardère's box. Lots of other people were there, including the actor Alain Delon, who I have known for thirty years, ever since he promoted a professional boxing contest at Roland Garros in 1973 between Carlos Monzon and Jean Claude Bouttier. It was the year

I won the title there, and I was invited along. Alain is one of those people that either likes you immediately or doesn't. And if he doesn't, he'll tell you. The first time I met him, he kissed me straight away, so I knew I was OK. Coincidentally, my house in Bazoches was in the village next to his own country house, so we'd see each other occasionally down there.

After the soccer match, we went back to Jean-Luc's house – palace, really – for dinner. I put Amalia in a taxi, because I had to stay behind a bit longer to talk to people, and I told the driver the address. I completely forgot that Amalia had no money. The driver got lost, and Amalia of course had absolutely no idea where she was going. Hell, she'd never been outside Romania. In the end the driver found the house, and somebody paid for Amalia's taxi. When I arrived a little later, she told me: 'Don't ever do that to me again!' A woman who knew her mind. I loved that.

She then did the greatest thing, which makes me laugh to this day. She got fed up with coming back home, either to my Paris apartment or to my Bucharest house, and hearing all the messages on the answerphone from women. Usually along the lines of: 'Hi, Ilie, it's x. Just to say I've changed my phone number. My new number is . . .' She deleted every single message before I got to it. I didn't realize at first. I just thought I was getting less pestered by women I'd met in passing over the years and who stupidly I'd given my number to. Then, Amalia went through my address book and changed every woman's number by one digit, so that I could not possibly know what the number should be. Again, when I finally realized, I thought that was so funny. By then, I was in love with her and committed to her, and to tell the truth she has never needed to doubt me since we've been together. She wouldn't stand for it anyway – and I know it!

CHAPTER FOURTEEN

1999–2002

Blair was very tense as he stood there waving my racket around. I had told him his was quite light and that he should try mine as it was heavier.
'Are you sure? Can I try?'

By 1999, I had reached a stage in life where I wanted to give something back to the game that had been so good to me. I could never have imagined, as a shy, skinny kid growing up behind the Iron Curtain in the Fifties, all the opportunities that I would be given, thanks to tennis. What I also realized was that somehow, over the last fifteen years, through all the people I had met, through the profile I still had, and through a certain amount of good fortune, I was one of sport's survivors: I was still able to play, and was being paid to do so, which was great; I was given opportunities to work in areas outside tennis; and I had met a fantastic young woman who wanted to share her life with me. I was a very lucky guy.

So in 1999 I decided to re-enter politics – tennis politics, this time – and that was a whole new experience as well. The President of the ITF, the Australian Brian Tobin, had resigned, after eight years in the job, and elections were due in the Netherlands the week after Wimbledon. As President of my Federation, I was eligible to stand, so I put forward my candidacy. I felt I had something to offer as a president of the ITF. As with the mayoral election for Bucharest, my candidacy was nothing to do with gaining power or money; I just wanted to make a contribution to tennis. I thought it was important to have a former player – and a top player as well who had achieved something in the sport – as president. This had never happened before. A former player would understand the issues facing current players as well as those of the game's organization.

My candidacy surprised quite a lot of people who still, after all these years, thought that I hadn't taken the game seriously because of the way I had played. Of course I had been serious, because you have to be in order to become the best in the world, to be number 1. But I have sometimes come up against their assumptions that I cannot take things seriously off court as well. People who know me understand that when I do something I work hard – I do it professionally and properly, as I showed when I stood for mayor. I don't behave like a prima donna, arrive late for meetings, that sort of thing. If I say I'll be somewhere at a certain time, I'll be there. I treat people with respect, and I do my best.

There were other candidates for the ITF presidency, including the presidents of the Swedish Federation and of another European federation, plus an Italian, Francesco Ricci Bitti. He'd never been involved in tennis at a high level. He'd worked for a phone company in Italy and said he'd played third-division tennis. In the end, the Swedish and the other European guy pulled out. That left me and Ricci Bitti to fight on behalf of the European countries. I decided I was going to continue to stand, at the risk of splitting the vote and Europe failing to get an ITF president.

At the meeting before the election, in Helsinki, I made a

speech setting out my ideas. I suggested that there should be a players' council, made up of the likes of Stefan Edberg and Boris Becker, for the men's game, and Chris Evert and Martina Navratilova, for the women's. They would act as a link between the ITF and the other players, because today's players have no idea what goes on at the ITF. Nor did I, when I was a player. Everybody thought that was a good idea, but nothing happened.

I also believed the ITF should redistribute differently all the money they make from the grand slams and other events. Currently, each federation gets the same amount of money. The year before, mine had received a grand total of less than $3,000. So I said: 'The ITF should use the money it distributes to each federation to pay for one proper tennis centre in one country. I'm not saying Romania. It could be Bulgaria, Hungary, Russia. It would be much more useful than paying these small amounts to all these countries.'

Even with Romania's small amount, we now have Wimbledon junior boys' champions of 2003 in singles and doubles, and a world number 1 junior in the boys. Think what we could do if resources were more pooled? It's not as if the ITF doesn't have the money. They have beautiful, luxurious offices in Roehampton, in London, and they spend millions of dollars per year running those offices and paying staff. They could halve those costs if they really wanted to. The grand slams each contribute several million dollars to the ITF, and every ITF-sanctioned tournament around the world pays a tax to the ITF. I pay if I run such a tournament in Romania. So the ITF receives a lot of money. How much actually goes back into the sport?

Also, I said that the top players, like Pete Sampras (who was number 1 at the time, in 1999) should be sent to poorer nations to promote the sport in those countries. Today's players just earn money, and they don't realize how much tennis has given them. 'I admit I was the same when I played and it's only now that I appreciate how good tennis has been to me,' I added. Poorer countries who could not afford to pay for television coverage of the big events should be given it for free or virtually nothing – again, to promote the sport. Because its popularity in some of the richer countries is actually going down and we cannot afford for that to happen, we need to find more and more markets as well as more and more countries to produce champions.

My speech lasted for twenty minutes. At the end of it, some people applauded, others did not. Then we all went away and gathered again in Amsterdam the week after Wimbledon to elect the new president. I have to say, it was worse than normal politics. I could see little groups of people, huddled in corners, speaking to each other. I was by myself, though Christian Bimes, the President of the French Federation, came over now and again. Then, I was told we had to do a presentation about what we'd done in our life. 'Why didn't you tell me that?' I asked the organizers. 'Oh, we wrote to your Federation, maybe they didn't pass on the information.' Ricci Bitti had his all beautifully prepared. So I said to a girl from the ATP: 'Right, I'm going to write down quickly all about me and you're going to make me 500 copies. Now. And I'll pay for it.' So that's what I did. Anyway, despite my best efforts, Ricci Bitti was elected. And guess who came running up to him the minute his name was read out? The other European president. He hugs and kisses him. And guess who's now on the ITF board? He is. And I'm not even on the board.

There was one measure that I proposed, though, that was accepted, and for that I'm really pleased. I proposed that the elections should be held every four years. Unbelievably, before that, the president was elected indefinitely. So Tobin had been there for eight years and his predecessor, Philippe Chatrier, thirteen. So now, at least, the president gets to keep on his toes and has to be properly re-elected, which is what happened in 2003.

In the meantime, I carry on doing what I can for my Federation and coming up with new ideas. For example, I think we should twin federations, rich ones with poor ones. I have now suggested with Christian Bimes, who is a close friend of mine, that our two federations are twinned, and now he helps me. I have two kids who went to Paris for two months to practise. He gives me old balls and nets for the kids in Romania, because otherwise they just get thrown away. For us, they're perfectly good. All this should happen automatically, as a result of ITF initiatives.

I said to Ricci Bitti last year: 'I have a junior champion.' He just said: 'Oh, that's great.' I felt like saying: 'Yeah, it's great for you to say it's great. What would be greater would be if you supported the federations properly.' We support these kids ourselves, we go to the banks. Société Générale, who are in Romania, they helped us, Tiriac helped us. And now, thanks to that, we have managed to put together ten, fifteen tournaments. We have all these kids coming from Bulgaria, the Ukraine, Russia, it's unbelievable – no thanks to the ITF. Still, now that I get to go to these meetings, I see how they work, because before, as a player, I couldn't go and had no idea what went on. Now I understand why nobody from the game can get in. For them, it's all a question of power and bureaucracy. They don't want players to get involved. They like to keep it the way it has always been, spending the money in the way they think is best. And that makes me upset. Because of that, once again, I was not afraid to speak the truth.

In 2001 Jean-Luc Lagardère, who I had known for many years, appointed me chairman and chief executive of three radio stations that he owned in Romania. One has since been sold off, and I now oversee the running of the two biggest privately-owned radio stations in the country: *Europa 1*, which is like France's *Europe 1*, also owned by Jean-Luc; and *Radio 21*, which is for younger people, like Radio 1 in Britain. The Lagardère group part-own that one. I love the atmosphere, I love having to learn how the business is run, and I have a fantastic team of people who run the stations on a day-to-day basis.

Jean-Luc was a fantastic guy. An industrialist with vision, he was an incredible friend and was like a father to me. He believed in Romania when no one else had faith in it, and he invested in it from the start. He loved tennis, and I used to play with him a lot at the Polo Club in Paris. At seventy-five years old, he was as fit and as energetic as a man twenty years younger. In fact, that's what killed him. Because he loved to play tennis, he insisted on having a hip-replacement operation on his second hip, because he didn't want to lay just doubles all the time. And that's when he suffered a massive auto-immune reaction to the blood transfusion. Within twenty-four hours, he was dead. That was in March 2003. His wife Bethy was overcome with grief, so she asked me to organize the pallbearers for the funeral. Henri Leconte, Christian Bimes, Cédric Pioline, and I carried the coffin into and out of the church near the Invalides, in Paris, where the funeral ceremony took place. Jean-Luc was then buried in Normandy, where he kept all his racehorses, his other passion.

I have a very good relationship with his son, Arnaud, who has now taken over the running of the Lagardère group, and I hope that, before long, our radio stations will start to make some profits. I very much want to repay the trust Arnaud puts in me. But doing business in Romania is tough. For a start, people are always trying to get something for less, or for nothing. It's part of the mentality. People come to me, and, because they are my friends, they'll say: 'I want to buy some publicity from your radio, but I want to pay less.' Amalia tells me to insist: 'Listen, there are rules here. If I give it to you for thirty and to the others for fifty, the guys in Paris are going to go crazy.' But I have to admit that abroad I can shake hands with somebody on a deal and trust them. In Romania, that's not the case. When I came back in the mid Nineties, I was very surprised about the promising and not delivering. That disappoints me about people in my country, and they are slower to change than I would like.

There was a homeless down-and-out in New York, called Bill, who lived on the corner of the street I lived in. Every morning, when my son was small, I'd take him to school, and we'd go past Bill. Nicky started to get friendly with him, and he started to ask me for a dollar to give to 'my friend Bill'. So I'd give him a dollar. Then, time goes by and Nicky starts to say: 'Dad, give him a pair of your tennis shoes.' So I'd give him the shoes. Then it became a tracksuit. And so on. Eventually, Bill was entirely sponsored by Adidas. Though I think he sold the stuff, because he never wore it. He was a really scruffy old man, with a dirty long beard and holes in his shoes. Then, one day, another homeless guy came up to him, when Nicky and I were with him, and shouts over:

'Hey, Bill, howya doing?'

'I'm just great, man! Just great!' he says with a big smile on his face.

And Bill goes: 'Hey, Joe, howya feeling, man?'

'Just great, too!' replies Joe.

These people, they're unbelievable. They're almost dead, but they have an attitude that says they're fine. They never showed life was going badly. Pride keeps them going.

I'm afraid to say that in Romania it's usually: 'Somebody please help me.' That's a throwback to the Communist days, when you got something for nothing. That's one of the things I immediately liked about Amalia when I met her. She was not afraid to work to make money. Whereas in Romania, to have four jobs like she had, that's seen as something to be ashamed of. They don't understand that it's a way of making a better living.

I still get letters the whole time from people begging me for money, people I don't know, cranks who invent crazy stories, who keep coming back. People are shocked sometimes that I don't want to come to their lunch or function for nothing, as if I'm a charity. Amalia has to tell them all to go away. Even when they promise money, as with the ad campaign I did a few years ago for the Romanian arm of an upmarket clothing company, they never pay. Amalia chased and chased. Nicky had also been used in the campaign, so in the end she suggested they might just send him some nice clothes instead of paying. But they never did, and I never got paid a cent. Before, people used to take advantage of me too much, because I was not good at saying 'no' to them. Now, Amalia takes care of all that.

Right from the start, she also had the courage to tell me things that people never had. She reorganized my life, my business life, my emotional life, because it was a mess. She hired this woman from my bank in France to sort out all my finances, to pay all my bills. I was paying my service charge twice on my apartment in Paris, that sort of thing. I didn't have time to look at everything closely. Amalia, with her maturity and intelligence, saw that things weren't right, and she stepped in early to sort me out. I didn't marry her for that, but it was certainly a big bonus.

I have been lucky, because since the early 1990s there has been a good seniors' circuit around the world, which I enjoy playing when I can. The tournaments have a great atmosphere, and all the players enjoy meeting up and entertaining the public. All the four majors have seniors' doubles tournaments, and so far I have won two of them: the US Open (with Tom Okker) and the French Open (with Peter McNamara). It's funny because I won the same two as a 'junior' in my twenties.

Some of the best tournaments are in Britain. The end-of-year tournament at the Royal Albert Hall is our favourite; for me, it also brings back fantastic memories. And in the summer, before Wimbledon, I enjoy playing at the exclusive Hurlingham Club, the setting for all those pre-Wimbledon tea parties I used to attend with Dominique. I only play doubles now, but many of the seniors' tournaments have singles events as well, and in those the guys are still competitive. They still want to play well, they still badly want to win, but they want to show the public they can entertain as well, that they're having more fun than the current players.

The player who takes it all 110 per cent seriously, though, is John McEnroe. If he doesn't win a match, he goes crazy, on court and off it afterwards. Most people in the public think he's putting on an act when he starts hitting balls at the linesmen, missing their heads by a few centimetres. But he's not. He gets really mad at himself, at the officials if they make a mistake, at the crowd if they make a noise. He's hardly changed over the years. Although people often said he took over from me in his behaviour, I don't agree, because I never thought he was really like me. There was more aggression in him, he was threatening on court, and I think he really scared officials sometimes because he could get quite violent. He'd break things, hit balls at people. I know I went too far as well, but I also joked around. With him, there was no humour. Back then, I could understand it. But now, he's still like that. I remember at the Royal Albert Hall tournament in 2002, he lost to ex-Wimbledon champion Michael Stich, and he went crazy on court. When he came off, everybody stayed out of his way. Just like the old days. Nobody wanted to be in the dressing room when he came off after losing.

Now, McEnroe's created this new image for himself and this new career as a commentator, and I have to say I think he's the best in the business. He's very professional, he explains the tactics, and he describes the players well. People who don't know much about tennis really understand the sport better thanks to him.

Another great character of our seniors' tour is a guy who hardly even played the proper circuit when he was younger: Mansour Bahrami, who is Iranian and about ten years younger than me. He remembers ball-boying for me at the Tehran tournament I played during the Shah's reign. It's possible. I don't remember him, because he didn't have his famous moustache then. Or maybe he did, because I think he was born with it. After the Iranian revolution, he was prevented from leaving the country and only made it out to France when he was in his thirties, with barely a few francs in his pocket. At first, he was just doing exhibitions with me in France, and he was unbelievable. He can do things with the ball that are incredible. He practises them like crazy and, to stay superfit, he also practises with young kids, chasing after every ball they hit him. So I said to him: 'You must go to the States.' And, little by little, he got invited to tournaments around the world. Now, thanks also to his great sense of humour, he is one of the most popular players on the seniors' tour. He's such a great, generous guy that, over the years, we have become very close friends.

In the summer of 2003, we found ourselves being driven up the M1 motorway to Manchester by Henri Leconte. We were playing a tournament there at a place called Mottram Hall. I was in the back and neither Mansour nor I had our glasses, so we couldn't see where we were heading. Henri said: 'It's OK, I know the way, because the guy from the tournament told me. Trust me.' So there we are in this Mercedes, with Henri – French – driving at 160 kmph, with one finger, and in the driving rain. Of course we didn't buy a map. No. Not until we'd got completely lost. Then we bought one. We went about 80 km past Manchester. I remember at one point seeing a sign for Blackpool.

Eventually we stop, pull off the motorway, and the guy at the petrol station tells us we have to turn round and go back the other way. Then, there's a fork. One way goes to Southport, the other to Manchester. So we take the one to Manchester. It's still raining, and by now it's dark. We've been going for three or four hours already. Then it gets worse. We arrive near Manchester but Mottram Hall is actually about 10 km outside. We call the chap at reception, and he gives us wrong directions. We call him two, three more times, and each time he says, in his clipped British accent: 'You're 5 km away, sir.' Probably we'd been in front of Mottram Hall twice already, but we hadn't noticed. It wasn't as if we'd never been there before – between us we must have visited half a dozen times, but not in the dark, not when it was raining and especially not when Henri was driving. In the end, it took us another two hours to do those last 10 km, and we got there about midnight. I think we'd gone round and round in circles all that time. It was really like one of those jokes that starts: 'Have you heard the one about the Frenchman, the Iranian, and the Romanian driving up to Mottram Hall?'

By 2001, I felt it was time to end my marriage to Alexandra. I had been with Amalia since 1998, and when you feel good with somebody you want to be with them all the time. I knew she was the best thing for me, that we had a real future together, and there was nothing or nobody that was going to change the situation. Not even my kids. They understood anyway. I'm not saying that made it any easier, nor the fact that I'd gone through a divorce once already. But the pretence had gone on long enough, and it was better to sort things out, for everybody's sake.

From my previous experience, I knew it was essential to try and make it as painless as possible for everybody. Because he was older than his sister, my son Nicky was more upset than Charlotte about the divorce. He didn't say much to me, but one comment he did make was: 'What am I going to say to the other kids at school if you divorce? I don't want you to divorce. They're going to tease me.' I explained to him that I wasn't the only divorced parent in the school – on the contrary – but it was still tough for him to accept.

Of course, when our lawyers got involved things got worse. Both were from New York, both women, and neither of them wanted to give an inch. And the longer it went on, the better they got paid. They were fighting the whole time, and I have to say I thought Alexandra's lawyer was unreasonably tough. She didn't answer communications from my lawyer, she didn't agree to any suggested terms of settlement, she tried to dig for money where there wasn't any. This dragged on for months. Then the months turned into a year, then over a year. It was costing both of us a lot of time, money, and emotion. And it was difficult for Alexandra to understand what I was telling her: that, because I'd been through it once already, I knew it was really important to try to resolve things nicely. She agreed, but then her lawyer would get all pushy again. I have never blamed Alexandra, and she always let me see the kids whenever I wanted, so I can never fault her for that. But until January 2003, when the divorce was finally pronounced, the lawyers kept fighting.

If Amalia had not been there, I'm not sure I could have seen the whole thing through. She was fantastically well organized. She would send any documents they asked for, including papers from my first divorce. She'd calm me down when I got angry or depressed about things, and she persevered until the end. Thank God she was there. Now she jokes: 'I'm the one who got you divorced, I'm the one who married you. But that's it. We stop there.'

The other reason I wanted to sort out my private life was that it was tough on Amalia to be with me while I was still married. For her to be suddenly in the public eye was not easy anyway, and while my situation was still unclear to the outside world it was not much fun for her. People would look at her and not take her seriously. They thought she was just another girlfriend, that the thirty-year age gap was too big and that it couldn't last. They knew nothing about her, nothing about how good she was for me, nothing about all her qualities. I don't care too much what people say about me – I'm used to press attention – but I wanted to change things for her.

I have consciously stayed in touch with the world of tennis. I like still to be in contact with people, for them to recognize me. And I appreciate my popularity more now than when I was number 1. Then it was: 'Oh, yeah, great', but you're in the middle of it, so it's just normal for you. I wasn't pinching myself every five minutes to remind myself how much people loved me. Now, though, I really like it. I go to the grand slams, I play in their seniors' events, I watch the matches, I give interviews, and the TV cameras still pick me out in the crowd. And that's great. I have to say I love that. I attend every day of the French Open, where, as President of my Federation, I sit in the presidential box and talk to all the guests. Roland Garros feels like my second home.

That's where I met Bill Clinton, in 2001, when he came to watch André Agassi. Bill and I had coffee together and he was very talkative, though I do remember that he spent the whole time looking over my left shoulder. There was a nice-looking blonde who was in fact the daughter of the French ex-tennis champion, Jean-Noel Grinda, the owner of Le Privé nightclub I used to go to. She was about 2 m tall, with incredibly long legs, and Bill was just looking at her 'LIKE THAT' and at me 'like this'. It was like: 'You're my date tonight.'

His successor at the White House, George W. Bush, was completely different with me. When Romania joined NATO in 2002, he came to our country, and our President and Prime Minister hosted a big reception for him. I was invited, as well as the gymnast Nadia Comaneci and the footballer Gheorghe Hagi. When Bush walked in, he made straight for me and started to talk to me, rather than greet the President. He knew all about me: he told me he knew I was born in 1946 like him, in July like him, but that my birthday was on the nineteenth and his on the sixth. 'That makes me thirteen days wiser,' he joked, 'except I don't think so.' He then asked me about Connors, and who threw the racket furthest, me or him. 'Connors, of course,' I replied, pretending to be annoyed. I told him I'd played tennis against his dad, when he was vice-president and he'd come to Romania.

We probably spoke for about ten minutes, non-stop. He was very charming, very relaxed, even though about 95 per cent of the people in the room were his bodyguards, and security was really tight. But afterwards, everybody was shocked that he'd spent so much time with me and not the President of Romania. 'Do you know the guy?' they wondered. 'No, I've never met him before in my life.'

So being well known has allowed me to meet all sorts of completely different people. Sometimes, it also has a few minor advantages. I used to be embarrassed by them, but now I'm more comfortable, partly because they happen much less often to me. In 2003, I was returning from New York, and I did get special treatment, which I was very grateful for. I had a lot of extra luggage, even though I was travelling business class, where your allowance is bigger. I had raided Gap for my newborn daughter, and I also had the Warhol print that I was bringing back to Bucharest, so I ended up with more than $100-worth of excess luggage. That's fine. But then the woman at the Air France counter said, in that typically officious manner: 'Security won't allow you to carry onto the plane your bag, all your rackets, plus the Warhol.' So I explained that there was nothing else I could do, and she finally said: 'OK, I'll make an exception, because of who you are and you have a frequent flier card. A hostess will accompany you to the gate.'

So we get to the security check, and there's this enormous queue snaking round. The hostess takes me straight to the front of the queue where they're X-raying the luggage and making us all take our shoes off. Immediately, the security guard stops us right there.

'What's all this?' he snaps.

'My manager told me to allow Mr Nastase on as a VIP with his hand luggage,' goes the hostess.

'VIP? What's that?' he barks back. So I'm on the point of turning around to go to the back of the queue, because that wouldn't have bothered me at all, and everybody's looking at me. Then he spots the rackets.

'You a player?'

'I used to be, sir,' I answer politely.

'OK. But that's the last time. Don't do it again.'

I was just trying to take my shoes off when he waves me through: 'It's OK, don't bother.' It just shows, though, that there's one rule for people like me and one for everyone else. I know it shouldn't be like that, but I've seen it happen regularly over the years and I've finally come to accept it.

Now that I'm getting older, I appreciate that I'm lucky to be here. It's good to grow up, have kids, and get older, because some people don't make it. I have friends of mine, like Arthur, Vitas, and Horst Dassler (the owner of Adidas who was a close friend). They never made it to my age. I think of them, and how unfair it is. They should be here. I look at Muhammad Ali now with his illness, and how he used to be, and that's terrible too.

Yes, my body is not what it used to be, and in my business physical ability is the main thing. Sure, when I look at pictures of what I was like when I was twenty, then I get depressed and think, my God, I've changed. But I avoid doing that, because as always I don't think there's any point in looking backwards. And I'm not special. Why shouldn't I get old? As Arthur said: 'Why not me?' I can have the same problems and illnesses as everybody else. Athletes are the same as those women who are famous for their beauty. They have got to accept getting old, otherwise they go crazy and become desperate. That's when those women start to have facelifts or botox injections. Their faces don't move any more, and they just start to look weird. Or they have breast implants. That would be the one thing that would keep me away from a woman, knowing she had false breasts. I hate that. So, no, I'm not bothered about ageing. If I really was, I'd do more about it.

To be honest I'm lazy about staying in shape, and I was never somebody who went into gyms to work out, and I'm hardly going to start now. I was never one for practice, either. Half an hour would do me on match days. I remember Tiriac telling me that Vilas, once, hadn't practised for three days. 'Yes, and what's the problem?' I asked, surprised. 'Well, it will take him another three days just to get back to the same level.'

That's one of the good things about the seniors' events. They keep me playing and moving around. It's important to the public that I look OK when I play. They don't expect us seniors to play brilliantly, so unless I play really badly they're happy. But if you look really fat, and on top of that you can't get a ball over the net, then you're embarrassed. So I keep playing tennis and try to watch my weight a bit.

I have always had a good appetite, though. When I was young, I burned it off. Now I have to be more careful. My favourite foods – French and Italian – I could have every day, as well as Romanian food, but none of them is very good for staying slim. And good food goes with good wine. I started to like wine when I lived in France, in the Burgundy region. Burgundies are my favourite wines, and when they're good they're difficult to refuse. I never drink excessively; usually it's just a couple of glasses every few days, although people are always saying: 'Come on, have a drink.' But, if somebody told me tomorrow I couldn't drink any more alcohol, it wouldn't bother me.

My best advice for not getting old is never to take up golf. I've tried it a few times. The first was when a French filmmaker made a documentary about me and Ion when we got to the Davis Cup final in 1972. They made us do various sports, including riding on horseback – which we both hated – and playing golf. We'd never done that. After five minutes, I remember parring the first hole. The film crew were amazed; Tiriac less so. Because another time he had put me on ice-hockey skates just to show me how good he was – he'd played for Romania at the 1964 Olympics – and after five minutes I was chasing after him on the ice. So he knew I had a good eye for the ball, and good balance and coordination.

People are always trying to get me to take up golf, but I've always resisted. I'll take it up when I'm really old and can't do anything else. That's what I told this American guy I was sitting next to on the plane a couple of years ago. I was flying over to the US Open and he was next to me in first class. I was trying to sleep. First the hostess comes, asks me if I want a drink. 'No'. I try to go back to sleep. Next, it's 'How about lunch?' So I wake up, have lunch, and the guy starts to talk to me about tennis and sports in general. He plays golf, he tells me. So I start to discuss golf, though I was quite bored by then because he wouldn't stop talking.

'Have you ever played?' he asks me.

'No,' I reply, trying to discourage the conversation.

'Why not?'

I want to get rid of him by this stage, so I say: 'Because I'm still fucking my wife.'

The guy was so shocked. He couldn't believe what he'd heard. That hit him right between the eyes.

'What do you mean?' he managed to ask.

So I explain that I'm still young, I'm still having sex, I want to have babies, and as soon as I get very old and very shaky, then I'll take up golf. He stopped talking to me after that.

Unfortunately, the thing that does happen to me as I get

older is that I think more and more about death. I never thought about it when I was young. Everybody is like that, especially once they have children. You want to live, to be there for them, and yet nothing can protect you from death, not even money. I remember Sting said he hoped to die without fear, to accept that it's normal. I'm not sure that's possible. I just want to die without suffering. And I try not to think about it, because otherwise I can't do anything. I can't live a normal life. I accept that I'm not what I was physically at the peak of my career, but my little worries about death and ageing are nothing compared to the big tragedies that have taken place over the years. That puts things into perspective for me.

What I realize now is that, however bad things are, with time you forget. It's unbelievable how much a human being can take. How much you can forgive, how much you can forget. Horrible things can happen, the Holocaust, Hiroshima, 9/11. Who could believe there could be 9/11? I was in New York at the time, because it was just after the US Open. I was due to play a tournament in Central Park with McEnroe and Noah, and I was staying at the Waldorf Astoria hotel, just nearby, where I'd been during the Open. Amalia and I woke up that morning hearing lots of sirens, but in New York that's normal. She then switched on the TV and said: 'Look, there's this crazy movie on TV,' because both towers had been hit by the time we got up. When we realized what had happened, we went out onto the street, and immediately Amalia gave blood. There was this great feeling of solidarity between all the nations. It didn't matter if you were Chinese, American, or whatever.

But life goes on after these disasters, and unfortunately, however bad the suffering, we gradually forget about them. They should keep reminding people why these disasters happened, particularly in America, where the young have no idea about history. This upsets me for the future. They need to make sure these things never occur again, but sadly people in politics are not in it for the right reasons. They talk and never do much.

That's why, for me in Romania, the best way I can achieve something, make a difference, is through business, through employing people and helping them. Being well known gives you a voice, it gives you opportunities to make things happen. And that's what I have concentrated on doing over the last few years, as well as staying involved in tennis wherever possible. That has given me satisfaction and a better perspective on life; it has made me calmer and more at peace with myself.

As well as my radio work, I'm starting up a tennis academy in Bucharest, which will be our biggest tennis centre in the country. I have the land and the planning permission, and the idea is to build a big club that is partly private and partly a centre for all our best junior players to come and practise, because such a facility does not yet exist in Romania. The idea is that the money raised by the private club funds the tennis project for the youngsters.

Incredibly, I have run into problems with the name: the Ilie Nastase Tennis Academy. When I tried to register it as a trademark, I discovered that there was a guy operating from a PO Box in Switzerland who had already registered the very same name. In fact, I'd started to come across people who would say they'd booked an hour's lesson with me at the Academy. 'What academy?' I'd go. They'd explain. But as this guy runs things from a PO Box, I have no way of tracking him down, and I can't retrieve my own name. I'll still go ahead with the name for my academy, though. Let the guy sue.

I also do some charity work. My main involvement is with the Laureus Sports Awards. We are thirty-three members – I was a founder member – all ex-champions from all sorts of different sports. The likes of Mark Spitz, Emerson Fittipaldi, Daley Thompson, Gary Player, and Nadia Comaneci are members. We get about $15 million sponsorship money per year from Cartier and Mercedes, and those members from rich countries have to raise the same amount as well. Then we do one big sports project in one of the poorer countries and help projects in the richer ones as well. Each year, we concentrate on a different country. So in 2003 it was Morocco, in 2002 it was India (Kapil Dev is a member), and before that South Africa. In addition, we each have to visit at least one project a year. In past years, I have been to Lyon, where we funded sports facilities in a school for handicapped children, and also to Harlem, where I played basketball with the handicapped kids. Nadia and I would now like to do something in Romania.

Every year, we have an awards ceremony in Monte Carlo, where we present various categories: best athlete, best comeback, best wheelchair athlete, and so on. In 2002 and 2003, Nelson Mandela came to speak at our awards, which added to its reputation. This is a project that I'm proud to be involved with and that I feel does help some people. I'm especially pleased because every year its profile is getting higher, and we are able to raise more money.

In summer 2002, before the men's singles final at Queen's Club in London, I played in a charity exhibition match. Most years I took part in it, and this time I thought I was playing with Pat Cash, Peter Fleming, and Peter McNamara, the Aussie doubles specialist. When I arrived at the club, they said that this year they had decided to make it more fun by inviting a comedian, Alistair McGowan, and another personality – but they couldn't tell us who. Pat and I didn't ask, because frankly we didn't care. It wouldn't matter who it was. I was sitting in the dressing room with Pat, about half an hour before we were due on, when suddenly we saw a lot of police with their dogs checking every corner, the bathrooms, everything. Suddenly, Tony Blair appeared – he was our fourth man. I was a bit surprised, especially as he started to get changed right there in front of us, chatting to us while his bodyguards hung around. Blair was very tense as he stood there, waving my racket around. I had told him his was quite light and that he should try mine, as it was heavier. 'Are you sure? Can I try?' So we went to hit on the indoor wooden court for about ten minutes. He then admitted he never played doubles, only singles, and asked me what he should do in doubles.

'You just serve, come to the net, put your racket up, and volley.'

'Yeah, easier said than done!' he laughed nervously.

So he kept my racket – which he still has – and I made sure he had the Head logo well painted on the strings, because I knew it would be all over the papers the next day. He took Pat Cash as a partner, and I played with Alistair. I have to say, Blair plays well. He can serve, hit the volley, and he's got a good forehand. Alistair plays well too. Blair kept joking during the match: 'Oh, come on guys, you're too nice to me. I know you can hit harder.' Although he won, he knew he wasn't playing so well that he could say he'd really beaten Nastase. Afterwards, we had a drink in the dressing room, he had a shower, and he stayed and talked to me and Cash. He's a real tennis fan, and he was asking me lots of questions about Connors and Borg. I was then asked by the press how I'd lost to the Prime Minister: 'I'm not stupid, I want to be allowed to leave the country!'

At Christmas 2002, Amalia told me we were expecting our first child together. This could not have come at a better time, and, although it was something we had both been hoping would happen, it was still fantastic to hear the news. My life was settled again, both professionally and personally, and knowing that I was going to be a parent again was really exciting. A new chapter was about to begin for me.

CHAPTER FIFTEEN

2003–2004

Somehow, I seem to find myself with three surprisingly sensible kids. I'm not sure it's much thanks to me, although they do say that kids rebel against their parents.

Amalia's pregnancy went very well until the summer. In the new year, we had learned that the baby was a girl, and we were both really happy at that. Amalia thought I would have preferred a boy, but I kept telling her that, as long as the baby was healthy, I didn't care one way or the other.

The baby was due about 10 August, so until then I carried on with my tennis and other professional commitments. I played seniors' tournaments all over Europe, including the French Open and Wimbledon, and Amalia based herself in Paris where she was due to give birth. By the time Roland Garros came round in May, she was suffering really badly from the hot weather and was desperate to have the baby.

We had decided to get married before the baby's birth. I would have liked the wedding to be on 19 July, my birthday, but I was playing an exhibition match in Germany that day, so instead we arranged it for the seventeenth. My daughter Nathalie came over from southern Spain, where she was living at the time. Amalia's parents came from Romania, and we invited about thirty friends, including Tiriac, Mansour Bahrami, and one of my two witnesses for my wedding, Christian Bimes.

It was a beautiful sunny late afternoon when our little party set off on foot from my apartment, round the corner from the Mairie of the 16th *arrondissement*, where the civil ceremony was to take place. Nathalie held my hand all the way, while Amalia walked close by with her parents and a few friends. I wasn't nervous for what I was about to do. I was nervous about Amalia having the baby right there, because she was enormous by then and the baby was kicking her very hard. But I was also really happy that my first child was with me, supporting me on this day, as well as some of my oldest and closest friends. It was particularly good to have Ion there, because this was the first marriage of mine that he had attended, so it was about time he came. We had asked his son Ion-Ion, who is exactly the same age as Amalia, to be another witness, and in fact later that year he also became godfather to our daughter.

The mayor, Monsieur Taittinger, of the Taittinger champagne family, married us, then we all went off, after a glass or two of his champagne, to the restaurant at Roland Garros, where the dinner took place. The weather was perfect, we had drinks on the lawn and a fantastic dinner before heading off, with Mansour and his wife, to the Etoile nightclub, near the Arc de Triomphe, for a final bit of partying. Amalia avoided the dancefloor, though, in case she suddenly found herself giving birth in front of everybody. It had been a great day, and yet the best was still to come. The birth of our baby.

Ten days later, and two weeks before the due date, I set off for Montpellier, in south-west France, where I was playing a couple of exhibition matches with Mansour, Henri Leconte,

Yannick Noah, Mats Wilander, and Bjorn Borg. Not long before, Bjorn himself had had a baby with his third wife, and Amalia and I had been to their wedding the summer before in Sweden. The night before leaving for Montpellier, I'd stayed up late to iron all the tiny baby clothes we had bought and washed, in preparation for the baby's arrival. It's not that Amalia had asked me to do it; it's just that I'm quite a tidy person anyway, and I was so excited about the birth that I had decided to prepare the entire pile of pink and white clothes before I left. I was only going to be away for a couple of days, and this was my final trip before the birth, so I was happy and relaxed when I left the next day, 27 July.

But at nine o'clock the following morning, I got a call from Amalia's doctor. 'Don't worry', he said worryingly, 'everything's fine, but Amalia went into labour in the night and she's now in the delivery room.' 'What happened? No, no, I want to be there!' When I finally managed to speak to Amalia, I was almost in tears. I had so wanted to be there for the birth. I had not been at the birth of any of my children, and I had planned that this time would be different. But it was too late. There was no way I could have made it back in time. Amalia, as ever, was so calm. Her mother was there, she said, she'd be fine, so I should just try to play my match and come back after that.

It's an understatement to say that I found the next few hours difficult. But I had no choice and, later that afternoon, I went onto court with Mansour, Henri, and Yannick. This match was being filmed by the local TV station, so I had to give a good performance. While we were warming up, my mobile rang at the courtside. I rushed over. It was Amalia's doctor. With the cameras filming me, he announced to me that Amalia had given birth at 2.15 p.m. to a little girl, weighing 3.2 kg (7 lb 2 oz). She had had a Caesarean section in the end (which she told me afterwards she was really pleased about), because the labour had not progressed properly. Both she and the baby were fine. I was so excited, I started jumping around the court, telling everybody the news, while the other guys were leaping all over me, congratulating me. It was a fantastic way of hearing about the birth, and I now have the videotape of that moment to remind me of it forever.

I took the first flight back to Paris the next morning and went straight to the clinic. I poked my head round the door of the room where Amalia and the baby were, and crept in, thinking they might be asleep. Amalia was awake. When I saw my daughter for the first time, I was overwhelmed. 'She's so tiny, she's so tiny,' I kept saying. She was a beautiful pink colour and was completely perfect. I'd forgotten how tiny and fragile newborn babies looked, and how incredibly moving it was to see your child for the first time.

We named our baby Alessia, and four days later we proudly took her home. It was then that we realized the heat wave that was already gripping France was going to be a real problem for a very young baby. For days, the thermometer had not gone below 36°C, and for several days in early August Paris and the whole region around it reached an unbelievable 42°C. We tried taking Alessia to our house in Bazoches, thinking it would be cooler in the country, but it was even hotter there. So, after a day there, we returned to Paris. We spent hours wandering around an air-conditioned shopping mall, to keep the baby cool, with shoppers surprised to see Amalia up and about, only a week after giving birth. I also drove Alessia around Paris in my air-conditioned car, because there was not the slightest breath of wind, and Alessia was so red and hot she was very uncomfortable. The heat wave was a real problem for many vulnerable people, and many old people died because, like babies, they were unable to control their body heat and became dehydrated very quickly.

After two weeks, we had had enough. The temperatures were not going down, so we returned to Bucharest. We had not planned to go until the end of August, but the temperatures there were 'only' in the low thirties.

Newly married and newly a father again, I went off to the 2003 US Open at the end of August and won the super seniors' tournament with Tom Okker. This rounded off a really good summer for me. My hip might give me problems, and I might be heavier than I used to be, but who cares? I had added another major to my name, and I could proudly say that I was the best fifty-seven year old around! I also saw my kids Nicky and Charlotte in New York. All along, they had been great about the arrival of Alessia. I know it's not easy for them, but they know that having another child does not make any difference to how much I love them. They're such great kids. Charlotte, who's now fourteen, is very mature and organized, and she works hard at school. Nicky is also organized and happy to work. Every summer, during his school holidays, he goes to work for a month in a hotel in Santa Fe, where Alexandra has family. He wants to work, he tells me, and he saves the money in his bank account. That's good for me because it shows he has the right mentality, the American mentality, that work is a good thing. Now he's seventeen he could easily be saying: 'Send me some money, Dad', like some kids would. I have to say Alexandra did a really good job in bringing them up.

They have known from the beginning that they were adopted, and they're very cool about it and very open about telling people. I remember overhearing Charlotte saying to Mansour, who was having dinner with us during that 2003 US Open: 'Did you know that me and my brother were adopted by my father?' She was keen to tell him all about it. I pretended not to hear, but I was very moved all the same.

They always tell me that they don't want to know who their birth mothers are. They say: 'You're my real father and mom is our real mom, and that's it.' My son told me he could not dream of having a better family and that he didn't want to know his birth parents, because it would only make him upset. If one day he changes his mind, though, I'd encourage him to go and find out. I've told him that it will never be a problem for me. But I think at the moment he doesn't plan to do it, at least not when I'm alive, in case it upsets me as well as him. Maybe once I'm no longer there, he'll do it.

Unlike some kids adopted by well-known people, mine were not affected by my name, because they never saw me competing and I was not in the spotlight when they were growing up. In fact, they'll say: 'Dad, my principal told me that you were a bad boy on the court.' 'No, no, he's got the wrong guy. He's thinking of Tiriac probably,' I reply. They know about me, that I was number 1, but they don't know how famous I was. They just hear things from other people.

Nathalie gets on very well with Nicky and Charlotte and has no problems with them. Again, I'm incredibly lucky because they all love each other, even though they don't see each other very often and certainly not as often as I would like. I'm now closer to Nathalie than I have ever been, which is great as it could so easily have been the other way round. I might have been close to her when she was young and now she might not want to know me, because that happens too to people. It doesn't matter what you do or don't do to your kids. There are no guarantees of how they'll work out or how your relationship will be with them.

I think Nathalie sees my faults but has the maturity to rise above them. She knows nobody's perfect, and she knows – I hope – how much she means to me and how proud I am of her. She got a really good education, which is important, and, after studying languages at the Sorbonne for a couple of years (she speaks fluent Spanish and English), she went back to live and work in Spain, where Dominique had been living for some years. She is now based in Paris and is working in PR for the French Tennis Federation, which she loves because she feels very at home in that world, although she doesn't play tennis. She has never made use of her name, or spent the money that Dominique and I put aside for her.

Somehow, I seem to find myself with three surprisingly sensible kids. I'm not sure it's much thanks to me, although they do say that kids rebel against their parents. So if their dad was always rushing around the world and had a crazy life, maybe it's not surprising that they're happy just to be normal kids. No matter what happens, I will always be proud of them and they will always be my kids, even when they're all grown up. And, no, umpires and linesmen around the world can relax: none of them will ever be a tennis player. Although, of course, there is Alessia . . .

Tennis has changed so much since I was playing, so if she takes up the sport she will play it in a very different way. In my day, there were all these small differences in the grip. The semi-Western grip for the forehand, then the Eastern grip on the backhand, with the 'v' of the hand on the left of the grip. All that's gone now. They say put the racket on the ground, pick it up and off you go. That's your grip. That's the grip I would teach Alessia, not mine. Otherwise, she won't have a chance; she won't be able to hit topspin like everybody else, because that's the future.

Of course, one of the main reasons the game has become

like ping pong is that the rackets have changed so much. If we'd had these rackets thirty years ago, we would have played very different tennis, that's for sure. The talent is the same, through all the eras. Even the girls whip the rackets now, because they are much lighter, and as a result they can hit hard. Someone like Justine Henin-Hardenne, who's built like a rake, hits the ball incredibly hard. With wooden rackets, you had to prepare much earlier; you couldn't move the racket head through as quickly or go for the winner as much. We played in slow motion compared to these guys today. But the rackets made us more complete players then, because we had to learn to drop-shot, volley, lob, and defend. Technique, finesse, and intuition were more important than in today's game.

I played my best tennis with a wooden racket because I could control the ball better. We all played with this fantastic racket, the Dunlop Maxply – Laver, McEnroe, me. These days I use a big Head racket and it's easier to play with, now I'm old. I haven't lost the touch, but I have less control. With a wooden racket, if I missed, I did so by a small amount. Now, if I miss, it's by a larger amount, because you cannot control the rackets as much. With all due respect to McEnroe, who would like to go back to wooden rackets, I don't think you can go back. Nobody would want it – not the players, not the public, and especially not the women and the amateur players, because for them the larger, lighter rackets have been great.

It's the same with changing the rules. That's something McEnroe and other people have been talking about, to make the game more attractive. We've discussed all this at the ITF. Ideas like having one service only and no let cords. But if you touch one rule, you can change all the rules. Both those ideas, for me, would be out of the question. It would change completely the way the game was played. Having one serve only would make players even less willing to take a risk on a first serve. Now, it's 'will he go for an ace, or go for placement?' If he misses, you then have the excitement of what he will do with the second serve. What sort of spin and direction will he go for? Similarly, if you had to play the ball, even if it was a let, it would be crazy, because sometimes the ball really drops just the other side of the net.

But all sports have changed, not just tennis, and none of them would go back to what they were. As well as the equipment, players in all sports have also become physically better prepared. The combination of those two things mean that sports have speeded up. That's why, in tennis, it's pointless to compare champions like Laver, Borg, McEnroe, and Sampras. Maybe in ten years' time they'll say Sampras was not fast enough – although I don't think anybody will ever equal his seven Wimbledon wins. I can't see how any player will be able to dominate like that again.

I used to love watching Pete, who was just a fantastic player with a great all-round game. One day, he came up to me in the locker room and said:

'Hi, Mr Boring, how are you?'

'What do you mean?'

'You said I was boring,' he replied.

'I never said that,' I protested.

Pete claimed that once, some years before, somebody asked me what I thought about the game, and I'd replied that he, Sampras, was boring. He also said that he had seen a match between me and Laver in California, years ago, when he was a kid. I don't know what happened, but at one stage apparently I gave the finger sign – one of the many Romanian peace signs I enjoyed showing on court. He told me that this was not a good example, but that he liked the way I played, with all the excitement. So now, whenever he sees me, he calls out: 'Hi, Mr Boring, did you get fined again?'

I like Agassi and the way he's stayed up there with all these young kids. But one day, I must have been a bit pissed off with him about something, because I told him: 'When you win, you bow to the crowd and blow kisses to them. But it's no good, because when you lose you don't do that. It means nothing if you've won. If you lose and you do that, then it means something.' But Agassi, when he loses, he's like everybody else. He's mad. When he lost at the 2003 US Open, in the semis to Juan Carlos Ferrero, I happened to be in the dressing room because I was playing my semi in the seniors' tournament. He came in, and he went crazy. He started wiping his face with his socks, because he didn't know what he was doing any more. And he didn't talk to a single person in his team.

Andy Roddick has an amazing talent, but he doesn't have the kind of game I like to watch, with all those service winners being banged down past the opponent. Obviously, he doesn't care whether I go and watch his matches or not, he just wants to win and that's fine. But if he's going to win 6–1, 6–1, and blast serves all day, then I'm not going to go and watch, and I'm not sure how many other people will as well. It's like a movie. It might be great, but if it's not my sort of film I won't go and see it.

It's the same with clay-court tennis. Although I was brought up on clay, I'm not interested in watching two guys slugging it out from the back of the court until one of them puts the ball in the net. That's why I enjoy watching a player like Roger Federer, who has a lot of talent and plays crazy shots like I used to. I'm hoping, now that he has won Wimbledon, that a few more kids might want to copy the way he plays and use a single-handed backhand that gives a greater variety of shot. Because most of them now just sit on the baseline, with that big grip on the forehand and the double-handed backhand, and they just smash the ball. It's not nice to watch, even though it's efficient. Generally, the players I like to watch are those that put excitement and passion into their tennis and who play a good, varied game: players like the Russian Marat Safin and the Moroccan Younes El Aynaoui, as well as Tim Henman, who has got a great serve-volley game.

People in Britain ask me why they cannot produce world-class players and why there has not been a British Wimbledon champion since Fred Perry. I used to think it was unbelievable, as I flew into Heathrow, to look down and see all these soccer pitches, rugby pitches, cricket pitches, even tennis courts – but with hardly anybody on them. Maybe that is the problem. The British kids take them for granted. We don't have anything like those facilities in Romania, so we appreciate every bit of sports land. Our kids play wherever they can, they practise with whatever balls they are given. I'm not saying this is the best way to become a good player, but maybe it helps. The real motivation has to come from each individual kid, from within. If he really wants it, he can't be stopped. Of course, if he has a great coach and great facilities, it might happen quicker, but mainly it's the person who plays the sport who has to believe and want it.

In Britain, Tim Henman and Greg Rusedski, in their very different ways, both want it badly. Greg is a nice guy, whatever anybody says and whatever he may have done. But he's not British and I'm sure he doesn't see himself as that either. He's not 'made in England' like Tim.

I like Tim. Mr Nasty, he sometimes calls me. Every year,

we play backgammon together at Wimbledon. He thinks he can beat me, but I'm a champion backgammon player, so I always win. In fact, he doesn't know anything about backgammon. Luckily, he knows a bit more about tennis. Despite his appearances, Tim is very determined, and he has a good game, which I like to watch. It's unfortunate that he hasn't succeeded on grass with the game he has. But it can still happen. He won a big tournament in Paris in the autumn of 2003, one of the 'Super 9', and that result can be all it takes to give him that extra bit of confidence. It's unbelievable the difference that can make to a player, because the dividing line between winning a big tournament like Wimbledon and coming very close, like Tim has on several occasions, is very thin. It can all be down to a bit of luck, a good draw, and a bit more confidence. Also you have to remember that Tim was playing for a long time during the years that Pete Sampras was dominating the tournament. So who knows? I believe Tim can still win Wimbledon.

I have to say, though, that I sympathize with him about the huge pressure on him from the media. It's like when I used to play Davis Cup in Romania. If they really wanted to help him, the media would leave him alone during the tournament. Instead, the whole of Wimbledon is taken up by the papers and the television following him around the whole time. Anybody who is interviewed during that time is asked whether he can win – and God forbid if anybody criticizes his chances. Every day it's: 'My God, Tim is playing. What time? Is that good? Is that bad? What court is he on? Is that good? Is that bad?' Everything is analysed in minute, ridiculous detail. It's crazy. Then, the rest of the year, they forget about him and about tennis. They forget that there are three other grand slam tournaments that he plays. Nobody bothers about them.

When he's interviewed, I understand why Tim gives some boring answers. They were probably stupid questions anyway. I would have done the same. It's his way of staying concentrated, of handling the pressure, the media, the sponsors, the public. But he couldn't change his image, even if he wanted to. He couldn't suddenly start smashing his rackets on court, swearing. He'd be unable to play. I once said to him, when people were accusing him of being boring: 'Come on, Tim, give them shit. Tell the umpires to fuck off.' But he just laughed, because he knows he cannot. It's not in his personality.

Away from the cameras, he's a lot more fun and relaxed than people imagine. He's a bit like me, he's two different people off and on court. And he has done a lot for British tennis. Before him, nobody talked much about the sport in his country. When he's retired, people will realize that and maybe appreciate him a bit more. He deserves it.

Everybody says that tennis is ugly now. OK, but you can't force the players to play in a way that pleases the public. In my case, it happened, though it wasn't on purpose. You can't plan for that. But you could improve the way the men dress. They should get rid of the baggy clothes. I think it would look nice if they had shorter shorts, and I think the female fans would appreciate it. Anyway, the players look smaller in these baggy clothes and you can't see how strong and athletic they are. I hate that. I also hate when they have their shirt hanging out. There should be a rule about having to have your shirt tucked in. Finally, they should ban those baseball caps. I know it's the fashion and everybody wears them away from the courts as well, but it's not even as if they just wear them when it's sunny. They wear them the whole time, indoors, even. All the caps do is make the players faceless and anonymous.

All the players today are surrounded by minders, and they never come near the public. That's a shame, too. We used to walk around everywhere, and everyone had access to us. I can understand why it's become like that, and again it's the same in all commercial sports, not just in tennis. It's not that the players don't want to speak to their fans, but it's their managers and the tournament directors who don't want them to, in case somebody comes and attacks them. Also, because the money and the stakes are so high now, the guys have to be so dedicated and have to train so hard that they don't have the time or the energy to mix with people. They hardly ever go out into the real world. People want a rapport, though. They want to come not just to see you play but maybe also to talk to you a bit, to get your autograph, your photograph, something. I remember at Wimbledon one year having an ice cream with a guy I'd never met before. I got talking to him, and he was asking me how many tournaments I'd played, how many I'd won. It was normal for us to mix with the public. That's why they now remember us so well and come to watch us play the seniors' tournaments. There's no longer any contact between today's players and the fans. The cars just pick them up outside the dressing room, and away they go. The public never even sees them.

This lack of contact also means that the players have no sense of their responsibility towards the public. They have no sense that with success you have some duty towards those who pay and contribute to that success. If I play a tournament and get a guarantee of $250,000, I think it's normal to do a clinic or something. It's to do with promoting the tournament, with helping others. Some players just take the guarantee, play, lose, then go. Of course, the fault also lies with the organizers, who want the best players, the best sponsors, then let the guys get away with it. And their managers only care about getting the biggest fee. They don't care about telling the players they should put something back into the game by doing the clinic.

I think now the ATP is trying to make the young players more aware that it shouldn't be just take, take, take. It tells tell them they have a responsibility, as professional players, with the image they give to the public. Also, the ATP is trying to get them to plan ahead financially and decide what they're going to do when they've stopped playing. Because the ones who never get into the top ten or twenty – the vast majority – they're going to be pleased to get a pension cheque every month. Even I now get a pension. Every month, I get a small cheque through the post. After all those years of fines to the ATP, I think I've earned it!

When I was starting out, I never thought about the money. Never. I wanted to do well, for me. That's what motivated me. It didn't matter that I didn't have the right equipment or the right coach. I had the desire to keep improving. And I just loved to play. I'd practise for hours. I'd do only topspin lobs, say, for half an hour. I'd say to my practice partner: 'Stay at the net, I'm going to give you 100 lobs.' Systematically. But I wouldn't just have him sitting there at the net. I'd say to him: 'Make me run.' So I'd hit them from different positions and move him about as well. Otherwise, it's no good, you can only hit them if they're in the right place. And I'd run and run, even if the balls were out.

I just wanted to win – and badly. I took the game seriously, but in a way that nobody could understand. Having fun on court did not mean, in my mind, not caring whether I won or lost. It was my way of expressing myself, showing my passion and emotions. If I had not cared about getting good results, I would not have practised like I did in the early years; I would never have won as many tournaments as I did, and I would certainly never have had the arguments I did on court. After all, why bother to get angry if you don't care whether you win or lose? But I could never have been made to change. I know that would have been impossible. And, by being myself, I made more of a mark on the sport than if I had been a good boy and kept my mouth shut, and my emotions inside me.

One memory does sum up the way I was on court and how I think many people will remember me. It was in July 1975 and I was partnering Arthur Ashe in a tournament in Louisville, Kentucky – population ninety-nine per cent black. The ATP had just brought out a rule that doubles partners had to play in matching colours. I was in the locker room with Connors and Eddie Dibbs, that crazy, pugnacious player from Miami, who liked to joke around off court, and they were saying: 'Nasty, you're going to get fined because you're white and he's black'. So they found a tin of shoe polish and set about blacking me up, legs, face, everything. We're in the bathroom, and Arthur is pacing around in the dressing room, calling out: 'Where's Nasty, where's Nasty?' Finally, without Arthur seeing me beforehand, I walk out on court, with a towel on my head and 6,000 black faces looking at me. I take the towel off, Arthur takes one look at me, and he cannot stop laughing. He is crying so much we cannot play for at least five minutes. Luckily the public thought it was funny as well, especially when the polish melted in the heat and turned my clothes all black.

So when I look back, I don't regret anything. That's pointless, anyway. I stayed sane off court, even if I was sometimes crazy on it. I didn't spend all my money, abuse alcohol or drugs. Maybe I had too many women, too many wives? Yes, I could have won more, but I think I achieved a lot of things in a short time. I was number 1 for most of 1973. I won two majors and four Masters. I won a lot of great matches and enjoyed many others, even some that I lost. I had a lot of fun and touched a lot of people, and for better or worse not many people stayed indifferent to me. I know that I have been unbelievably lucky to have had the life I had. It could have been a lot worse. And it could have been so different.

I used to have this dream that came all the time during Wimbledon. Finally, I win this son-of-a-bitch tournament, and I take my trophy and go all around the stadium, bowing to people and giving the finger to everybody. Then I take my rackets and break them in my hands. I throw them in the river, and I stop playing tennis forever. Just like that.

CAREER STATISTICS

Career Highlights

1946	Born 19 July, Bucharest
1959	Wins first junior national tournament in Cluj
1963	First trip abroad to Sofia, Bulgaria
1966	Plays first Davis Cup tie, against France, first French Open and first Wimbledon Ranked no.7 in Romania
1967	Wins first tournament abroad at Cannes
1969	Romania reach Davis Cup Challenge round. Ranked no.1 in Romania
1970	Wins Italian Open Wins French Open Doubles with Tiriac and Wimbledon Mixed Doubles with Casals
1971	Finalist at French Open Romania reach Davis Cup Challenge round Wins first Masters title in Paris
1972	Finalist at Wimbledon. Wins Wimbledon Mixed Doubles with Casals Becomes engaged to Dominique Grazia Wins US Open Romania reach Davis Cup final Wins second Masters title in Barcelona Marries Dominique, first in Brussels, then in Bazoches-sur-le-Betz, France, December
1973	Wins Italian Open Wins French Open Wins Wimbledon Doubles with Connors In August, ranked no.1 in the world in first ever official rankings Stays at no.1 for 40 weeks Wins third Masters title in Boston

1974	Finalist at Masters tournament, Melbourne
1975	Daughter Nathalie born, 12 March
	Wins fourth Masters title in Stockholm
1976	Finalist at Wimbledon
1977	Made Major in Romanian army
1980	Separates from Dominique
1982	Divorce pronounced
1984	Marries Alexandra King, September
	Retires from international tennis
1987	Son Nicky born, 1 July
1990	Daughter Charlotte born, 14 March
1996	Candidate for election of Mayor of Bucharest
	Elected president of Romanian Tennis Federation
1998	Official separation from Alexandra
1999	Candidate for election of president of the International Tennis Federation
2001	Appointed chairman and chief executive of Europa 1 and Radio 21, Romania's two largest private radio stations
2003	Marries Amalia Teodosescu, in civil ceremony in Paris, July
	Daughter Alessia born, 28 July
2004	Made Colonel in Romanian army
	Marriage to Amalia blessed in church, in Paris, June

Singles and Doubles Record

1965 Ranked No.9 in Romania

1966 Played 11 tournaments. Won 1 Singles and 3 Doubles
SINGLES: *Won Bucharest International.*
DOUBLES: *Won Nottingham, Travemuende, Bucharest. R/up French (all with Tiriac).*
WIN/LOSS RECORD: B.Butcher, J.Kodes, B.Montrenaud, M.Riessen, G.Sara, 1–0; C.Zeeman 1–1; I.Tiriac 1–2; R.Crealy, P.Darmon, C.Drysdale, K.Fletcher, F.Jauffret, T.Koch, L.Pawlik, J.Saul, W.Tym. 0–1. Ranked No.7 in Romania.

1967 Played 20 tournaments. Won 3 Singles and 6 Doubles
SINGLES: *Won Cannes, Travemuende, Romanian Nats. R/up Alexandria, Carlton, Riccione.*
DOUBLES: *Won Belgian, Senigallia, Travemuende, Viareggio, Mamaia and Romanian Nats (all with Tiriac).*
W.Bungert, D.Contet, J.P.Courcol, E.Drossart, Z.Franulovic, W.Gasiorek, M.Holecek, P.Hombergen, R.Howe, V.Korotkov, R.Kuhlmey, J.Leschley, S.Likhachev, J.E.Lundquist, P.Marmureanu, F.Pala, H.Pohmann, R.Russell, M.Sangster, M.Sonbol, P.Strobl, S.Tacchini, R.Taylor, 1–0; P.Curtis, I.Tiriac, 1–1; C.de Gronkel, C.Drysdale, I.El Shafei, J.Gisbert, G.Maioli, A.Metreveli, B.Montrenaud, M.Mulligan, J.Pinto-Bravo, H.Plotz, M.Santana, G.Stilwell, 0–1; J.Kodes, N.Pietrangeli, 0–2. Ranked No.2 in Romania.

1968 Played 20 tournaments. Won 3 Singles and 8 Doubles
SINGLES: *Won Viareggio, Mamaia, Romanian Nats. R/up Parioli (Rome), Reggio Calabria.*
DOUBLES: *Won Calcutta, Bombay, New Delhi, Parioli, Catania, Viareggio, Mamaia (all with Tiriac), Belgrade (Holecek).*
E.Castigliano, M.Di Domenico, S.Dron, P.Marmureanu, 2–0; J.Alexander, W.Bowrey, P.Curtis, P.Dent, G.di Maso, E.di Matteo, M.Elvik, J.Fassbender, Z.Franulovic, W.Gasiorek, B.Jovanovic, T.Lejus, G.E.Maggi, S.Minotra, J.Paish. O.Parun, B.Phillips-Moore, J.Pinto-Bravo, A.Stone, P.Toci, D.Viziru, M.Werren, 1–0; R.Crealy, M.Mulligan, 1–1; E.Mandarino, A.Metreveli, J.Mukerjea, T.Okker, N.Pietrangeli, 0–1; P.Lall, M.Riessen, I.Tiriac, 0–2. Ranked equal No.1 in Romania.

1969 Played 31 tournaments. Won 8 Singles and 6 Doubles
SINGLES: *Won East India HC, Indian HC, Indian Nats, Barranquilla, Ancona, Travemuende, La Corogne, Budapest. R/up Palermo, Stockholm Inds.*
DOUBLES: *Won East India HC (Lall), Indian HC (Marmureanu) Indian Nats (Marmureanu), St Petersburg (Franulovic), Palermo, Bastad, Ancona (all with Tiriac).*
I.Gulyas, J.Kodes, 3–0; P.Lall, M.Rybarczyk, 2–0; M.Cox, S.Smith, 2–1; G.Andrew, J.Arilla, S.Baranyi, J.C.Barclay, P.Beust, M.Carlstein, I.Crookenden, E.Davidman, P.Dent, V.Dhawan, E.Drossart, S.Dron, B.Fairlie, W.Gasiorek, T.Gorman, T.Koch, G.Maioli, V.Marcu, P.Marzano, A.Metreveli, S.Misra, G.Mulloy, H.Plotz. H.Pohmann, R.Ruffels, M.Santana, M.Sonbol, R.Taylor, J.Ulrich, T.Ulrich, G.Varga, H.Zahr, V.Zednik, 1–0; P.Barthes, I. El Shafei, Z.Franulovic, J.Mukerjea, T.Nowicki, N.Spear, I.Tiriac, 1–1; A.Roche, 1–2; A.Ashe, A.Gimeno, G.Goven, C.Graebner, R.Holmberg. R.Lutz, S.Matthews, M.Mulligan, J.Newcombe, M.Orantes, N.Pilic, G.Stilwell, 0–1; K.Rosewall, 0–2. Ranked No.1 in Romania.

1970 Played 30 tournaments. Won 4 Singles and 9 Doubles
SINGLES: *Won US Inds, Italian Open, Naples, Catania. R/up Palermo, Belgian Open, German Open, Romanian Nats.*
DOUBLES: *Won Philadelphia Inds, Reggio Calabria, Catania, Palermo, Italian Open, Belgian Open, French Open, Western Open (USA), (all with Tiriac), Naples (Pala). Also won Wimbledon Mixed (Casals).*
N.Kalogeropoulos, 4–0; R.Crealy, A.Gimeno, J.McManus, M.Mulligan, B.Phillips-Moore, H.Plotz, G.Stilwell, R.Taylor, I.Tiriac, 2–0; I.Gulyas, 2–1; T.Addison, H.Akbari, T.Akbari, G.Battrick, B.Bertram, J.Borowiak, A.Bouteleux, R.Carmichael, E.Castiglano, L.Coni, I.Fletcher, T.Gorman, G.Goven, F.Guzman, R.Hewitt, R.Howe, J.Hrebec, P.Jemsby, J.Kodes, J.Kukal, M.Lara, M.Leclerq, J.Lloyd, V.Marcu, A.McDonald, R.McKinley, J.Osborne, J.Paish, F.Pala, O.Parun, A.Pattison, N.Pietrangeli, P.Proisy, F.Robbins, A.Roche, T.Ryan, T.Ulrich, S.Warboys, A.Zugarelli, 1–0; C.Richey, 3–3; J.Alexander, A.Ashe, A.Panatta, N.Pilic, 1–1; Z.Franulovic, 2–2; J.Cooper, P.Hutchins, H.Kary, D.Lloyd, P.Marmureanu, D.Ralston, K.Rosewall, N.Spear, 0–1; J.Fillol, C.Graebner, R.Laver, T.Okker, 0–2.

1971 Played 28 tournaments. Won 11 Singles and 8 Doubles
SINGLES: *Won Ancona, Omaha, Richmond, Hampton, Nice, Monte Carlo, British Indoors, Swedish Open, Champions Cup (Sweden), Istanbul, Pepsi Grand Prix Masters (Paris). R/up French Open, Madrid, Belgian Open, South American Open.*

DOUBLES: *Won Omaha, Nice, Monte Carlo, Belgian (shared), Madrid, Swedish, Istanbul, (all with Tiriac), South American (Franulovic)*
F.Froehling, G.Gorman, T.Koch, 4–0; J.Leschley, 3–0; Z.Franulovic, 3–2; B.Jovanovic, J.Kukal, E.Mandarino, J.Newcombe, M.Orantes, P.Proisy, C.Richey, R.Ruffels, R.Russell, 2–0; J.Kodes, S.Smith, 2–1; W.Alvarez, A.Ashe, S.Baranyi, R.Barth, J.Bartlett, O.Bengtsson, J.Borowiak, W.Bungert, J.Clifton, J.Connors, P.Cornejo, R.Crealy, P.Curtis, M.Di Domenico, E.Drossart, T.Edlefsen, R.Emerson, O.Escribano, J.Fillol, W.Gasiorek, A.Gimeno, F.Hemmes, M.Holecek, J.Hordijk, F.Jauffret, K.Johansson, R.Keldie, C.Kuhnke, P.Lall, R.Laver, J.Loyo-Mayo, V.Marcu, B.Mignot, J.Mukerjea, J.Mulligan, T.Nowicki, T.Okker, L.Olander, C.Pasarell, A.Pattison, J.L.Rouyer, M.Santana, J.Shalem, J.Stabholz, 1–0; R.Carmichael, R.Taylor, I.Tiriac, 1–1; C.Graebner, 2–2; P.Barthes, C.Drysdale, G.Goven, 0–1.

1972 Played 32 tournaments. Won 12 Singles and 9 Doubles
SINGLES: *Won Baltimore, Omaha, Monte Carlo, Madrid (Melia), Nice, Düsseldorf, Canadian Open, S.Orange, US Open, Seattle, Dewar Cup, Commercial Union Grand Prix (Barcelona). R/up US Indos, Hampton, Wimbledon, Swedish Open.*
DOUBLES: *Won Omaha, Kansas, Hampton, Italian Open, Canadian Open (all with Tiriac), Melia (Smith), German Open (Kodes), Düsseldorf (McMillan), Edinburgh (Howe). Also won Wimbledon Mixed (Casals) and r/up US Open Mixed (Casals).*
T.Gorman, 9–1; J.Connors, 6–0; S.Baranyi, J.Fassbender, F.Pala, 3–0; M.Orantes, 3–2; C.Barazzutti, G.Battrick, M.Belkin, C.Dibley, P.Dominguez, P.Gerken, I.Gulyas, J.Fillol, B.Jovanovic, G.Masters, A.Pattison, P.Proisy, P.Szoke, I.Tiriac, T.Ulrich, 2–0; P.Barthes, T.Edlefsen, J.Gisbert, C.Graebner, A.Panatta, 2–1; T.Akbari, A.Amritraj, M.Anderson, K.Andersson, A.Ashe, J.C.Barclay, J.Bartlett, B.Borg, M.Burgener, E.Castigliano, M.Collins, J.Cooper, P.Cornejo, I.Crookenden, J.Clifton, C.Drysdale, H.Engert, H.Elschenbroich, I.Fletcher, B.Gottfried, L.Hoad, J.Hrebec, T.Kakulia, N.Kalogeropoulos, H.Kary, T.Koch, A.Kurucz, B.,Mackay, A.Mayer, F.McMillan, K.Meiler, A.Metreveli, R.Moore, J.Muntanola, A.Olmedo, J.Osborne, O.Parun, J.Pinto-Bravo, H.Rahim, R.Ramirez, C.Richey, N.Spear, S.Stewart, F.Stolle, B.Taroczy, R.Taylor, J.Velasco, J.Zabrodsky, 1–0; R.Hewitt, J.Kodes, 2–2; O.Bengtsson, R.Tanner, 1–1; P.Cramer, A.Gimeno, T.Okker, 0–1 S.Smith, 1–4.

1973 Played 32 tournaments. Won 16 Singles and 13 Doubles
SINGLES: *Won Omaha, Calgary, Merrifield, Barcelona (TC Polo), Monte Carlo, Madrid, Florence, French Open, Italian Open, Queen's Club, Gstaad, Istanbul, Western Open, Barcelona (Godo Cup), Paris Inds, Commercial Union Grand Prix Masters (Boston). R/up Hampton, British Hd Cts, Dewar Cup.*
DOUBLES: *Won Monte Carlo, British Hd Cts, Istanbul, Paris Inds (all with Gisbert), Calgary (Estep), Madrid (Norberg), Hampton, Charleston (Graebner), Godo and Melia (Okker), Wimbledon, S.Orange, Stockholm Inds (Connors). R/up French (Connors).*
J.Connors, 4–1; P.Cramer, M.Estep, J.Gisbert, F.Jauffret, J.Kodes, R.Moore, M.Orantes, N.Pilic, P.Proisy, 3–0; A.Panatta, 3–1; J.Alexander, P.Bertolucci, J.B.Chanfreau, P.Dupre, J.Fassbender, B.Fairlie, J.Hrebec, N.Kalogeropoulos, E.Mandarino, A.Metreveli, J.Paish, J.Pinto-Bravo, J.Singh, S.Steart, R.Taylor, M.Vasquez, 2–0; A.Amritraj, G.Battrick, M.Caimo, R.Case, E.Castigliano, J.Cooper, M.Cox, P.Dent, E.di Matteo, P.Dominguez, H.Elschenbroich, I.El Shafei, R.Emerson, H.Fitzgibbon, I.Fletcher, N.Fleury, J.Ganzabal, G.Goven, J.Guerrero, Z.Guerry, J.Higueras, M.Holecek, H.Hose, T.Kakulia, R.Kreiss, M.Lara, G.Masters, R.Maud, I.Molina, M.Mulligan, J.Newcombe, W.N'Godrella, O.Palmer, B.Phillips-Moore, H.Plotz, H.Rahim, M.Riessen, J.L.Rouyer, T.Sakai, S.Siegel, J.Simpson, G.Stilwell, R.Stockton, P.Szoke, J.Thamin, I.Tiriac, P.Toci, A.Zugarelli, 1–0; B.Borg, P.Gerken, T.Gorman, O.Parun, S.Smith, 1–1; B.Gottfried, C.Graebner, A.Mayer, K.Meiler, A.Pattison, R.Ramirez, 0–1; T.Okker, 3–4.

1974 Played 29 tournaments. Won 9 Singles and 4 Doubles
SINGLES: *Won Kingston, Richmond, Washington Inds, Portland, British Hd Cts, Cedar Grove, Madrid (Melia), Barcelona (Godo Cup), Hilton Head. R/up Toronto, Hampton, Monte Carlo, Italian Open, Commercial Union Grand Prix Masters (Melbourne).*
DOUBLES: *Won British Hd Cts, Godo (Gisbert), US Clay Cts, Dewar Cup (Connors). R/up Italian (Gisbert)*
G.Goven, R.Taylor, 4–0; H.Solomon, 3–1; R.Crealy, R.Dowdeswell, F.McNair, M.Orantes, N.Pilic, K.Warwick, 2–0; C.Barazzutti, P.Barthes, B.Borg, B.Gottfried, T.Okker, R.Ramirez, M.Riessen, A.Stone, 2–1; V.Amritraj, R.Barth, O.Bengtsson, P.Bertolucci, M.Claitte, P.Dominguez, C.Drysdale, P.Dupre, J.Fassbender, I.Fletcher, J.Gisbert, T.Gorman, G.Hardie, J.Higueras, J.Hrebec, L.Johansson, T.Koch, A.Korpas, M.Lara, R.Laver, A.Mayer, J.McManus, F.McMillan, A.Metreveli, M.Mulligan, J.Newcombe, A.Panatta, U.Pinner, O.Parun, B.Prajoux, H.Rahim, R.Reid, M.Robinson, R.Ruffels, E.Scott, S.Smith, E.Van Dillen, J.Velasco, 1–0;

J.Alexander, F.Jauffret, R.Maud, A.Pattison, R.Stockton, R.Tanner, 1–1; G.Vilas, 1–2; W.Brown, J.Connors, J.Kodes, C.Richey, 0–1.

1975 Played 31 tournaments. Won 10 Singles and 5 Doubles
SINGLES: *Won Barcelona, Valencia, Madrid (Melia), S.Orange, Dutch Round Robin, Hilton Head, Graz, Helsinki, Commercial Union Grand Prix Masters (Stockholm), Uppsala. R/up Swiss Inds, Tucson, Louisville, Canadian Open, Charlotte.*
DOUBLES: *Won US Inds, S.Orange, US Open, Hamilton (all with Connors), Melia (Kodes). R/up Italian (Connors).*
M.Orantes, 4–3; P.Dent, I.El Shafei, W.Fibak, H.Kary, V.Pecci, 3–0; B.Borg, 3–2; J.Andrew, M.Cox, E.Dibbs, J.Higueras, S.Krulevitz, R.Laver, I.Molina, A.Munoz, B.Phillips-Moore, H.Pohmann, M.Riessen, G.Stilwell, B.Taroczy, I.Tiriac, 2–0; R.Ramirez, 2–1; Anand Amritraj, Ashok Amritraj, B.Andersson, O.Bengtsson, P.Bertolucci, D.Crawford, J.Delaney, C.Dibley, P.Dominguez, R.Dowdeswell, Z.Franulovic, J.Gisbert, T.Gorman, B.Gottfried, J.Lutz, R.Machan, E.Mandarino, W.Martin, G.Mayer, F.McNair, B.Mignot, Z.Mincek, B.Mitton, R.Moore, M.Mulligan, R.Norberg, T.Okker, J.Pinto-Bravo, H.Rahim, M.Robinson, A.Stone, R.Taylor, S.Turner, E.van Dillen, J.Velasco, T.Waltke, 1–0; J.Alexander, A.Panatta, K.Rosewall, S.Stewart, G.Vilas, 1–1; V.Amritraj, J.Connors, J.Fillol, J.Hrebec, J.Kodes, K.Meiler, P.Proisy, C.Richey, 0–1; A.Ashe, 1–2; V.Gerulaitis, 0–2.

1976 Played 30 tournaments. Won 9 Singles and 1 Doubles
SINGLES: *Won Atlanta, US Inds, La Costa, WCT Avis Challenge Cup, Nottingham (shared), Pepsi Grand Slam, S Orange, Caracas Round Robin, Argentine Round Robin. R/up Baltimore, Hampton, Caracas, Stockholm, Wimbledon, Hong Kong.*
DOUBLES: *Won Stockholm WCT (Metreveli)*
R.Laver, G.Vilas, 4–0; J.Connors, 4–1. J.Borowiak, R.Stockton, 3–0; A.Panatta, 3–2; J.Alexander, M.Cahill, J.Fillol, Z.Franulovic, W.Martin, S.Menon, R.Moore, J.Hrebec, C.Pasarell, H.Rahim, E.Van Dillen, 2–0; M.Orantes, H.Solomon, R.Tanner, I.Tiriac, 2–1; L.Alvarez, V.Amritraj, J.Andrews, S.Ball, O.Bengtsson, P.Dent, C.Dibley, M.Edmondson, I.El Shafei, B.Fairlie, P.Fiegl, P.Fleming, C.Hagey, H.Kary, C.Kirmayr, J.Kodes, Tom Gullikson, C.Lewis, J.Loyo-Mayo, J.Lloyd, E.Montano, P.Parun, H.Pohmann, R.Reid, M.Riessen, W.Scanlon, S.Smith, N.Spear, A.Stone, B.Taroczy, B.Walts, K.Warwick, 1–0; A.Ashe, B.Mitton, R.Ramirez, K.Rosewall, 1–1; V.Gerulaitis, T.Gorman, B.Gottfried, 0–1; W.Fibak, 1–3; B.Borg, 3–4.

1977 Played 22 tournaments. Won 3 Singles and 4 Doubles
SINGLES: *Won Mexico WCT, WCT Challenge Cup, Aix-en-Provence. R/up Rotterdam, Virginia Beach, Rye.*
DOUBLES: *Won St.Louis, Earls Court, River Oaks (all with Panatta), Aix-en-Provence (Tiriac)*
J.Kodes, R.Moore, A.Panatta, 3–0; V.Gerulaitis, 3–2; V.Amaya, C.Drysdale, W.Fibak, J.McEnroe, F.McMillan, T.Okker, 2–0; J.Alexander, L.Alvarez, L.Baraldi, B.Boileau, R.Cano, R.Case, M.Cox, J.Feaver, Z.Franulovic, Tim Gullikson, Tom Gullikson, R.Hewitt, J.Higueras, J.Hrebec, R.Laver, B.Manson, W.Martin, K.Meiler, A.Pattison, B.Prajoux, P.Proisy, J.Richer, R.Tanner, E.Teltscher, 1–0; C.Barazzutti, K.Rosewall, 1–1; V.Amritraj, B.Borg, P.Dent, E.Dibbs, B.Gottfried, G.Goven, F.Jauffret, H.Pfister, A.Roche, R.Stockton, 0–1; W.Scanlon, 1–2; J.Connors, 1–3; G.Vilas, 1–5.

1978 Played 21 tournaments. Won 2 Singles
SINGLES: *Won Miami, WCT Challenge Cup. R/up WCT Houston, Barcelona, WCT Forest Hills Invitational, Gunze Open.*
P.Fleming, 4–0; M.Fishbach, Z.Franulovic, Tom Gullikson, F.McMillan, R.Stockton, 2–0; C.Barazzutti, R.Benavides, P.Bertolucci, M.Cox, E.Dibbs, C.Dibley, R.Fagel, J.Fillol, F.Fukai, J.Higueras, P.Kronk, S.Krulevitz, M.Lara, G.Masters, S.Mayer, G.Ocleppo, C.Pasarell, K.Richardson, C.Richey, S.Stewart, B.Teacher, E.Teltscher, V.Winitsky, J.Yuill, A.Zugarelli, 1–0; J.Alexander, J.McEnroe, T.Moore, R.Tanner, 1–1; A.Ashe, B.Borg, T.Gorman, B.Gottfried, J.James, R.Lutz, T.Okker, B.Taroczy, K.Warwick, 0–1; R.Ramirez, 1–2; V.Gerulaitis, 0–2.

1979 Played 21 tournaments. Won 0 Singles and 5 Doubles
SINGLES: *R/up Cleveland.*
DOUBLES: *Won Sarasota (with Krulevitz), WCT Monte Carlo (Ramirez), Cincinatti (Gottfried), Atlanta (Moore), Tel Aviv (Okker). R/up Braniff World of Doubles (Stewart), WCT Birmingham (Okker), Johannesburg (Moore), Italian Open (Clerc).*
S.Birner, J.Damiani, R.Fisher, Z.Franulovic, E.Friedler, A.Gimenez, F.Gonzales, Tom Gullikson, J.James, B.Kleege, J.Kriek, D.Joubert, G.Malin, A.Maurer, R.Meneschincheri, T.Moore, B.Nunna, L.Palin, S.Stansbury, L.Stefanki, V.Winitsky, J.Yuill, 1–0; P.Fleming, Tim Gullikson, 1–1; M.Orantes, A.Panatta, 1–1; J.Alexander, E.Dibbs, C.Dibley, P.Dominguez, R.Gehring, B.Gottfried, G.Hardie, R.Lutz, J.McEnroe, S.Smith, R.Tanner, T.Waltke, A.Zugarelli, 0–1; J.Connors, V.Gerulaitis, R.Meyer, 0–2.

1980 Played 18 tournaments. Won 0 Singles, 0 Doubles
SINGLES: *R/up Dubai.*
DOUBLES: *R/up Stowe (Vermont) with F.Taygan*
J. Alexander, V.Amaya, B.Boileau, P.Dominguez, J.Feaver, J.Kriek, O.Parun, M.Riessen, J.Sadri, R.Stockton, 1–0; A.Mayer, 1–1; B.Borg, J.Connors, E.Dibbs, P.Fleming, V.Gerulaitis, S.Glickstein, I.Lendl, J.P.McEnroe, P.Rennert, Rocavert, S.Smith, B.Teacher, G.Vilas, B.Walts, 0–1; V.Amritraj, W.Fibak, 0–2.

1981 Played 26 tournaments. Won 0 Singles, 3 Doubles
SINGLES: *R/up Nancy, Bologna*
DOUBLES: *Won Nancy (with A.Panatta), Basle (J.-L.Clerc), Paris Indoors (Y.Noah)*
C.Zipf 2–0; B.Drewett, M.Davis, S.Glickstein, Kirchhubel, P.McNamara, G.Moretton, P.Proisy, T.Smid, H.Solomon, R.Tanner, B.Taroczy, F.Taygan, 1–0; E.Teltscher, G.Vilas 1–1; J.Alexander, F.Buehning, R.Cano, J.Delaney, V.Gerulaitis, H. Guenthardt, Tom Gullikson, H.Ismail, J.Kriek, R.Lewis, J.P.McEnroe, T.Moor, Y.Noah, M.Purcell, C.Roger-Vasselin, N.Saviano, S.Smith, 0–1; A.Mayer, 0–2

1982 Played 26 tournaments. Won 0 Singles, 0 Doubles
DOUBLES: *R/up Bournemouth (with H.Leconte), Venice (J.-L.Clerc)*
M.Estep, B.Gottfried, J.-L.Clerc, J.Kriek, Z.Kuharsky, T.Moor, Popp, F.Taygan, 1–0; L.Bourne, J.Connors, M.Davis, G.Forget, V.Gerulaitis, A.Gomez, P.Hjertquist, C.Lewis, J.McEnroe, P.McNamara, P.McNamee, T.Smid, B.Taroczy, V.Van Patten, 0–1 *Records incomplete.*

1983 Played 13 tournaments. Won 0 Singles, 1 Doubles
DOUBLES: *Won Kuwait (with V.Amritraj), r/up Caracas (A.Gomez)*
P.Cash, J.Hervet, T.Hogstedt, C.Motta, 1–0; P.Fleming, J.Kriek, M.Purcell, G.Vilas, 0–1 *Records incomplete*

SUMMARY

- 1st player to be ranked number 1 when ATP official rankings first produced, August 1973.
- Number 1 for 40 consecutive weeks
- In 1972, was top earning player with $176,000
- In 1973, was top earning player with $228,750
- In 1976, first European to exceed $1 million in career prize money.
- Total career earnings $2,076,761
- In the Open era, one of five players to win more than 100 pro titles, 88 singles and 80 doubles (39 with Tiriac).
- Among the all-time winners of both singles and doubles titles, only Nastase and McEnroe appear in the top 10 list of each.

Davis Cup Record

Year	*Romania Opponent*	*Venue*	*Romania Win–Loss result*	*Nastase Singles results*	*Nastase Doubles result*
1966	France	A	1–4	Lost P.Darmon 1–6 2–6 2–6	Lost
				Lost F.Jauffret 1–6 3–6 6–8	(w Tiriac)
1967	Belgium	H	4–1	Won P.Hombergen 6–3 5–7 6–1 6–0	Won
				Won E.Drossart 6–2 5–7 10–8 6–2	(w Tiriac)
	Spain	H	2–3	Lost M.Santana 6–0 3–6 3–6 3–6	Won
				Lost J.Gisbert 3–6 6–4 7–9 4–6	(w Tiriac)
1968	Denmark	H	4–1	Won T.Ulrich 6–4 6–4 6–2	Lost
				Won J.Ulrich 6–2 11–9 4–6 4–6 6–4	(w Tiriac)
	Norway	A	5–0	Won M.Elvik 6–2 6–3 6–1	Won
				Won F.Prydz 4–6 6–0 8–6 6–0	(w Tiriac)
1969	UAR	H	3–2	Won M.Sonbol 6–4 6–0 6–4	Won
				Lost I.El Shafei 2–6 6–1 3–6 1–6	(w Tiriac)
	Israel	H	5–0	Won E.Davidman 6–0 6–2 6–4	Won
				Won J.Stabholz 6–2 6–2 6–0	(w Tiriac)
	Spain	A	4–1	Won J.L.Arilla 6–4 8–6 6–2	Won
					(w Tiriac)
	USSR	H	4–1	Won T.Lejus 4–6 6–3 6–2 6–2	Won
				Won A.Metreveli 6–4 6–2 7–5	(w Tiriac)
	India	H	4–0	Won J.Mukerjea 6–2 6–4 4–6 4–6 6–1	Won
					(w Tiriac)
	GB	A	3–2	Lost G.Stilwell 4–6 6–4 1–6 2–6	Won
				Won M.Cox 3–6 6–1 6–4 6–4	(w Tiriac)
	USA	A	0–5	Lost S.Smith 6–4 6–4 4–6 1–6 9–11	Lost
				Lost A.Ashe 2–6 13–15 5–7	(w Tiriac)
1970	Iran	A	4–1	Won H.Akbari 6–2 4–6 6–2 6–3	Won
				Won T.Akbari 10–8 6–0 6–8 5–7 6–3	(w Tiriac)
	Greece	H	5–0	Won N.Kalogeropoulos 6–2 7–5 6–4	Won
					(w Tiriac)
	Yugoslavia	A	2–3	Lost Z.Franulovic 3–6 6–3 2–6 1–6	Won
				Lost N.Spear 5–7 6–8 2–6	(w Tiriac)
1971	Israel	A	5–0	Won J.Shalem 6–1 6–2 6–3	–
				Won J.Stabholz 6–0 6–0 6–1	
	Holland	H	5–0	Won J.Hordijk 6–2 6–2 6–3	Won
					(w Tiriac)
	Yugoslavia	H	4–1	Won Z.Franulovic 7–5 6–2 6–3	Won
				Won B.Jovanovic 4–6 6–4 ret.	(w Tiriac)

Year	*Romania Opponent*	*Venue*	*Romania Win–Loss result*	*Nastase Singles results*	*Nastase Doubles result*
	Germany	H	5–0	Won W.Bungert 6–2 6–3 6–2	Won
				Won C.Khunke 6–0 6–4 6–4	(w Tiriac)
	India	A	4–1	Won J.Mukerjea 6–3 6–3 6–4	Won
				Won P.Lall 6–3 8–10 6–1 6–1	(w Tiriac)
	Brazil	A	3–2	Won E.Mandarino 6–4 6–1 6–1	Lost
				Won T.Koch 6–4 6–0 8–6	(w Tiriac)
	USA	A	2–3	Won F.Froehling 6–3 6–1 1–6 6–4	Won
				Lost S.Smith 5–7 3–6 1–6	(w Tiriac)
1972	Switzerland	H	5–0	Won M.Burgener 6–1 6–2 6–3	Won
					(w Tiriac)
	Iran	H	5–0	Won T.Akbari 6–1 6–1 6–3	Won
					(w Tiriac)
	Italy	H	4–1	Won C.Barazzutti 7–5 6–2 6–0	Won
				Won A.Panatta 4–6 6–0 6–3 6–1	(w Tiriac)
	USSR	A	3–2	Won A.Metreveli 6–4 6–0 6–4	Won
					(w Tiriac)
	Australia	H	4–1	Won C.Dibley 6–3 6–0 6–2	Won
				Won M.Anderson 6–2 6–2 4–6 6–3	(w Tiriac)
	USA	H	2–3	Won T.Gorman 6–1 6–2 5–7 10–8	Lost
				Lost S.Smith 9–11 2–6 3–6	(w Tiriac)
1973	Holland	A	3–2	Won J.Hordijk 6–3 6–3 6–2	Won
				Won T.Okker 6–4 6–2 6–4	(w Haradau)
	New Zealand	H	4–1	Won O.Parun 6–1 8–6 6–2	Won
				Won B.Fairlie 4–6 6–0 6–3 6–0	(w Santeiu)
	USSR	H	3–2	Won T.Kakulia 6–0 6–3 6–0	Lost
				Won A.Metreveli 6–0 6–2 6–4	(w Santeiu)
	USA	A	1–4	Won M.Riessen 6–2 6–4 6–2	Lost
				Lost S.Smith 7–5 2–6 4–6 6–4 3–6	(w Santeiu)
1974	France	H	3–2	Won P.Barthès 6–2 6–2 6–3	Won
				Lost F.Jauffret 6–2 4–6 3–6 2–6	(w Tiriac)
	Italy	A	2–3	Won C.Barazzutti 9–7 6–0 6–1	Lost
				Won A.Panatta 6–0 6–0 7–5	(w Tiriac)
1975	Spain	A	2–3	Won J.Higueras 6–0 8–6 4–6 6–1	Lost
				Won M.Orantes 6–2 6–2 6–4	(w Tiriac)
1976	Austria	A	4–1	Won P.Fiegl 6–1 6–3 7–5	Won
				Won H.Kary 6–3 7–5 6–1	(w Marcu)
1977	Belgium	H	5–0	Won J.P.Richer 6–2 6–2 6–2	Won
				Won B.Boileau 6–1 6–4 6–1	(w Tiriac)

Year	*Romania Opponent*	*Venue*	*Romania Win–Loss result*	*Nastase Singles results*	*Nastase Doubles result*
	Czecho-slovakia	H	3–1	Won J.Kodes 6–2 6–2 6–4	Won
				Won J.Hrebec 6–2 1–0 ret.	(w Tiriac)
	GB	H	4–1	Won J.Feaver 6–1 6–2 4–6 6–4	Won
					(w Tiriac)
	France	A	2–3	Lost F.Jauffret 6–3 6–0 4–6 3–6 1–6	Won
				Won P.Proisy 6–4 4–6 8–6 6–1	(w Tiriac)
1978	–	–	–	Nastase suspended, so did not play	–
1979	Belgium	A	4–1	Won B.Boileau 6–3 6–4 6–2	Won
				Won T.Steavaux 6–0 6–4 6–4	(w Marcu)
	W.Germany	H	4–1	Won P.Elter 6–4 6–4 6–2	Won
				Won M.Wuenschig	(w Haradau)
	Sweden	H	2–3	Won S.Simonsson 7–9 5–7 7–5 6–3 6–3	Lost
					(w Marcu)
				Lost B.Borg 3–6 0–6 0–6	
1980	Yugoslavia	A	5–0	Won Z.Ilin 12–10 6–3 4–6 6–3	Won
				Won Z.Petkovic 6–2 6–1 6–2	(w Segarceanu)
	Austria	H	3–2	Won H.Kary 6–1 7–5 6–4	Won
				Won R.Reininger 6–3 6–3 6–3	(w Segarceanu)
	GB	A	3–2	Won C.J.Mottram 6–3 6–2 6–4	Lost
				Won J.Feaver 7–5 8–6 2–6 2–6 6–4	(w Dirzu)
1981	–	–	–	Nastase suspended, so did not play	–
1982	Chile	A	2–3	Won B.Prajoux 1–6 9–7 6–4 6–8 6–2	–
				Lost P.Rebolledo 7–5 4–6 1–6 3–6	
	Mexico (relegation round)	A	3–2	Won F.Maciel 6–4 2–6 6–4 10–8	Won
				Lost R.Ramirez 2–6 1–6 3–6	(w Segarceanu)
1983	Chile	H	5–0	Won R.Acuna 2–6 6–3 6–2 6–4	Won
				Won H.Gildemeister 2–6 6–4 6–2	(w Segarceanu)
	Australia	A	0–5	Lost M.Edmonson 6–4 3–6 12–14 2–6	Lost
				Lost P.Cash 3–6 3–6	(w Segarceanu)
1984	USA	H	0–5	Lost J.McEnroe 2–6 4–6 2–6	Lost
				Lost J.Connors 4–6 4–6	(w Segarceanu)
1985	Denmark	H	2–3	–	Lost
					(w Segarceanu)

SUMMARY

- Nastase played 146 Davis Cup rubbers, second only in the all-time list to Nicola Pietrangeli (164).
- He has played 96 singles rubbers, with a win–loss aggregate of 74–22, again second to Pietrangeli and ahead of third-placed Manuel Santana (69–17).
- He has played 50 doubles rubbers, winning 35 and losing 15, which places him third in the all-time doubles table, behind Pietrangeli and Orlando Sirola. In partnership with Ion Tiriac, he won 27 and lost 7.

Major Championships Results and World Rankings

Year/Tournament	*Round reached*	*Opponent*	*Score*	*World Ranking*
1966				–
French Open	3	Drysdale	6–3 4–6 4–6 2–6	
Wimbledon	1	Koch	2–6 0–6 0–6	
1967				–
French Open	3	Kodes	4–6 5–7 3–6	
Wimbledon	1	Curtis	4–6 4–6 2–6	
1968				–
French Open	2	Crealy	6–4 6–8 5–7 2–6	
1969				–
French Open	1	Matthews	3–6 6–0 6–0 4–6 6–8	
Wimbledon	3	Graebner	5–7 6–8 4–6	
US Open	4	Rosewall	1–6 5–7 6–4 3–6	
1970				6
French Open	1/4F	Richey	5–7 7–9 6–4 3–6	
Wimbledon	4	Graebner	3–6 0–6 6–4 3–6	
1971				10
French Open	Final	Kodes	6–8 2–6 6–2 5–7	
Wimbledon	2	Goven	4–6 4–6 2–6	
US Open	3	Carmichael	3–6 3–6 6–7	
1972				3
French Open	3	Panatta	6–1 7–9 4–6 3–6	
Wimbledon	Final	Smith	6–4 3–6 3–6 6–4 5–7	
US Open	Won	Ashe	3–6 6–3 6–7 6–4 6–3	
1973				1
French Open	Won	Pilic	6–3 6–3 6–0	
Wimbledon	4	Mayer	4–6 6–8 8–6 4–6	
US Open	2	Pattison	7–6 6–2 3–6 4–6 4–6	

Year/Tournament	*Round reached*	*Opponent*	*Score*	*World Ranking*
1974				10
French Open	1/4F	Solomon	4–6 4–6 6–0 6–3 4–6	
Wimbledon	4	Stockton	7–5 4–6 3–6 8–9	
US Open	3	Tanner	6–4 7–6 5–7 4–6 4–6	
1975				7
French Open	3	Panatta	6–3 3–6 0–6	
Wimbledon	2	Stewart	6–8 8–6 2–6 6–1 3–6	
US Open	1/4F	Orantes	2–6 4–6 6–3 3–6	
1976				3
Wimbledon	Final	Borg	4–6 2–6 7–9	
US Open	1/2F	Borg	3–6 3–6 4–6	
1977				9
French Open	1/4F	Gottfried	6–4 6–3 2–6 2–6 3–6	
Wimbledon	1/4F	Borg	0–6 6–8 3–6	
US Open	2	Barazzutti	4–6 4–6	
1978				16
Wimbledon	1/4F	Okker	5–7 1–6 6–2 3–6	
1979				50
French Open	1	Orantes	6–4 4–6 1–6 2–6	
US Open	2	McEnroe	4–6 6–4 3–6 2–6	
1980				79
Wimbledon	3	Fleming	4–6 6–3 6–7 6–7	
US Open	2	Solomon	2–6 2–6 2–6	
1981				73
French Open	3	Moor	3–6 2–6 1–6	
Wimbledon	1	A.Mayer	4–6 6–4 6–4 4–6 4–6	
US Open	1	Purcell	6–3 3–6 4–6 6–3 3–6	
Australian Open (played in December)	1	Lewis	4–6 3–6 2–6	
1982				118
French Open	2	Forget	1–6 7–5 4–6 6–1 7–9	
Wimbledon	1	Bourne	1–6 3–6 6–3 4–6	

Year/Tournament	*Round reached*	*Opponent*	*Score*	*World Ranking*
US Open	4	Connors	3–6 3–6 4–6	
1983				169
French Open	3	Vilas	1–6 2–6 1–6	
US Open	1	Fleming	6–7 4–6 6–2 6–2 6–7	

NB: From 1973 onwards, the world rankings are those of the official ATP year-end computer rankings. Prior to that date, as official rankings did not exist, those given are compiled from World Tennis, Rothmans Year Book, and Tennis Australia, Asia, and the Pacific.

Career Win–Loss Record (up to 31 December 1983)

These records exclude one-set matches, Team Tennis and exhibition matches.

Opponent	*W–L*
Addison, T	1–0
Akbari, H	1–0
Akbari, T	2–0
Alexander, J	11–5
Alvarez, L	2–0
Alvarez, W	1–0
Amaya, V	3–0
Amritraj, An.	3–0
Amritraj, Ash	1–0
Amritraj, V.	2–5
Anderson, M	1–0
Andersson, B	1–0
Andersson, K	1–0
Andrew, G	1–0
Andrew, J	2–0
Andrews, J	1–0
Arilla, J.L	1–0
Ashe, A	5–6
Ball, S	1–0
Baraldi, L	1–0
Baranyi, S	5–0
Barazzutti, C	5–3
Barclay, J.C	2–0
Barth, R	2–0
Barthès, P	5–4
Bartlett, J	2–0
Battrick, G	4–0
Belkin, M	2–0
Benavides, R	1–0
Bengtsson, O	5–1
Bertolucci, P	5–0
Bertram, B	1–0
Beust, P	1–0
Birner, S	1–0
Boileau, B	2–0
Borg, B	10–11
Borowiak, J	5–0
Bourne, L	0–1
Bouteleux, A	1–0
Bowrey, W	1–0
Brown, W	0–1
Buehning, F	0–1
Bungert, W	2–0
Burgener, M	1–0
Butcher, B	1–0
Cahill, M	2–0
Caimo, M	1–0
Cano, R	2–0
Carlstein, M	1–0
Carmichael, R	2–1
Case, R	2–0
Cash, P	1–0
Castigliano, E	5–0
Chanfreau, J.B	2–0
Claitte, M	1–0
Clerc, J-L	1–0
Clifton, J	2–0
Collins, M	1–0
Coni, L	1–0
Connors, J	16–12
Contet, D	1–0
Cooper, J	2–1
Cornejo, P	2–0
Courcol, J.P	1–0
Cox, M	6–1
Cramer, P	3–1
Crawford, D	1–0
Crealy, R	6–2
Crookenden, I	2–0
Curtis, P	3–1
Damiani, J	1–0
Darmon, P	0–1
Davidman, E	1–0
Davis, M	1–1
De Gronkel, C	0–1
Delaney, J	2–0
Dent, P	7–1
Dhawan, V	1–0
Dibbs, E	3–4
Dibley, C	5–1
Di Domenico, M	3–0
Di Maso, G	1–0
Di Matteo, E	2–0
Dowdeswell, C	3–0
Dominguez, P	5–1
Drewett, B	1–0
Dron, S	3–0
Drossart, E	3–0
Drysdale, C	4–3
Dupre, P	3–0
Edlefsen, T	3–1
Edmondson, M	1–0
Elschenbroich, H	2–0
El Shafei, I	6–2
Elvik, M	1–0
Emerson, R	2–0
Engert, H	1–0
Escribano, O	1–0
Estep, M	4–0
Fagel, R	1–0
Fairlie, B	4–0
Fassbender, J	7–0
Feaver, J	2–0
Fibak, W	6–5
Fiegl, P	1–0

Player	Record
Fillol, J	6–3
Fishbach, M	2–0
Fisher, R	1–0
Fitzgibbon, H	1–0
Fleming, P	6–3
Fletcher, I	4–0
Fletcher, K	0–1
Fleury, N	1–0
Forget, G	0–1
Franulovic, Z	16–5
Friedler, E	1–0
Froehling, F	4–0
Fukai, F	1–0
Ganzabal, J	1–0
Garcia, T	1–0
Gasiorek, W	4–0
Gehring, R	0–1
Gerken, P	3–1
Gerulaitis, V	3–12
Gimeno, A	3–2
Gimenez, A	1–0
Gisbert, J	7–2
Glickstein, S	1–1
Gomez, A	0–1
Gorman, T	18–4
Gottfried, B	5–6
Goven, G	6–3
Graebner, C	4–7
Guenthardt, H	0–1
Guerrero, J	1–0
Guerry, Z	1–0
Gullikson, Tim	3–1
Gullikson, Tom	6–1
Gulyas, I	7–1
Guzman, F	1–0
Hagey, C	1–0
Hardie, G	1–1
Hemmes, F	1–0
Herrera, J	1–0
Hervet, J	0–1
Hewitt, R	5–2
Higueras, J	6–0
Hjertquist P	0–1
Hoad, L	
Hogstedt, T	1–0
Holecek, M	3–0
Holmes, N	1–0
Homberg, R	0–1
Hombergen, P	1–0
Hordijk, J	1–0
Hose, H	1–0
Howe, R	2–0
Hrebec, J	8–1
Hutchins, P	0–1
Ismail, H	0–1
James, J	1–1
Jauffret, F	5–3
Jemsby, P	1–0
Johansson, K	1–0
Johansson, L	2–0
Joubert, D	1–0
Jovanovic, B	5–0
Kakulia T	3–0
Kalogeropoulos, N	7–0
Kary, H	6–1
Keldie, R	1–0
Kirchhubel	1–0
Kirmayr, C	1–0
Kleege, B	1–0
Koch, T	8–1
Kodes, J	16–8
Korotkov, V	1–0
Kreiss, R	2–0
Kriek, J	4–2
Kronk, P	1–0
Krulevitz, S	3–0
Kuharsky, Z	1–0
Kuhlmey, R	1–0
Kukal, J	3–0
Kurucz, A	1–0
Lall, P	3–2
Lara, M	4–0
Laver, R	9–2
Leclerq, M	1–0
Lejus, T	2–0
Lendl, I	0–1
Leschley, J	4–0
Lewis, C	1–1
Lewis, R	0–1
Likhachev, S	1–0
Lloyd, D	0–1
Lloyd, J	2–0
Loyo-Mayo, J	2–0
Lundquist, J	1–0
Lutz, R	1–3
Machan, R	1–0
Mackay, B	1–0
Maggi, G.E	1–0
Maioli, G	1–1
Malin, G	1–0
Mandarino, E	6–2
Manson, B	1–0
Marcu, V	3–0
Marmureanu, P	3–1
Martin, W	4–0
Marzano, P	1–0
Masters, G	5–0
Matthews, S	0–1
Maud, R	2–1
Maurer, A	1–0
Mayer, A	4–4
Mayer, G	1–0
McDonald, A	1–0
McEnroe, J	3–5
McKinley, R	1–0

McManus, J 3–0
McMillan, F 6–0
McNair, F 3–0
McNamara, P 1–1
McNamee, P 0–1
Moretton, G 1–0
Meiler, K 2–2
Meneschincheri, R 1–0
Menon, S 2–0
Metreveli, A 4–2
Meyer, R 0–2
Mignot, B 2–0
Mincek, Z 1–0
Minotra, S 1–0
Misra, S.P 1–0
Mitton, B 2–1
Molina, I 3–0
Montano, E 1–0
Montrenaud, B 1–1
Moor, T 3–2
Moore, R 10–0
Motta,C 1–0
Mukerjea, J 2–2
Mulligan, M 8–3
Mulloy, G 1–0
Munoz, A 2–0
Muntanola, J.I 1–0

Newcombe, J 4–1
N'Godrella, W 1–0
Noah, Y 0–1
Norberg, R 1–0
Nowicki, T 1–0
Nunna, B 1–0

Ocleppo, G 1–0
Okker, T 9–10
Olander, L 1–0
Olmedo, A 1–0
Orantes, M 17–8
Osborne, J 2–0

Paish, J 4–0
Pala, F 5–0
Palin, L 1–0
Palmer, O 1–0
Palmieri, S 2–0
Panatta, A 16–7
Parun, O 7–1
Pasarell, C 4–0
Pattison, A 6–2
Pawlik, L 0–1
Pecci, V 3–0
Pfister, H 0–1
Phillips-Moore, B 6–0
Pietrangeli, N 1–3
Pilic, N 6–2
Pinner, U 1–0
Pinto-Bravo, J 5–1
Plotz, H 4–1
Pohmann, H.J 5–0
Popp 1–0
Prajoux, B 2–0
Proisy, P 10–1
Purcell, M 0–2

Rahim, H 6–0
Ralston, D 0–1
Ramirez, R 9–6
Reid, R 2–0
Rennert,P 0–1
Richardson, K 1–0
Richer, J.P 1–0
Riessen, M 9–3
Robbins, F 1–0
Robinson, M 2–0
Roche, A 2–3
Rocavert 0–1
Roger-Vasselin, C 0–2
Rosewall, K 3–6
Rouyer, J.L 2–0
Ruffels, R 4–0
Russell, R.A 3–0
Ryan, T 1–0
Rybarczyk, M 2–0

Sadri, J 1–0
Sakai, T 1–0
Sangster, M 1–0
Santana, M 2–1
Sara, G 1–0
Saul, J 0–1
Saviano, N 0–1
Scanlon, W 3–2
Scott, E 1–0
Shalem, J 1–0
Siegel, S 1–0
Simpson, J 1–0
Singh, J 2–0
Smid, T 1–1
Smith, S 8–10
Solomon, H 6–2
Sonbol, M 2–0
Spear, N 3–2
Stabholz, J 2–0
Stansbury 1–0
Stefanki, L 1–0
Stewart, S 5–1
Stilwell, G 5–2
Stockton, R 8–2
Stolle, F 1–0
Stone, A 5–1
Strobl, P 1–0
Szoke, P 3–0

Tacchini, S 1–0
Tanabe, K 1–0
Tanner, R 7–5
Taroczy, B 5–2
Taygan, F 2–0
Taylor, R 13–1
Teacher, B 1–2

Teltscher, E	3–1	Varga, G	1–0	Yuill, J	2–0
Thamin, J	1–0	Vasquez, M	2–0		
Tiriac, I	13–8	Velasco, J	3–0	Zabrodsky, J	1–0
Toci, P	2–0	Vilas, G	9–12	Zahr, H	1–0
Turner, S	1–0	Viziru, D	1–0	Zednik, V	1–0
Tym, B	0–1			Zeeman, C	1–1
		Waltke, T	1–1	Zipf, C	2–0
Ulrich, J	2–0	Walts, B	1–3	Zugarelli, A	3–1
Ulrich, T	5–0	Warboys, S	1–0		
		Warwick, K	3–1		
Van Dillen, E	4–1	Werren, M	1–0		
Van Patten, V	0–1	Winitsky, V	2–0		

Nastase has a winning record against the five players against whom he played the most matches:

	Played	*W–L*
Connors, J	28	16–12
Orantes, M	25	17–8
Kodes, J	24	16–8
Panatta, A	23	16–7
Gorman, T	22	18–4

All Ilie Nastase career records up to and including 1978 compiled by Joe McCauley and reproduced by kind permission of Richard Evans.

INDEX

ACKNOWLEDGMENTS

from Debbie Beckerman

Richard Evans, for generously being the middle man. Without you, this would never have happened.

Ion Tiriac, Dominique Nastase and Nathalie Nastase, you all gave unstintingly of your time. I am deeply grateful.

Susanna Lea, Rebecca and Nicky, your support and enthusiasm were crucial.

Michael Doggart and Tom Whiting, publishers *extraordinaires.*

Christian Bimes, thank you for letting Ilie and me camp out in your offices.

Tim Phillips, many thanks for your kindness and hospitality. Audrey Snell, at the Wimbledon Library, your help was invaluable.

Penny, Dad, and especially Keith. You know how important you were. Nicholas and Nathasha, thanks for your understanding.

Amalia, what on earth would I have done without you? I don't know where to begin to thank you!

Ilie, finally. Your generosity, patience and sense of humour throughout have been incredible. As Ion memorably said to me: 'Nastase doesn't have two lungs, he has two hearts.' This is your story.